THE
DARKNESS OF GOD

THEOLOGY AFTER HIROSHIMA

JIM GARRISON

WILLIAM B. EERDMANS
PUBLISHING COMPANY
GRAND RAPIDS, MICHIGAN

© Jim Garrison 1982
First published 1982 by SCM Press Ltd., England
First American edition published 1983 through special
arrangement with SCM Press by Wm. B. Eerdmans
Publishing Company, 255 Jefferson Ave. S.E., Grand
Rapids, MI 49503

Library of Congress Cataloging in Publication Data

Garrison, James.
The darkness of God.

Originally published: London: SCM Press, 1982.
Includes bibliographical references and index.
1. Atomic warfare — Religious aspects — Christianity.
2. God — History of doctrines — 20th century.
3. Hiroshima-shi (Japan) — Bombardment, 1945.
4. Eschatology. I. Title.
BR115.A85G38   1983   261.8'73   83-1415
ISBN 0-8028-1956-7

Thus says the Lord:
Behold, what I have built
   I am breaking down,
and what I have planted
   I am plucking up –
   that is, the whole land.
And do you seek great things
      for yourself?
   seek them not;
For, behold, I am bringing evil
      upon all flesh,
      says the Lord;
   But I will give you your life
      as a prize of war in all
      places to which you may go.

Jeremiah 45.4,5

Dedicated to
Eric Hutchison who brought me to an understanding
of our antinomial experience of God.

I wish to express a special note of thanks as well
to John Robinson and Dorothy Emmet
for their constant help along the way.

CONTENTS

I   Introduction: The Darkness of God   1

II The Inherited Tradition   9

    A. The Problem of God in the Modern Age   9
    B. The Doctrines of the *Summum Bonum* and *privatio
       boni*   21
       1. Evil defined   21
       2. The doctrines of the *Summum Bonum* and *privatio
          boni*   23
       3. Summary   27

III The 'Mighty Acts of God'   29

    A. Process Thought and the Philosophy of Whitehead   29
    B. Hartshorne's Dipolar Theory of the Godhead   37
    C. Panentheism   44
    D. The Question of Evil   50
       1. Hartshorne's treatment of evil   50
       2. Evaluation   52
    E. Divine Action   54
    F. Summary   58

IV The Historical Event: The Atomic Bombing of
    Hiroshima   61

    A. The Event   61
    B. Comment   68
    C. The Plutonium Culture   72
       1. Nuclear technology and nuclear weapons   72
       2. Nuclear technology and the technotronic society   86

V   The Confessional Heritage: Apocalyptic and the Wrath
    of God   92

    A. Introduction   92
    B. Classical Apocalyptic   93
    C. The Evil Forces in the World   99
    D. The Wrath of God   103

VI The Synthesis of Hiroshima and Apocalyptic   118

  A. Introduction   118
  B. Jung's Description of the Psyche   124
      1. The psyche as objectively real   124
      2. The unconscious   126
      3. The archetypes   129
      4. God and the unconscious   137
      5. God and the Self   138
      6. Life in God: The process of individuation   140
  C. Jung and Process Panentheism   147
  D. Wotan   152
  E. An Answer to Job   160
      1. The context   161
      2. The question of Job   166
      3. Comment   168
  F. *Theologia Crucis*   171
  G. The Revelation of John   178
  H. Modern Thought on the Antinomy of God   183
      1. Theological comment   183
      2. The contribution of Jung   188
  I. Apocalypse Now   193
  J. The Paradox of Apocalypse   198

VII Conclusion: Hiroshima as Gateway to Christ Crucified 202

  Notes   216

  Index   236

I

Introduction: The Darkness of God

Why is it that after several thousand million years of evolving life on planet earth, our species – in our generation – has brought this life to the verge of extinction through thermonuclear war?

This seems to me to be the single greatest question of our age. We are the product of a life process which over the aeons of time has evolved beauty, diversity, creativity and freedom. And yet we are now on the brink, the very brink, of bringing down the fires of nuclear destruction upon that which has taken thousands of millions of years to build. Why?

Any answer almost pales beside the question. Indeed, if Einstein is right, we are virtually incapable of articulating an answer, for what occurred when we split the atom, he said, was a leap in technology that changed everything in the world – save our mode of thinking. And thus we drift towards 'unparalleled catastrophe'. We are as infants playing with dynamite.

This inability to come to grips with the problem of humanity's imminent self-destruction is one that permeates even the Christian church, that body which was mandated by our Lord to be the light of the world. Karl Barth pointed this out in 1959, when he declared that the most vital issue confronting Christianity was the inability of the church to take a definite stand against nuclear weapons. He asserted that their very existence posed a challenge to the core of the Christian faith. He recognized that humanity itself was being threatened with global annihilation and yet at the same time he witnessed the comparative silence of the religious leaders. This incongruity caused him to ask in an article published in *Christianity Today*: 'How do you explain the fact that the large Christian bodies cannot pronounce a definite yes or no on the matter of atomic war?'

In 1960, Herman Kahn's major work, *On Thermonuclear War*,

was published. In it, he starkly detailed both Soviet and American nuclear capabilities and the consequences of various nuclear exchanges. Two years later, he wrote a sequel, *Thinking the Unthinkable*, in which he said that the biggest criticism he had received about his previous work was not about its factual assertions concerning the American and Soviet capabilities of annihilating the human race but that the book had been written at all. People, he said, were outraged and offended that he had even brought the subject up.

Two decades have passed since Barth's question and Kahn's stark description of nuclear war, and while various churches have issued encyclicals, adopted position papers, and occasionally even lobbied for cuts in military expenditures, it has amounted to little more than pious chatter. Meanwhile, the spiralling nuclear arms race continues unabated. It is estimated that the two super-powers alone have in their nuclear arsenals the equivalent of five tons of TNT for every man, woman and child on the planet.

Through these nuclear weapons we have created a world of buttons which can be pressed at need, with the underlying assumption that they will not have to be pressed if one threatens clearly enough to press them. Through them we have perverted the very word 'peace' to mean little more than a balance of terror, a terror which has been anaesthetized by a new vocabulary of 'credible first-strike capability', 'limited theatre nuclear forces', 'surgical strikes', 'reciprocal fear of surprise attack', 'calculated pre-emption', and even 'striking second-first'. Nuclear weapons have created a world where chance has all but been squeezed out with fail-safe systems and built-in controls. The new computerization of nuclear weapons technology is even relegating the human factor to near-obsolescence, so that if the end must come, it may well do so not by human decision but by the malfunction of a silicon chip. And yet it is human beings who are fashioning these computers and who have created a world of such suspicion and fear that each side only feels it has ensured its own 'national security' if it has convinced the 'enemy' that it has not only the means but the will to destroy it utterly before it is itself utterly destroyed. Only thus, it is argued, will the nuclear weapons remain unused. Human trust has become so poisoned that it is only out of the thicket of mutual assured destruction that we believe we can pluck the flower of safety.

The danger is so obvious, yet words are inadequate to describe the danger we are in. It is not only that the United States and the Soviet Union seem to be on a collision course and that rational communication between them has broken down; it is that the ultimate sanction behind their conflicting policies is arsenals of such mass destructiveness that were even a fraction of them used, civilization itself, if not planetary life, would be terminated.

Yet perhaps because everything is dangerous, nothing seems frightening, and we have gone on piling weapon upon weapon, missile upon missile, bomber upon bomber until the levels of destructiveness have ceased to be meaningful. Like lemmings rushing to the sea, like children marching to the tunes of the Pied Piper, we have built these arsenals as though we were victims of a compelling nightmare, hypnotized and magnetized by the dreamlike quality of our ability to push all life into the abyss of death.

Unless we can shake ourselves from our fixation with the mask of death, we may well all wear it. The need to act, therefore, to speak out, becomes ever more pressing; yet permeating most of the Christian church is a peculiar psychic paralysis that inhibits meaningful and effective action. This paralysis, I believe, is due to the fact that the church has no conceptual framework within which to interpret the experience of Hiroshima and its aftermath. I shall be arguing that our inherited theistic notion of God is inadequate in a secular world 'come of age', and that the doctrines of the *Summum Bonum* and the *privatio boni*, by which the church has dealt with the problem of evil, are unable to help Christians cope realistically with the overwhelming power of evil confronting them. The nuclear problem, in terms of both atoms for war and atoms for peace, is so new that the theological framework of the past simply cannot comprehend the problem, much less the consequences or solution. What is required is a new conceptualization of both humanity and Divinity to match a phenomenon that is both new in our history and potentially destructive of it. This study is a first step towards the conceptual shifts necessary to enable Christians to come to grips with an issue that threatens not only the existence and future of our species but the planet itself.

We are being confronted in our day with an event inside our historical reality that is at once numinous and revelatory. We are in the midst of Emmanuel, 'God with us', and are being given deeper insights into the ancient truth our tradition has long echoed, that God acts in history to reveal the divine will for our salvation. What I shall be focussing on, therefore, is not so much the threat of species death which the nuclear age implies but the *salvific potential* of the Hiroshima event.

The path to wisdom that Hiroshima challenges us to take is to the good of life itself. We are being summoned to direct our energies, not to the greatest material good of 'our group' at the expense of others, but to the life process itself, which creates and sustains us all. This is to say, we must concentrate upon the creative *source* of life and values rather than upon specific values as they are expressed through the narrow provincialism of a particular group. Although the stakes are global, however, this plea for redirection is not a novel call to a wayward humanity; it is and has been the substance of the Judaeo-Christian tradition. Indeed, it was a fundamental aspect of the mission of Jesus himself to break down the separateness and exclusiveness of the individuals and groups he encountered so that they could be receptive to the kingdom of God and openly responsive to one another. He taught them to love their neighbour as themselves, particularly the neighbour oppressed by the guilt induced by orthodox legalisms and social ostracism. As Henry Wieman puts it, Jesus 'split the atom of human egoism';[1] his presence was like a catalyst inducing creative transformations in the persons who believed in him.

Wieman amplifies this observation concerning Jesus with a note that has striking similarity to the concept we shall be dealing with in relation to Hiroshima:

> The creative transformation power was not in the man Jesus, although it could not have occurred apart from him. Rather he was in it. It required many other things besides his own solitary self. It required the Hebrew heritage, the disciples with their particular capacity for this kind of responsiveness, and doubtless much else of which we have little knowledge. The creative power lay in the *interaction* taking place between these individuals. It transformed their minds, their personalities, their appreciable world, and their community with one another and with all men.[2]

What occurred in the group surrounding Jesus was the elevation of a creative event, happening within the bounds of their history, to a place of dominance and centrality in their lives. They understood and believed the creative event to be Emmanuel, and they were willing to open up the walls of their separateness to the transforming power of Christ and the all-encompassing community of fellow-believers. Their leap of faith was in their willingness to incorporate a newly-enacted historical event within their confessional heritage and in allowing their old modes of understanding to be opened up to the freedom of spirit at work in the new event. They experienced thereby a new dimension of human possibility and could give witness to the fact that the Christ event had produced a new order of human awareness and potentiality.

We are being confronted in our day with the same necessity to transform our old modes of understanding if we are to be saved. We must first of all be willing to recognize that what is occurring is Emmanuel – God with us. To make this leap in consciousness, however, will be as difficult for us today as it was for the Pharisees and Sadducees, steeped and secure as they were in their orthodox legalisms, to make concerning Christ two thousand years ago. Even as the early believers were able to see the handiwork and overall control of God in the midst of the crucifixion and resurrection of Christ so, too, must we be willing to perceive God at work in the atom bomb. This is perhaps the most difficult statement of this entire study, that we must see the handiwork of God in the atom bomb, but I believe it is true.

Hiroshima confronts us as never before with the imperative to take the wrath of God seriously. We must be willing at long last to give up our monopolar prejudice concerning God being merely an expression of the *Summum Bonum* and capable of only love and mercy and 'goodness'. We must recognize that God is the God of all possibilities; that is to say, God utilizes all the instruments of power, including the blinding of those involved in the divine plan, including the deliberate and intentional committing of what we experience as intrinsic evil, and including the ruthless disregard for any claims of covenantal morality. Ultimately what we are witnessing in our day is a great attempt on the part of the Godhead to reveal deeper dimensions of the divine pleroma, and to compel us to explore even more deeply the mystery of Christ crucified.

The second point we must recognize, in order fully to appreciate the Hiroshima event, is that with the power of mass destruction in our hands, we have taken upon ourselves that last category attributed to God in the traditional view: the determination of apocalyptic judgment. What the apocalyptists believed was fixed by the counsel of God and brought to pass by divine will and action alone is now something within the realm of human decision. This means that we must internalize theologically both the terror and the salvation of the traditional Judaeo-Christian concept of apocalypse as something that will not be done *to* us by divine fiat alone, but as something that might well be done *by* us through our own decision, God working divine wrath through our arrogance.

If the termination of the human species is to come, or if the historical process is to be mutated beyond recognition, it is our hands which will push the button, it is our wrath which will condemn us to final judgment, for it is our technology and consciousness which have given us the power of absolute destruction. Hiroshima humanized the eschaton. This is the basic shift I believe we must internalize in order to begin to come to terms with the nuclear age: that the referent for the apocalypse is no longer God alone but humanity as well.

To assert that Hiroshima represents an era of new dimensions of human power, while at the same time asserting that it points us to the darkness of God at work in Christ crucified, may sound contradictory. But it is not: it is complementary. Both are happening simultaneously and must be kept in a dialectical tension if we are to give any sense at all to the claim I shall be setting forth: that the relational encounter between God and humanity is that of co-creation. Both God and humanity cohere relationally in a single event that draws each according to its degree of freedom and affects each according to its respective vulnerability. Hiroshima is the nexus point in our day when God and humanity meet to reveal deeper dimensions within the reality of both. As such, therefore, Hiroshima is numinous, holding forth to the eyes of faith the ambiguity involved in all creative events.

I shall proceed to examine these areas, as well as to clarify and substantiate in greater detail the assertions I have made concerning the numinosity of Hiroshima, in the following steps:

1. In order to assert that God acts in our midst, I must delineate an ontology of God. I examine the possibilities for an ontology within the context of philosophical theology. I shall present those aspects of our confessional heritage which I believe are essential to a Christian ontology, particularly the notions of God as having both cosmic and historical dimensions; of God as creative; and of God as One who acts in our history to affect our salvation (Chapter II).

I bring these claims into a synthesis with the modern philosophical assertions of process thought. I shall argue that process thought articulates affirmations about the God of our forebears in a way that is acceptable to a secular world come of age while at the same time not abrogating the distinctive claims of the Christian faith. I explicate this ontology under the term *process panentheism* (Chapter III). It is an ontology that understands God as a dual transcendence; God and the world as integral to one another; God and humanity as joined together in a co-creative relationship that impinges upon and changes both; and God and humanity as possessing both light and dark dimensions.

Correlative with an ontology of God is an ontology of divine events. I shall articulate a *hermeneutic of engagement* that sees divine events as the confluence of certain historical events judged to be numinous, with the confessional witness of the believing community. In terms of this study, the historical event will be the Hiroshima event, and the category within the confessional witness upon which it impinges that of apocalyptic, that area of Christian belief dealing with the 'end of time'.

2. I shall then examine both the Hiroshima event (Chapter IV) and the classical Judaeo-Christian assertions concerning the Apocalypse (Chapter V).

3. The synthesis of Hiroshima and apocalyptic will occupy the major portion of this work. As Hiroshima has humanized the eschaton, I shall explore the human *psyche* itself in order to gain further insight into those forces within us that bear on war and peace (Chapter VI). What we shall discover is that it is within the psyche that God affects us directly; that our images of God are formed; and that our work of co-creation with God takes shape. My examination of human psychic life will be done through the empirical methodology of Jungian depth psychology, which in its description of the psyche offers a way not only into understanding the tensions within both the Godhead and humanity that *produced* Hiroshima, but also into a new understanding of the relation between Divinity and humanity that may point us towards a *solution* to the crisis Hiroshima is compelling us to face.

I should like to make two points before proceeding. The first concerns my understanding of philosophical theology. I shall draw freely from the Christian tradition as well as from modern process and panentheistic thinking and depth psychology. I have been careful not to superimpose the biblical tradition upon our modern world view; nor have I taken process thought or depth psychology as more normative than the biblical tradition. Rather, I have attempted to present both as variables in an understanding that sees the 'givenness' of Christianity as something that must be qualified. Philosophical theology seeks a relational synthesis between the distinctive claims of the Christian faith and the assertions of modern philosophical and scientific theory. This relational synthesis must at all times remain in creative tension. To do this requires the awareness that true tension only exists between two things which are internally related. If there is no relation, there is only dichotomy and compartmentalization, an error made all too frequently in the history of both theology and philosophy in their perceptions of each other. My use of philosophical theology assumes the internal relatedness between scripture and the modern world.

The second point I wish to make is that this work is not a systematically worked-out theological discourse. It is much more the subjective confession of a young man who has realized he may well be part of the last generation of human beings to inhabit this earth. In some ways, therefore, the chapter on the Hiroshima event and the advent of nuclear weapons (Chapter IV) should be read first, as the magnitude of what nuclear weapons mean forced me to come to terms with the vicariousness of life. The terror and the hope this thought has instilled within me, both in my dreams and waking reflections, have opened my eyes not only to seeing the scriptures anew but to those aspects of contemporary thought which can inform both scripture and human survival.

My endeavour to understand has humbled me. I have learned that to seek God is like holding a light in the darkness. As the light increases, the circumference of the darkness also expands. The more light, therefore, the more darkness. The more we know God, the more of God there is to know, thus making anything we say of only momentary significance, like the flicker of a candle against the vastness of the night.

II

The Inherited Tradition

As I mentioned in the Introduction, there are two aspects of the Christian tradition in particular which are integral to the psychic paralysis the church seems to be trapped in today in the face of nuclear war. The first is our inherited theistic notions concerning God; the second is the doctrines of the *Summum Bonum* and *privatio boni*. In an era when history has entered the Age of Overkill Christians have not had a concept of God relevant to the secular world; nor have they had an adequate concept of the reality of evil to aid them in dealing with the overwhelming presence of evil that nuclear weapons represent.

Without undue elaboration I shall examine these two areas. They will be briefly stated here, for as the thesis unfolds each will be dealt with in greater depth and detail.

A. THE PROBLEM OF GOD IN THE MODERN AGE

What we are concerned with is *Heilsgeschichte*, with the witness of the believing community to the actions of God in history.

To speak of a God who acts in our history today, however, is fraught with difficulties. The history of thought between the times of the biblical writers and the present century has been a long and tortuous one, and many of the assumptions made then – particularly concerning a God who was completely distinct from and unaffected by the creation, who ruled over history as a feudal monarch – are no longer tenable in an age of scientific rationalism. As Arnold E. Loen states the matter: 'Formerly, man was conscious of living in a world whose order pointed to God and in which God acted directly. Today that is no longer true; we are neither conscious of God in the cosmic order nor of his direct activity.'[1]

Modern discussion concerning the absence of God has not come about *de novo* but is the product of centuries of realignment in human self-perception in the West, a realignment which Dietrich Bonhoeffer asserted began in the thirteenth century. Perhaps the most important catalyst in this change has been the Enlightenment; indeed, Heinz Zahrnt asserts that the primary reason why the question of God is so radicalized in our day is due to the fact that 'the final and ultimate encounter between the Enlightenment and Christian faith has come about'.[2] The Enlightenment has claimed many victims, he says, 'but the greatest and most notable was God. Because he was the greatest, and the loftiest, he fell the furthest.' As de Lubac puts it: 'We have witnessed during the last few centuries the rationalistic evaporation of God.'[3]

The Enlightenment has been summarized perhaps most succinctly by Kant in his essay 'What is the Enlightenment?' In it he stated that it fundamentally concerned 'man's leaving behind the immaturity for which he himself was to blame'. The challenge now, he said, was for each person 'to make use of his reason without anyone else's guidance'.[4] The impact of this perspective, as with the rest of Kant's thinking, has been enormous. According to Nicholas Berdyaev, the importance of Kant's contribution to the Enlightenment lies in the fact that he 'makes an end of the metaphysics of the naturalistic rationalistic type, metaphysics which are derived from the *object*, from the world, and he reveals the possibility of metaphysics based on the *subject*, of a metaphysics of freedom.'[5] It is precisely Kant, he says, who 'makes existential metaphysics a possibility'.

This shift from a naturalistic rationalistic metaphysic to one much more subjective and hence existential has been known more generally as the process of secularization. It has been due not so much to an intentional revolt against God or the old metaphysic as to a movement in human thought which has gradually extended the horizons of knowledge and understanding to the point where God is no longer a necessary category of explanation for what happens in the world.

The world view of classical religion understood that God was the *causa prima*, the first cause, of everything in the world. This first cause was encountered within what took place in the natural world in the form of *causae secundae*, i.e. God was mediated in the world by secondary causes. After the Enlightenment science extended the causal nexus to all phenomena, thereby 'explaining' the world in a 'natural' way and without recourse to an external agent. God was therefore forced out of the dimensions of secondary causes and forced to lose ground in the areas of human society and natural existence. As science has progressed and explained more and more by empirical observation and logical deductions, functions formerly fulfilled by God are being increasingly emptied of divine content. The *causae secundae* have simply become autonomous, resulting in what Max Weber has called the 'disenchanting of the world'[6] and the creation of a world view in which the *prima causa*, the Divine itself, is no longer discernible.

The process of secularization has been the result of a whole series of different but related factors. Perhaps of paramount importance was the effect of the Copernican Revolution, which removed the earth from being the centre of the universe. The paradoxical result of this was to make the human being the new referent, an anthropocentric revolution symbolized most profoundly by Descartes' famous phrase *cogito ergo sum*. If the only support one can find to confirm his or her existence is the act of thinking, then it follows that any truth discerned in the rest of existence is relative to the human subject knowing that truth. All truth in the Cartesian schema, therefore, must be submitted to human judgment, a process in which direct common-sense experience is amplified by conscious reflection. It is a process, too, in which any discussion concerning God is not believed because 'the Bible tells me so' but because it accords with human subjective judgment. The Enlightenment, therefore, began a process in which humanity no longer felt the need to justify itself before God; it was God who had to justify the Divine existence to humanity.

This shift has had a direct impact on almost all metaphysical thinking in the West. Prior to the Enlightenment, both practical and theoretical knowledge was predicated upon the assumption of a cosmic dualism derived from a synthesis of Hellenic and Judaeo-Christian thought. In this world view there stand in polarity two distinct worlds, each thought of as possessing substantial existence: the supernatural and the natural, the spiritual and the physical, the heavenly and the earthly, the Ideal and the concrete. Although there were numerous different and contradictory beliefs and schools of thought concerning this duality of existence, it was generally agreed that the higher, supernatural, spiritual realm was somehow transcendently better, somehow more real than our physical, natural, terrestrial world below. The process of secularization, however, has largely dissolved the 'higher' realm, absorbing it within the 'lower' one – which is now the only realm accepted as real. Hegel spoke for many when he wrote: 'Apart from some earlier attempts, it has been reserved in the main for our epoch to vindicate at least in theory the human ownership of the treasures formerly squandered on heaven.'[7]

Perhaps the most direct result of the Enlightenment and subsequent secularization has been in terms of a revolution in authority. Prior to the Enlightenment, authority was understood by and large as being handed over horizontally (paradosis) from the early Christian fathers and/or being handed down vertically by God through revelation – God and the church fathers generally being understood as in agreement. The Enlightenment subjected this schema to comprehensive scrutiny and much of it has dissolved and been replaced by an understanding of truth as historically conditioned and therefore mutable. This anthropocentric and subjective understanding of truth and authority has had the consequence of laying stress on the concepts of relativization and pluralism and on a corollary call for tolerance. As Lessing put it: 'Religion is not true because the evangelists taught it, they taught it because it is true. Written traditions must be explained on the basis of the inner truth of religion, and all written traditions are incapable of giving it truth if it possesses none.'[8]

This refusal to believe in something merely because of a claim of divine inspiration or ecclesiastical authority has resulted in a state, according to Karl Jaspers, in which 'no one who speaks of God does so in an official capacity, but speaks on the same level as anyone else, with no claim to authority, and counting only on the human power to convince'.[9]

The revolution in religious authority has been accelerated by criticisms of religion coming from the social, economic and ideological spheres. As science destroyed the concept of a heaven above with a patriarchal God penetrating into 'his' vassal state, so the Marxist critique, done via a penetrating economic and social analysis, came to the conclusion that religion was not even being helpful in the world below; it was rather an 'opiate' that needed to be discarded if the peoples were to liberate themselves. This critique was made all the more devastating by Ludwig Feuerbach's assertion that 'theology is anthropology, that there is no distinction between the *predicates* of the divine and human nature, and, consequently, no distinction between the divine and human *subject*'.[10] This means, he said, that in the final analysis, 'religion, at least the Christian, is the relation of man to himself', an understanding which implies a concept of God as the product of human projection:

The divine being is nothing else than the human being, or, rather the human nature purified, freed from the limits of the individual man, made objective – i.e. contemplated and revered as another, a distinct being. All the attributes of the divine nature are, therefore, attributes of the human nature.[11]

What began to be seen of religion, then, was its anthropological character. While asserted to be from God, it was, in many dimensions at least, a manifestation of a particular culture or attribute of human nature. In our century the most forceful proponent of this viewpoint has been Sigmund Freud, who in *Future of an Illusion* argued that the image people hold of God is generally formed and structured by their experience of and need for a father figure.

The challenge of secularization is as serious as it is because for many people, theologians included, the general scientific method enunciated during the Enlightenment and since is not only the sole means of obtaining knowledge about the world as disclosed by our senses, it is the only method there is for obtaining any knowledge at all. The classic expression of this outlook goes back to David Hume's famous passage in *Enquiry Concerning Human Understanding* that all meaningful statements are either tautologies of formal logic and mathematics or putative statements of fact that can be proven or falsified by ordinary sense experience. Known generally as logical positivism, this method restricts all knowledge of reality to the general type of knowledge of which modern science is the refined and developed form.

Although widely criticized and reformulated, this attitude is still widely accepted and assumed in theological debate. For many, the issue is no longer whether theological statements can be made which do not conflict with science, but whether theological statements can be made at all. The reasoning followed is that if scientific knowledge is the only knowledge there is, then the claims of theology, in so far as they cannot be scientifically verified, cannot claim cognitive meaning. Such an attitude can be called 'secularistic' to distinguish it from the 'secular', which accepts the possibility of speaking in theological terms about God, albeit within contemporary modes of thought.

The secularistic outlook prompted several theologians in the beginning of this century to attempt a 'theology without God', most notably George Santayana, John Dewey, and Henry Wieman. Because a secularistic assumption was made, either openly or tacitly, the affirmation of God simply had to be surrendered in order to construct an acceptable theology. The result of this line of thinking in recent decades has been to take secularistic thinking to its logical conclusion: that 'God is dead'. By this is not meant a merely transitory subjectively experiential awareness of divine concealment but rather a public event rooted in historical space/time. Asserting that we are in a 'post-Christian era',[12] Gabriel Vahanian writes:

> The death of God is not an intellectual cry of merely iconoclastic value . . . God's absence, or the death of God itself, has become what a man directly experiences. It is no longer a theoretical declaration; it is a practical awareness by which authentic existence . . . is measured . . . God is dead, not in sheer intellectual scaffoldings, but in the down-to-earth give and take of the human condition.[13]

Thomas Altizer asserts the death of God for theological reasons, positing that the transcendent Deity literally dies with the incarnation of Jesus Christ. He writes:

> It is precisely because the movement of the Incarnation has now become manifest in every human hand and face, dissolving even the memory of God's original transcendent life and redemptive power, that there can no longer be either a truly contemporary movement to transcendence or an active and living faith in the transcendent God.[14]

Although refusing the label of a 'death of God' theologian, Paul M. van Buren has perhaps given the secularistic position clearest articulation. Emphasizing secular Christianity from the perspective of linguistic analysis, van Buren asserts that he wrote *The Secular Meaning of the Gospel*

> by a frankly empirical method which reflects the thinking of an industrialized, scientific age. It has taken certain attitudes characteristic of modern thought seriously and accepted them without qualification.[15]

Open about his debt to Hume, van Buren says that 'the empiricist in us finds the heart of the difficulty not in what is said about God, but in the very talking about God.'[16]

Although he goes on to assure us that the elimination of God from the gospel does no violence to the 'real' meaning of the Christian witness, I concur with Ogden's comment that 'faith in God of a certain kind is not merely an element in Christian faith along with several others; it simply *is* Christian faith, the heart of the matter itself'.[17] The very dynamic, therefore, which makes a secular interpretation of the Bible and the Christian tradition possible also makes a secularistic one impossible: 'The issue here is indeed either/ or, and all talk of a Christianity *post mortem dei* is in the last analysis, neither hyperbole nor evidence of originality but merely nonsense.'[18]

Besides it being nonsense, I believe the secularistic theologians have missed the entire point of secularism. It is not that God has been killed or died but that we are being forced to look for God somewhere else – *that* is what the Enlightenment adds up to. The only thing dead about God is our *image* of God. Karl Rahner is most insightful on this point:

> Because the world as a whole, while expressing *itself*, only speaks silently of God by leaving unsaid the ultimate word which is proper to it, it is possible to miss hearing this call of silence, it is possible to think that God cannot be found because one always encounters more of the world the further one's investigation penetrates into it. In reality, however, this experience is not the genesis of atheism, but the discovery that the world is not God.[19]

Calling the glib atheism of the secularistic theologians 'unpardonably naive' and the product of 'mass psychosis and a dogma of militant political *Weltanschauung'*, Rahner is much more concerned by the 'troubled atheism' of our day, an honest contemplation, he says, resulting from

> alarm at the absence of God from the world, the feeling of no longer being able to realize the divine, consternation at the silence of God, at God shutting himself up in his own inaccessibility, at the senseless secularization *(Profanwerden)* of the world, at the sightless and faceless materiality of the laws of the world up to the point where it is no longer merely a question of nature but of man – this experience which imagines that it must interpret itself theoretically as atheism, is a genuine experience of deepest existence . . . [20]

To the 'troubled atheist' Rahner urges not a rejection of God but an alternative perception of reality based upon the

> realization that God does not belong within the world-view, that the real God is not a Demiurge, that he is not the spring in the clockwork of the world, that wherever anything happens in the world which forms part of the 'normal' make-up of the world it is

always possible to discover for it a cause which is not God himself.[21]

As Buber observes, the problem is not God but in our relationship to God. Using the metaphor 'eclipse of God', he explains: 'An eclipse of the sun is something that takes place between the sun and our eyes, not in the sun itself.'[22] What we lack, he says, is 'only the spiritual orientation which will make possible a reappearance of "God and the gods", a new procession of sublime images', a point that has been taken up by several theologians seeking to explore beyond logical positivism. Much more honest, then, than the 'God is dead' theologians and the secularistic thinkers is someone such as the late Ronald Gregor Smith, who struggled to the end of his life with the question of God. A secular theologian to be sure who categorically rejected classical theism, particularly the notion of an impassible God transcendently impenetrable beyond our historical vicissitudes, he nevertheless did not negate God. In *The Doctrine of God*, left unfinished at his death, he wrote: 'The real audacity does not consist in declaring that God is dead but in daring at all to take that name on our lips.'[23]

The challenge of secularism must be met by realizing that secularism is the contemporary expression of a centuries-old reaction in the West against a particular metaphysical-theological tradition in Christianity. Although its negations are stark and seemingly unqualified, what makes it seem far from arbitrary is its critique of a very specific theism that has characterized Christian orthodoxy. This has been a theism whose 'crowning achievement', according to Ogden, 'is a supernaturalistic theism uniquely combining elements of classical Greek philosophy with religious insights derived from the Hebraic-Christian scriptures'.[24]

Tillich called this concept of God 'supranaturalism', a concept in which God is understood as the highest Being, existing individually, uniquely and independently of creation. Tillich himself speaks finally of a 'God above God' but he rejects in quite categorical terms the traditional theistic notions about God. This theistic notion 'must be transcended', he argues, 'because it is wrong. It is bad theology.'[25]

I agree with Tillich's assessment of traditional theism but I do not concur with his conclusion that it is wrong because it is bad theology. I prefer to view theism within the context offered by C. A. van Peursen, for whom the theistic concept of God falls within the ontological period of human thought, one of three ways, he says, in which humans have attempted to understand themselves and the rest of reality.[26]

The first way that humanity understood God was mythically, in which the inner and outer worlds were understood as continuous and interpenetrating. The second way was ontologically, in which reality was divided between natural and supernatural, subject from object. It was a system of categorization in which God and ethical values were given the status of ontological beings or were understood as eternal substances. Both classical physics and traditional theology fall within this category. Van Peursen points to a third way, however, which he asserts is more in tune with modern conceptions, namely that of functionalism, in which substances and supernatural entities are eliminated, and things are what they *do* or are understood by what can be done *with* them. Reality is seen not as a series of ontological substances but as a process of events interacting relationally. Within functionalism, God cannot be understood as a metaphysically distinct entity.

Theism, therefore, must be transcended rather than rejected. It must be transcended because it is not meaningful in terms of the scientific and philosophical structures through which twentieth-century humanity understands itself. Theism was a product of a world view articulated in the Graeco-Roman world where ontological categories were accepted as normative. The givens of our day, however, are the concepts of a world and humanity in evolving process. Our referent is much more 'becoming' rather than 'being', and therefore we conceive of the world and God in functional rather than ontological terms.

Because it is widely assumed that the reality of God stands or falls with traditional theism, to reject theism in the name of secularity has seemed to many to leave us with little but secularism itself. To abandon a system of thought, however, is not to abandon God. As de Lubac puts it,

Whenever it abandons a system of thought, humanity imagines it has lost God.

The God of 'classical ontology' is dead you say? It may be so; but it does not concern me overmuch. I have no inclination to defend the petrified constructions of Wolf. And if 'classical ontology' disappeared it was surely because it did not correspond adequately with being. Nor was its idea of God adequate for God. The mind is alive and so is the God who makes himself known to it.

'God is dead!' or so at least it seems to us . . . until, round the next bend of the road, 'we find him again, alive'. Once again he makes himself known, in spite of all we have left behind on the road, all that was only a viaticum for one stage of our journey, all that was only a temporary shelter till we had to make a fresh start . . .

God is never left behind among the dross . . . In whatever direction we go, he is there before us, calling to us and coming to meet us . . .[27]

What we must do now, then, given that the supernaturalistic conception of divine reality is no longer tenable, is to attempt an articulation that endeavours to be faithful both to the Christian faith and to a 'world come of age'. However, this challenge puts theology between an irresistible force and an immovable object. The irresistible force is the situation in which humanity finds itself: a secular age whose experience has been formed by the absence of the God of traditional theism; the immovable object is the message the church must proclaim if it is to remain Christian: that God is a God who not only is but also acts in history for our salvation. 'Ultimately,' says Zahrnt, 'both elements take the form of the question of the *content of reality* in belief in God', a task of two dimensions: theology 'must show the present day that God is *real*, and it must go on to speak credibly of this reality.'[28]

The problem we face in our day, therefore, is the problem of articulating statements about God in a way that is both intelligible to contemporary norms and consistent with the biblical witness. As Rahner puts it, the critical question is

. . . whether the church can so faithfully testify to the redeeming and fulfilling presence of that ineffable mystery whom we call God that the men of the age of technology, who have already made so many advances toward control of their world and destiny, can experience the power of this unspeakable mystery in their lives.[29]

In order to speak of God in a way in which modern humanity can experience the power of this 'unspeakable mystery', it is fundamental that we dispense with classical theism while remaining grounded in the biblical witness. This will be difficult because for centuries the notions of classical theism were considered to *be* the biblical witness. However, the God of the Bible is much more alive and versatile than the straitjacket of theism allows for. Dispensing with theism will allow us to return to the Bible and see deeper and more profound dimensions of the God we worship. What I wish to draw attention to before proceeding, therefore, is certain themes enunciated by the Judaeo-Christian confessional witness which will remain constant, for they form part of the distinctive claim of the Christian faith. This is to say that they can be reworked but not dispensed with.

What emerges as basic to the concept of God the Hebrews developed, and which the Christians later amplified, is that their God is at once the Cosmic Creator of heaven and earth and also inseparably linked with human history. Christians believe God is the Creator of the universe, the Sustainer of the world, the One who put the stars and the dawns in their places; Christians also believe that this Cosmic Creator is intimately involved with the details of human affairs, even to reside in the human heart. The importance of this is that the historical element gives the cosmic dimension placement in 'time'.

The Hebrews saw the connection between these two dimensions in terms of the Cosmogonic Creator being synonymous with the God of their forebears, Abraham, Isaac and Jacob. For them, God was an eminently social God who had made a covenant with them, the chosen people. The Christians believed that the nexus was between God and a chosen child within the chosen people, believing that in this child, Jesus, God had made a new covenant with humanity. What is clear for Judaeo-Christianity as a whole is that both aspects, the cosmic and the historical, are essential for any comprehensive ontology of God.

A second element in the Judaeo-Christian belief concerning God is in terms of divine creativity. 'In the beginning God created . . .' are the opening words of the scriptures, an understanding inherent even in the name 'Yahweh'.[30] God created the heavens and the earth; God created humankind; and God has been creatively active in human history even since – redeeming the people of Israel from Egypt, making the covenant with them at Sinai, leading them through the vicissitudes of their history to the promised land, exiling them for their disobedience, forgiving them and bringing them again to Israel, finally becoming incarnate in their midst as Christ Jesus.

The creative activity of God in history is not limited to working salvifically only amongst the chosen people. God works the divine will in all nations both to lift up and to destroy. This point is brought out most forcefully by Isaiah when he prophesies concerning the Lord's punishment of Israel. It is clear to the prophet that Assyria is a tool in the hands of God:

> Ah, Assyria, the rod of my anger,
>   the staff of my fury!
> Against a godless nation I send him,
> and against the people of my wrath I command him,
>   to take spoil and seize plunder,
> and to tread them down like the mire of the streets. (Isa. 10.5,6)

Isaiah is quick to point out that although Assyria is being used by God, Assyria is unaware of it. The Assyrians think they are defeating Israel by their own power, saying:

> By the strength of my hand I have done it,
>   and by my wisdom, for I have understanding. (13a)

Therefore, prophesies Isaiah, when the Lord has finished using Assyria to punish Israel, the Assyrians will in turn be punished for their 'arrogant boasting' and 'haughty pride'. (12)

> Shall the axe vaunt itself over him who hews with it,
>   or the saw magnify itself against him who wields it?
> As if a rod should wield him who lifts it,
>   or as if a staff should lift him who is not wood! (15)

God is sovereign over history, working the divine will creatively in our midst. It is a creative activity with both light and shadow dimensions before which the believers can only kneel in awe, filled with both reverence and trembling.

These themes will be greatly amplified as we proceed, for they must be understood if we are to perceive the handiwork of God in the atomic bombing of Hiroshima. What is important for our purposes here is to make clear that the assertion that God acts in history is the cornerstone of any Judaeo-Christian ontology of God.

Indeed, according to G. E. Wright in his book, *God Who Acts*, 'Biblical theology is a theology of recital or proclamation of the acts of God, together with the inferences drawn therefrom.'[31] This same point is emphasized by John Baillie:

> . . . one of the points in which there appears a remarkable breadth of agreement in recent discussion . . . is this: that God reveals himself *in action* – in the gracious activity by which he invades the field of human experience and human history . . . The Bible is essentially the story of the acts of God.[32]

What the Bible records, therefore, is the ongoing actions of a God who in different times and in different ways reveals deeper dimensions of the divine will for human history.

Two themes emerge, then, as fundamental to the Judaeo-Christian understanding of God: first that God works in both the cosmic and historical dimensions; and second, that God is creatively present and active in history to reveal ever deeper insights into the divine pleroma and to lead believers towards a deeper relationship with God.

These themes transcend the notions of theism and form the cornerstone to any Christian ontology of God. Because the God of theism is dead, however, these themes must be reworked anew and in a way that stays true to the distinctive claims of Judaeo-Christianity while remaining relevant to a secular world.

I shall offer such an ontology in the next chapter under the term 'process panentheism'. I use this term because I shall be drawing upon process thinking, which exemplifies van Peursen's category of functionalism most accurately, and upon the theological notion of panentheism, which sees God and the world as integral to one another but not synonymous. I shall expand this notion as to its psychological amplifications in Chapter VI with the depth psychology of Jung.

B. THE DOCTRINES OF THE *Summum Bonum* AND *privatio boni*

We have discussed the fact that because of the demise of theism in the modern era, Christians have not had an adequate concept of God to bear witness to. They also have not had an adequate concept of the objective reality of evil. This has been due to the traditional doctrines of the *Summum Bonum* and *privatio boni*, which, like theism, were developed in a world far removed from the present crisis of possible extinction through thermonuclear war.

Before discussing these doctrines, however, it is necessary to define what we mean by evil.

1. Evil defined

1. When the general term 'evil' is used it refers to that which either intends or causes destruction, decay, chaos, suffering or unhappiness in the world.

2. Writers commonly make a distinction between 'moral' evil and 'natural' evil, although different writers make different distinctions between these terms. Some draw the distinction between evil intended and evil undergone. 'Moral' evil is seen to refer to evil intention; 'natural' evil refers to all the suffering in the world. John

Hick bases the distinction upon the type of agent involved.[33] For him, 'moral' evil refers to that evil resulting from the misuse of rational freedom. It includes not only evil intentions but the effects of these intentions. Moral evil is understood as sin. 'Natural' evil refers to all evil done by non-moral agents. Writers who follow Hick's distinctions generally posit with him an absolute distinction between those agents possessing self-determining freedom and those who do not.

3. These definitions would appear to exclude evil from the deliberate intention of God. It is clear from Isaiah 45.7 that God creates evil; from Amos 4.6–12 and Revelation *passim* that God uses famine, drought and plague to work the divine will; and from Isaiah 10 that God commits moral evil through the use of the nations. God creates and uses moral evil; and yet God does not sin.

This paradox necessitates a re-evaluation of the traditional distinctions, including those of Hick. For my purposes, I will distinguish between evil done by the human ego and evil done by God or the Self, a point that will be taken up at length in Chapter VI. Moral evil is sin when it results from the misuse of rational freedom; however, it is ultimately creative when it is used by God for a greater good.

4. My use of the term 'evil' is based on the affirmation that evil is objectively and intrinsically real. Taking seriously the profound and startling assertion of Isaiah 45.7 that God creates evil, a strand of thought that runs throughout the scripture but is not easily assimilated into traditional theological concepts, I hold that evil, like good, comes from God and therefore is an objectively real phenomenon.

5. Intrinsic evil is invariably used instrumentally by God for a creative purpose. However, this does not negate the totally destructive reality of the intrinsic evil. Although some writers argue that when intrinsic evil is used instrumentally it is only 'apparent' or 'prima facie' evil,[34] I wish to stress the genuinely real character of the intrinsic evil: i.e., when evil occurs, it is just as objectively real as when good occurs. That intrinsic evil can be used instrumentally, therefore, should not be taken to mean that it becomes only apparently evil in the sense that it has no objective reality.

6. I am not here trying to resolve the mystery of the origin of evil. Rather, I am saying that the instant the mystery of iniquity begins to work in and through history, God is also at work – causally and instrumentally – so that the three strands – divine evil, the moral evil of human sin and the creative intention of God – are inextricably interwoven into a single whole. The crucifixion of Christ is a clear example, that indeed lies at the heart of my whole argument, of an

event simultaneously ordained and explicitly caused by God (Mark 14.21,27,36), brought about by human sin[35] and creatively transformed by God. It is a function of wisdom, given by the Holy Spirit, to learn slowly and painfully to discern between these strands.

2. *The doctrines of the* Summum Bonum *and* privatio boni

There is an enormous body of literature on these doctrines elsewhere, perhaps the most comprehensive recent study being John Hick's *Evil and the God of Love*.[36] My purpose here is to present only the essential content of these doctrines. Much more important is the critique of them which will follow as my argument develops. I will be arguing that they are deficient both in their refusal to acknowledge the genuine reality of evil and in their denial of a shadow dimension to God.

Because it was believed in the orthodox interpretation that the person of Christ reflected the complete manifestation of God, God could only be thought of as the *Summum Bonum*, i.e., God is totally perfect and good even as Christ manifested God to be. The corollary to this doctrine was that of the *privatio boni*, first propounded by Origen, who deprived evil of substance, characterizing it as a mere diminution of good.[37] The logic was simple: if God was total being, perfect being, then evil could not have its own existence outside the divine pleroma; it must be seen not as having substantive reality of its own but as being wherever good was not.

Irenaeus also embraced the doctrine of the *Summum Bonum*, stating in his refutation of the Gnostics that it was scandalous and reprehensible to suppose that within the pleroma of light there could be a 'dark and formless void'.[38] Neither God nor Christ could be a paradox; both must be pure light, primarily because of the fact that Jesus as the incarnation of God had manifested pure light. If Christ was pure light, without blemish, then God must be pure light, without blemish. This led to the axiom articulated by Tatian in the second century: '*Omne bonum a Deo, omne malum ab homine*;' i.e., 'Nothing evil was created by God; we ourselves have produced all wickedness.'[39]

As with the other Fathers, Augustine balances the doctrine of the *Summum Bonum* with that of the *privatio boni*, stating that 'those things we call evil . . . are defects in good things, and quite incapable of existing in their own right outside good things . . . Evil therefore is nothing but the privation of good.'[40]

Thomas Aquinas carried this tradition forward and with Augustine defined evil in generally negative terms, although he defined with a great deal more precision the Augustinian terms 'deprivation' and 'defect'; moreover, he was clearer than most concerning evil being a fact of existence.[41] For Aquinas, evil is 'the absence of the good which is natural and due to a thing'; therefore, 'evil is not a being, whereas good is a being'.[42]

The logic used is that

> good is everything appetible; and thus, since every nature desires its own being and its own perfection, it must necessarily be said that the being and perfection of every created thing is essentially good. Hence it cannot be that evil signifies a being, or any form or nature. Therefore it must be that the name of evil is signified by the absence of good.[43]

In this logic, Aquinas recalls the assertion of Aristotle in his *Topics*, that 'the thing is whiter, the less it is mixed with black'.[44] It is upon this metaphysical analysis that Aquinas constructs his theodicy, i.e., his defence of the righteousness of God in the face of the reality of evil.[45]

Roman Catholic writings since Aquinas generally have followed closely in the Thomist tradition, at least those writings of any kind of official standing. A contemporary representative of this is Abbé Charles Journet's *The Meaning of Evil*, which is quite explicit in stating that the notion of the *privatio boni*

> represents the most delicate and penetrating intellectual handling of evil which the mind can attain to, either on the metaphysical or theological plane. Evil is accorded a great deal of room, so that it can be seen to its full extent, and at the same time the metaphysical poverty of evil is laid bare. But with the affirmation that evil exists, yet lacks any substance, comes the triumph over the dilemma to which those succumb who either deny the reality of evil because of God's goodness and infinite power, or deny God's goodness and infinite power because of the reality of evil.[46]

The Augustinian tradition has been dominant also in Reformed and contemporary Protestant thought. Luther and Calvin both regarded Augustine as representative of the highest wisdom of the church before it 'succumbed' to the taint of mediaeval Scholasticism, although as Hick points out, they were Augustinian on the Pauline as opposed to the Neo-Platonic side of his thought.[47] Because of this, Hick suggests, owing to the fact that they had no contemporary heresy on the subject such as had confronted Augustine in Manichaeanism, Reformation theology had no general theory of the nature of evil as far as the problem of theodicy was concerned.[48] What they did emphasize, Calvin especially, was the Augustinian notion of the fall and depravity of humanity within a rather rigid concept of predestination. It was left to the eighteenth-century 'optimists' to revive the more philosophical aspects of the Augustinian theodicy, which had been carried over from antiquity via Neo-Platonism and articulated in the seventeenth century by the Cambridge Platonists.[49]

Like modern Catholic thought, contemporary Protestant thinking has by and large kept within the bounds of the doctrines of the *Summum Bonum* and the *privatio boni*. Hick calls these doctrines the 'majority report' of the Christian analysis of the problem of evil.[50]

Despite this 'majority report', I believe that the notions of the *Summum Bonum* and the *privatio boni* as traditionally articulated are not only a great hindrance to any attempt to appreciate truly the dimensions of the present world crisis but are not even fairly reflective of the biblical tradition itself. Furthermore, I believe that there is a clearly thought out, albeit less widespread, alternative tradition within Christianity which takes evil seriously as an objective reality and which does so not only because human experience demands it but also because the biblical tradition supports it.

The general points I shall be making concerning this alternative understanding are the following.

I wish to separate the notion of the *Summum Bonum* from that of the *privatio boni*, for the doctrine of the *privatio boni* deprived evil of its objective reality. Taking evil to be objectively real and as something created and used by God calls for a re-interpretation of the *Summum Bonum*. I realize that to say on the one hand that God creates evil (Isa. 45.7) and on the other that God is ultimately good, presents us with a seemingly insoluble contradiction. But while logically paradoxical, it expresses a profound element in the human experience of God and thereby opens up to us a fundamental insight: that God as experienced is antinomial.

Father Sergius Bulgakov defines antinomy thus:

> An antinomy simultaneously admits the truth of two contradictory, logically incompatible, but ontologically equally necessary assertions. An antinomy testifies to the existence of a mystery beyond which human reason cannot penetrate. This mystery nevertheless is actualized and lived in religious experience.[51]

This is to say that it is indeed true that 'God is light' as John 1.5

states; however, it is equally true that when this light is refracted through the 'prism' of human experience, it is composed of all the colours. The analogy is incomplete in that a prism does not refract black or darkness; nor does it yield the antinomial paradoxes that I shall argue are inherent in the experience of God. Nevertheless, it does offer a hint of how something can be both one thing (God as Supreme Good) and another (God as antinomial).

The emphasis here is upon the *experience* of God, for in the final analysis to assert Divinity as it is in itself to be the *Summum Bonum* is a statement of faith. I take Kant's point, and that of the modern physicists, that we cannot know the *Ding an sich* but only as it is mediated through our *a priori* categories of cognition.[52] To speak of God as the *Summum Bonum* is to articulate the metaphysical implications of our image of God, which are deduced from and shaped by experience and the necessity of human logic.

To say that God as experienced is antinomial is to say that God as experienced has been shown to possess light and dark dimensions and to be as savage and terrible as God is merciful and forgiving. The goodness of God, therefore, is not to be seen only in terms of the pure light and unblemished perfection of the person of Christ. Rather, the doctrine of the *Summum Bonum* is much more to be seen in the fact that God *creatively integrates* all aspects of reality, both the good and the evil, into an overall salvific unity. While possessing light and dark dimensions, therefore, God's will is ultimately benevolent, not malevolent.

This interpretation of the *Summum Bonum* requires an immense act of faith that in the power of God for life humanity can confront, integrate and transcend the evil willed by God and humanity alike. This faith is based on the experience of Christ crucified and risen and on the fleeting occasions of actual human experience, including, as we shall see, the experience of some of the survivors of Hiroshima and Nagasaki.

By using the terms 'creative integration' and 'salvific unity' to describe what I mean by the *Summum Bonum* I wish to stress that I am not trying to state a metaphysical ultimate. Rather, I am describing a process in which we are engaged and in which we experience the dynamic presence and leading of God. It is a process in which we experience the grace of God leading us inexorably towards an ever deeper and mutual co-inherence of God and humanity in Christ crucified.

The phrase in Colossians 3.3, that 'your life is hid with Christ in God' points towards what I shall mean by God being the *Summum*

Bonum. So, too, the words of Jesus in John 14.23, that 'If a man love me, he will keep my words: and my Father will love him, and we will come unto him, and make our abode with him.'

This co-inherence of humanity with God will be amplified in the discussion of process panentheism and depth psychology. What will emerge is an understanding of our relationship with God as something that embraces all the possibilities – both light and dark – and which is above all creative. To believe in God as the *Summum Bonum* is to believe that whatever the intrinsic good or evil in a situation, God's grace is sufficient to transform the situation into a creative advance in which both God and humanity deepen their vulnerability to and co-inherence with the other.

Although the doctrine of the *Summum Bonum* will be reinterpreted and that of the *privatio boni* discarded, I do so not because they are 'bad theology', to recall Tillich's condemnation of theism. To argue thus is to stand in judgment on the last two thousand years of the work of the Spirit in the church.

Rather, what will emerge as an important part of my overall argument is that these two doctrines, like theism in the way they were traditionally stated, were necessary to the times and mentality which articulated them. Moreover, they have served an indispensable role in preparing the church to face the implications concerning good and evil which I believe Hiroshima has made inescapable. That our generation is challenged to rework and move beyond these doctrines, therefore, is not to negate their critical role in bringing us to the present juncture.

3. Summary

Both the inherited notions of God and evil are deficient in aiding Christians in coming to terms with the spectre of nuclear annihilation. Because of this, Christians, as Barth pointed out, have remained psychically numbed to what nuclear weapons imply. What needs to be done, therefore, is to articulate both a new ontology of God and a realistic understanding of evil such that Christians can be equipped to deal with the present crisis. Hiroshima must be integrated into Christian experience or else Christians will remain powerless to prevent nuclear destruction from happening again.

I wish to turn now to a discussion of process panentheism, which offers an ontology of God consistent with the Judaeo-Christian witness of a God of both cosmic and historical dimensions who acts creatively and salvifically with the secular world because it draws upon the contemporary philosophical notions of a world in process and upon the modern theological attempt of panentheism to understand the world and God as interrelated but not synonymous.

Later, I shall amplify this understanding by drawing upon the depth psychology of Carl Jung. In this discussion I shall argue that the critical point of contact between God and humanity is in the depths of the human psyche. It is within the psyche that we articulate our images of God and commune with the Infinite, and that our work of co-creation with God takes shape.

III

The 'Mighty Acts of God'

A. PROCESS THOUGHT AND THE PHILOSOPHY OF WHITEHEAD

Any discussion of process thought must begin with the philosophy of Alfred North Whitehead, although so complex and elaborate are his many conceptual schemas that it is impossible to do him justice in a few short pages. What is possible, however, is to offer an overall view of his approach as a whole within which the discussion of an ontology of God can be set in context.

According to Victor Lowe, 'Whitehead's amazing philosophical achievement is the construction of a system of the world according to which the basic fact of existence is everywhere some process of self-realization, growing out of previous processes and itself adding a new pulse of individuality and a new value to the world.'[1] Fundamental to understanding Whitehead, therefore, is to realize that his was a connected and pluralistic universe. This is to say, to quote John Cobb and David Griffin, that 'Whiteheadian process thought gives primacy to inter-dependence as an idea over independence.'[2] No monist insisted more strongly than he that nothing exists separately from other parts; in fact, he often criticized monistic theories for not taking this perspective far enough.[3] For Whitehead, independent existence is an illusion, whether ascribed to God, a human being, a star or an electron. He was perhaps the first major thinker to take absolutely seriously the primary consequences of relativity theory, that things assumed to be independent in the Newtonian world view are in fact to be seen relationally in one continuum in which space and time are interlocked into a single four-dimensional reality.[4] To see any 'single' thing, therefore, is to understand all things as 'requiring each other'; only in this way, according to Whitehead, can one articulate a 'coherent' system.

On the other hand, Whitehead is equally struck by the plurality, the multiplicity, of individual existents. Therefore, Whitehead could equally appreciate a pluralist such as Leibniz even as he saw the point of a monist such as Spinoza. Whitehead, however, did not attempt a synthesis of monistic and pluralistic systems; rather, he sought to reconcile their insights into a new system which he named 'the philosophy of organism'.

Each pulse of existence is for Whitehead an 'actual occasion of existence'.[5] It requires the antecedent others as parts of its own make-up; and yet, while connected, each actual entity achieves a unique individuality, a finite synthesis and an ending which remains in the universe as one of an infinite number of settled facts from which the individual actual entities of the future will arise: 'the many become the one, and are increased by one'.[6]

This concept of Whitehead's gives rise to an understanding of the universe as evolving endlessly towards the production of new syntheses.[7] This dynamic and synthetic growth Whitehead terms 'creativity', a movement of 'eternal activity' by which 'the many, which are the universe disjunctively, become the one actual occasion, which is the universe conjunctively'.[8]

This perception, that all actual entities cohere relationally in a milieu of creative synthesis, yields the principle that there is ultimately one kind of actuality:

> 'Actual entities' – also termed 'actual occasions' – are the final real things of which the world is made up. There is no going behind actual entities to find anything more real. They differ among themselves: God is an actual entity, and so is the most trivial puff of existence in far-off empty space. But though there are gradations of importance, and diversities of function, yet in the principles which actuality exemplifies all are on the same level.[9]

Nothing is outside this process; the universe is composed entirely of these interrelated actual entities, from God to 'the most trivial puff of existence', and all cohere together to form new syntheses as evolution progresses. Whitehead's Categoreal Schema, therefore, begins with the three concepts, 'one'[10], 'many'[11] and 'creativity'[12]; all combined comprise the 'Category of the Ultimate'[13], a category which is the predicate to all other Whiteheadian categories.

'The Universe', he says, 'is thus a creative advance into novelty', the alternative being a 'static morphological universe'.[14] Put more concisely: '*how* an actual entity *becomes* constitutes *what* that actual entity *is* . . . Its "being" is constituted by its "becoming". This is the "principle of process".[15] As Hartshorne puts the matter: 'Reality consists of the becoming of unit-events'.[16] This notion is the basis for Whitehead's 'ontological principle':

> that every condition to which the process of becoming conforms in any particular instance, has its reason *either* in the character of some actual entity in the actual world of that concrescence, *or* in the character of the subject which is in the process of concrescence . . . This ontological principle means that actual entities are the only *reasons*; so that to search for a reason is to search for one or more actual entities.[17]

It is by the ontological principle that Whitehead asserts there must be an eternal actual entity whose active character makes a *possible* process into an *actual* process. This entity Whitehead calls 'God'; more specifically, this consideration denotes the 'primordial' aspect of God, which Whitehead defines as 'the lure for feeling, the eternal urge of desire'. It is that dimension which is 'the unconditional actuality of conceptual feeling at the base of things', a dimension which yields that aspect of the universe which is transcendent and permanent.

It is important to recall here Whitehead's famous statement that 'God is not to be treated as an exception to all metaphysical principles to save their collapse. He is their chief exemplification.' In articulating this principle, Whitehead put himself and process thought in direct opposition to classical Christian theism which had long understood God specifically as the exception to whatever metaphysical principles were applicable to the natural world.

A primary distinction between the two traditions can be seen in the concept of God as Creator. For Whitehead, God 'is not *before* all creation but *with* all creation',[18] a point which Tillich later clarifies by making a distinction in the tenses of the divine creativity:

> Since the divine life is essentially creative, all three modes of time must be used in symbolizing it. God *has* created the world, he *is* creative at the present moment, and he *will* creatively fulfil his *telos*. Therefore we must speak of originating creation, sustaining creation, and directing creation.[19]

This means in Whiteheadian thought that God is present in each and every concrescence (that is, an entity in the process of becoming) at its very inception in a dynamic participation in which God bestows a particular character upon the creativity of the universe. Not long before he died, Whitehead summarized this point in a conversation with Lucien Price:

> God is *in* the world, or nowhere, creating continually in us and around us. This creative principle is everywhere, in animate and so-called inanimate matter, in the ether, water, earth, human hearts. But this creation is a continuing process, and 'the process is itself the actuality' . . . In so far as man partakes of his creative process does he partake of the divine of God, and that participation is his immortality . . . His true destiny as co-creator in the universe is his dignity and his grandeur.[20]

Norman Pittenger has characterized this concept of Whitehead's as 'panentheistic in tendency',[21] pointing out that it means most fundamentally that 'relationship characterizes deity'.[22] God is integral to each moment of becoming and hence totally involved in the ongoing becoming of an evolutionary process that is open at every point to the actions of God. Central to the notion of God in Whitehead and process thought generally is the clear understanding that God is a God who acts in the historical process of becoming on behalf of creaturely endeavour.

As to how God acts in the universe, Whitehead again articulates an answer antithetical to traditional theism; indeed, he states quite specifically that the traditional notion is not even biblical but political:

> When the Western world accepted Christianity, Caesar conquered; the received text of Western theology was edited by his lawyers. The code of Justinian and the theology of Justinian are two volumes expressing one movement of the human spirit. The brief Galilean vision flickered throughout the ages, uncertainly . . . But the deeper idolatry, of the fashioning of God in the image of the Egyptian, Persian, and Roman imperial rulers, was retained. The Church gave unto God the attributes which belonged exclusively to Caesar.[23]

To replace this depiction of God as 'Monarch', Whitehead suggested the notion of 'persuasion': i.e., God offers to each occasion its possibilities of value. To understand how God works necessitates a perception of divine activity in which God establishes the 'germ' of divine purpose at the inception of the temporal process of the actual entity. This divine germ provides each entity with its 'subjective aim'. Without this action on the part of God the occasion's self-creation could never commence, for nothing comes from nothing in the Whiteheadian schema. Whitehead's position, there-fore, is that 'each temporal entity . . . derives from God its basic conceptual aim, relevant to its actual world, yet with indetermina-tions awaiting its own decisions'.[24] This latter point is emphasized by William Christian:

> The conditions an occasion may satisfy are given by the past actual world. The possibility it may realize is given by God. But the fact that it becomes at all, and that it becomes what it aims at, is not a necessary consequence of the past actual world, nor of God's primordial vision, nor of both taken together. This fact is the consequence of a 'self-creative act in which the concrescence actualizes its aim'.[25]

As Cobb puts the matter, 'by the way God constitutes himself he calls us to be what we can be and are not . . .',[26] giving us the 'subjective aim' of our existence; but whether we in fact actualize this aim is largely left to us.

This concept of persuasion as the operative way in which God acts obviously excludes the traditional theistic notion of divine omni-potence. God rather forms the subtle force 'by reason of which ideals are effected in the world and forms of order evolve'.[27] Any doctrine other than this would undermine both creaturely freedom and novelty in the temporal world, in which God and creation are directed towards each other and, in the mutual interaction between them, require and complement each other in a creative synthesis.

This is not to say that God's subtle persuasion in the life of human beings is something that can be taken lightly or easily disregarded. Quite the contrary: it must be stressed that the primordial nature of God which expresses the divine 'lure' is, as Loomer puts it, 'a stubborn and unyielding fact that must be taken into account'.[28] We can, of course, attempt to ignore this 'stubborn and unyielding fact', and given our egoistic distortions and defensive escapes, we usually do, but as the Psalmist points out, 'wherever I go, God is there'; we always encounter this inevitable presence either in fellowship or in wrath.

D. D. Williams has pointed out in this regard that, while certainly moving in the right direction, Whitehead's concept of persuasive agency does not altogether connote what is ultimately involved in divine action:

> When we turn to the question of how God acts upon the world we see that Whitehead has thrown important light upon some aspects

of this perplexing problem . . . But it still may be that Whitehead has underestimated the disclosure of the divine initiative in religious experience. I believe it can be shown that he has not carried through with his metaphysical method fully . . . It is precisely in that aspect of God which makes him a fully actual effective subject where Whitehead seems not to make clearly the affirmations which he needs to complete his doctrine. I suggest that it is because Whitehead has reacted so justifiably against the divine Monarch that he has given a partially inadequate account of the relation between God and the world.[29]

I concur with Williams' criticism of Whitehead on this point and in later discussion will be articulating a more adequate notion of 'divine lure'. Particularly in the section on Jung, there will be much discussion of the active presence of God within the human psyche.

For his part, Whitehead struggled to complete his theory of the Godhead by coming to grips with the paradox of the One and the Many, a double concern, he says, which involves conceiving 'actuality with permanence, requiring fluency as its completion; and actuality with fluency, requiring permanence as its completion'.[30] Whitehead's solution to this double challenge as applied to God is to articulate a 'consequent nature' of God to complement the Divine's 'primordial nature':

> God as well as being primordial, is also consequent. He is the beginning and the end . . . He is the presupposed actuality of conceptual operation, in unison of becoming with every other creative act. Thus by reason of the relativity of all things, there is a reaction of the world in God. The completion of God's nature into a fulness of physical feeling is derived from the objectification of the world in God. He shares with every new creation its actual world; and the concrescent creature is objectified in God as a novel element in God's objectification of that actual world.[31]

Thus, asserts Whitehead, 'analogously to all actual entities, the nature of God is dipolar'.[32] He seeks to make it clear, however, that 'God's conceptual nature is unchanged, by reason of its final completeness. But his derivative nature is consequent upon the creative advance of the world'.[33]

Because the temporal universe is a pluralistic dynamic of evolving entities and societies, creatively arising then fading away to become foundational to new occasions and societies of occasions, every new event, 'by reason of the relativity of all things', reacts on God and is felt by God. As has been discussed, the antecedent universe, synthesized and transformed by a novel prehension of feeling, constitutes the content of a temporal occasion. The consequent nature of God consists of these temporal occasions transformed in turn by the inclusive mode of feeling which is derived from the all-encompassing primordial nature of the divine. It is this inclusion of all temporal occasions into the consequent nature of the divine that enables the universe to be unified into a conscious and infinitely aesthetic harmony of feeling that is being continually renewed. Moreover, while individual occasions perish, after they have fulfilled their particular and inner purpose, they are absorbed into the creative advance of consequent Godhead, which in itself does not decay or perish. The theme of cosmology in Whiteheadian thought is 'the story of the dynamic effort of the World passing into everlasting unity and of the static majesty of God's vision, accomplishing its purpose of completion by absorption of the World's multiplicity of effort'.[34] The image that Whitehead suggests to exemplify this point is 'that of a tender care that nothing be lost', a dynamic in which God 'saves the world as it passes into the immediacy of his own life'.[35]

The depiction here is that of God and the world as standing over against one another, says Whitehead, a depiction which expresses the ultimate metaphysical truth

> that appetitive vision and physical enjoyment have equal claim to priority in creation . . . each is all in all. Thus each temporal occasion embodies God, and is embodied in God. In God's nature, permanence is primordial and flux is derivative from the World; in the World's nature, flux is primordial and permanence is derivative from God . . . Creation achieves the reconciliation of permanence and flux when it has reached its final term which is everlastingness – the Apotheosis of the World.[36]

This is not to say that either God or the world reach final completion; quite the contrary: 'Both are in the grip of the ultimate metaphysical ground, the creative advance into novelty. Either of them, God and the World, is the instrument of novelty for the other.'[37] Equally important is the fact that while God and the world are integral to one another, Whitehead does not suppose their equality. Their relationship is definitely asymmetrical with God remaining for ever the determiner and ultimate referent for all that is.

To explain more specifically how God and the world relate,

Whitehead develops a four-part schema.[38] First, there is the stage of 'conceptual origination', a phase which is infinite in its adjustment of valuation but deficient in actuality. Secondly, comes the temporal phase of 'physical origination' with its multiplicity of actualities and in which full actuality is attained. Thirdly, there follows the phase of 'perfected actuality' which derives the condition of its being from the two previous processes. In it 'the many are one everlastingly, without the qualification of any loss either of individual identity or of completeness of unity'. It is in this phase that immediacy becomes reconciled with objective immortality. Finally, the creative process completes itself as 'the perfected actuality passes back into the temporal world, and qualifies this world so that each temporal actuality includes it as an immediate fact of relevant experience'. Put theologically, says Whitehead, the fourth stage is 'the love of God for the world'; indeed, the entire process of universal becoming is a dynamic in which one discerns

> the particular providence for particular occasions. What is done in the world is transformed into a reality in heaven and the reality in heaven passes back into the world . . . The love in the world passes into the love of heaven, and floods back again into the world.[39]

In this sense, concludes Whitehead, we are in a flowing reality in which, while we are forced at times to know God as the 'void' and/ or the 'enemy', due largely to our own blindness and misdirection of will, we can understand God as 'the great companion – the fellow sufferer who understands'.[40]

The importance of Whitehead to my overall argument is that he offers a new way to understand the two notions I pointed to earlier as fundamental to any Judaeo-Christian ontology of God: first, that God has both cosmic and historical dimensions; and second, that God is creatively active in history. For Whitehead, God is both abstract (cosmic) and consequent (historical), eternally beyond time, space and causality and yet integrally involved with it. God's participation in history is in God's creative influencing of each and every event, instilling within each occasion the divine lure. Each entity completes itself according to its own degrees of freedom, but God is for ever moving and directing it according to divine purpose. Thus all creative advances in history are the result of God and humanity co-creating synchronistically.

B. HARTSHORNE'S DIPOLAR THEORY OF THE GODHEAD

This discussion of Whitehead is important background for the thinking of Charles Hartshorne, for the freshness of Hartshorne's approach is due to the fact that although he developed his process notions apart from Whitehead, his metaphysics are closely akin to the insights of Whitehead:[41] indeed, Hartshorne maintains that their common version of process philosophy represents a profound shift of perspective in Western metaphysics, a shift that sets his 'neo-classical' metaphysics in clear contra-distinction to the hitherto dominant classical metaphysical tradition.[42] What neo-classical metaphysics represents, he says, is a 'higher synthesis', a dynamic new perspective that says of any given category: 'this, yes, but not only this – nor only its contrary – but this as well as its contrary.'[43] As discussed, Whitehead conceived of God as an 'entity' and distinguished between the 'primordial' aspect of the Divine, independent of all particular created instances, and the 'consequent' aspect, that dimension both contingent and dependent upon the created order. Hartshorne calls this concept 'the principle of dual transcendence'[44] and refers to the two poles as God's 'abstract essence' and God's 'consequent states'.[45] It means that instead of distinguishing the Divine from the created order by terming Deity as necessary, infinite, independent, eternal – all the things which the creatures are not, the contrast is made in dual terms: 'God is, in uniquely excellent ways, *both* necessary and contingent, both infinite and finite, independent and dependent, eternal and temporal.'[46]

Put succinctly, Hartshorne's dipolar theory of the Godhead characterizes God as being on the one hand 'infinite, free, complete, primordial, eternal, actually deficient and unconscious',[47] and on the other as being 'determined, incomplete, consequent, everlasting (meaning incorruptible, all change being gain not loss), fully actual and conscious'.[48] The abstract essence of the Divine is fundamentally transcendent, 'limited by no actuality which it presupposes', while the concrete state 'originates with physical experience derived from the temporal world and then acquires integration with the primordial side'.

It is from the imperative Hartshorne feels to unite those polarities of divine existence into one all-embracing totality that he articulates his major critique of both classical theism and pantheism. For him, these classical conceptualizations were and are vitiated by a 'mono-polar prejudice' that has caused them to give 'a favoured status for one side of the ultimate conceptual contrasts, or a special disability for the other side'.[49]

An example of such monopolar prejudice can be seen in those theistic beliefs which have insisted that God is active rather than passive, necessary but not contingent, independent but not dependent, cause rather than effect. I will discuss the psychological reasons for this in Chapter VI. Hartshorne himself delineates numerous reasons for this monopolarity, the major one being that of an overdose of the Greek metaphysics of permanence and immutability, but says that in the final analysis all reasons reduce in some sense to experience: i.e., an unwillingness to project on to God those characteristics which Western cultural conditioning rejects: dependency, contingency, passivity. But why, asks Hartshorne, should it be considered more divine for God to act on the world than to be acted upon in return? Or to be changeless rather than evolving, independent of the universe instead of dependent on the very creation God loves?

'God is a being whose versatility of becoming is unlimited,' maintains Hartshorne, 'whose potentialities of content embrace all possibilities, whose sensitive responsiveness surpasses that of all other individuals, actual or possible.'[50] Only by the theory of dipolarity is this conception given justice, for only by embracing all possibility is it possible to say that 'God is thus the great "I am," the one whose existence is the expression of his own power and none other, who self-exists – rather than is caused, or happens, to exist – and by whose power of existence all other things exist.'[51]

This is not to involve God in contradictions; it is rather to perceive the polarities of reality as complementary aspects of a single totality. Thus God is temporal in one aspect of divine reality and eternal in another. Deity's actual knowledge is finite as it relates to the actual world at any given time, but infinite because it is cognizant of the potentiality inherent in all the actuality of existence. Similarly, God is necessary because God is the principle of possibility of all things, and yet God is also the contingent effect of all actualities; this is because God's actuality is altered with every change of the actual state of the world.

This theory of dipolarity does not involve Hartshorne in either a doctrine of two Gods or a radical dualism; rather, through the principle of 'dual transcendence' or 'categorical supremacy', God is understood as a 'radically unique individual in the most eminent sense',[52] although in principle different from all other aspects of being by virtue of being superior to them. Following Whitehead's assertion about God as being the 'chief exemplification' of the laws of nature, Hartshorne maintains that every category that applies either to the actuality or abstract existence of God applies as the supreme instance or 'supercase' of that category. He also uses the term 'surpassingness' to speak of God's unitariness and unique supremacy. His formula is that God is 'unsurpassable by another'.

It is in this sense, therefore, that Hartshorne is most insistent that his theory of dipolarity, while involving the notion of *complementary* aspects of Deity, is nevertheless radically monotheistic. The notion of polarity within our experience of God is an important one. That God is of complementary aspects, of both abstract and consequent dimensions, is a fundamental contribution of process thought to a relevant ontology of God, for it establishes philosophically the principle that polarity is an essential part of our experience of God. I shall be expanding the process notion of polarity in God in Chapter VI by arguing for a polarity of light and dark dimensions in the divine pleroma. I have already set forth this position in Chapter II with the phrase 'antinomial character' of God. The point that needs to be stressed at this juncture is that positing polarity in God does not negate a monotheistic belief in God; quite the contrary, it offers a notion of complementarity within God.

While affirming the monotheistic nature of the Godhead, Hartshorne is equally explicit in affirming that God's perfection must be a continually evolving and dynamic *process*.

Since evolution is a fundamental aspect of reality, Hartshorne posits it to be a fundamental attribute of God. But while exemplifying a dynamic common to all being, Divinity has unique ontological categories suitable only to one which is wholly its own pupil and wholly its own teacher. God is, so to speak, simultaneously the parent, teacher, educator and companion of the evolving actualizing God. It is not a dynamic in which the higher emerges from the lower or increased perfection arises out of imperfection, but rather one in which God's infinite reservoir of potentiality becomes an ever-expanding cornucopia of finite actuality. God's growth is a thrusting of more particularity out of the infinite abstraction present at creation. In one sense, therefore, God is growing into old age, while in another, God is growing back into youth. This is because as God becomes older in duration of time there are with each passing occasion new individual concretizations of possibilities never before actualized. Each new occasion reveals a novel dimension of the 'God of the Fathers'; a point that will be greatly expanded when we turn to a discussion of an ontology of events for the actions of God in history (in section E of this chapter) and, later, to a discussion of God and the human psyche in Chapter VI. New actualizations from the depth of ancient potentialities create the tension of movement within our experience of God, as the present for ever evolves into a more expansive future. This interplay between new events and ancient possibilities is central to what I shall be asserting in Chapter VI concerning the Hiroshima event: that it compels Christians to re-examine the potentialities inherent in the antinomial character of the cross.

It is the inextricable interweaving of God and the created order, along with the logical impossibility of conceiving total perfection, that compels Hartshorne to speak of the relative perfection of God. As there is an end neither to the creative process itself nor to the dynamic perfection of creaturely advance, so 'the infinity of possibilities in God's nature is inexhaustible in actuality even by divine power or any conceivable power. For each creative synthesis furnishes materials for a novel and richer synthesis'.[53]

The implications of this idea are integral to what Hartshorne conceives 'true religion' to be; it is not simply a contractual relationship in which one obeys a divinely decreed covenant, but most essentially 'contributing value to God' which God would otherwise lack. This is a genuine dependence on the part of the Creator, for to serve is to confer benefit in precisely the sense that the served will to some extent be dependent upon the server for the benefit rendered. 'In short', says Hartshorne,

> God with contingency but lacking dependence is not the God we can serve or, in what I think is the proper meaning, worship. Nor do I think such a God could be anything but an empty abstraction, far from the God of the Bible . . .[54]

In this doctrine, new meaning is given to the ancient religious assertion that 'the end of all creation is the glory of God'. 'Very literally,' suggests Hartshorne,

> We exist to enhance, not simply to adore and enjoy, the divine glory. Ultimately we are contributors to the ever growing divine treasury of values. We serve God, God is not finally a means to our ends. Our final and inclusive end is to contribute to the divine life.[55]

In the Hartshornian schema God is clearly an eminently social God, who not only corresponds in a complementary way to the social nature of all reality and joins it together with a loving all-inclusiveness, but also cannot realize the totality of the Divine Self apart from creaturely participation. In many ways, Hartshorne asserts, his dipolar theism is little more than an attempt to unpack the philosophical implications of that insight into God so clearly perceived by Israel and the church, that God is love; indeed, Hartshorne asserts 'perfect love' to be the final description of the generic nature of God and the ultimate reason for God's social involvement with creation. Hartshorne goes so far as to say that God *is* the love, or sympathy or sociality, which is manifested in the created order and compels God to accept creaturely participation. Since awareness or mind is the most developed expression of relationship, God as eminent mind/awareness is the most supremely related, most dependent being of all. In one of his most eloquent passages, Hartshorne stresses this point:

> It is appropriate for man to depend upon man, not for the supreme being to depend upon anything. But my proposition is that the higher the being the more dependence of certain kinds will be appropriate for it. One does not expect an oyster to depend for its joy or sorrow upon my joy or sorrow, as such, or even upon that of other oysters to any great extent. Sympathetic dependence is a sign of excellence and waxes with every ascent in the scale of being.[56]

Furthermore, if God is to be understood as the chief instance of the observations we make of reality, then the sociality of God must be understood as an absolute relativity; i.e., God is simply quite incapable of not sympathetically sharing all feelings. The divine experience is therefore the most eminent form of 'feeling of feelings', a point which Whitehead stresses as well, because of the fact that for him feeling is the basic characteristic of an actual occasion. Observes Hartshorne:

> The eminent form of sympathetic dependence can only apply to Deity, for this form cannot be less than an omniscient sympathy, which depends upon and is exactly coloured by every nuance of joy or sorrow anywhere in the world.[57]

This eminent sociality of God, then, necessitates two fundamental characteristics: first, that the immanent creativity of the Divine involves God continually in a *creative influencing* of created beings; and secondly, that this participatory creativity means that God is the supreme instance of being *creatively dependent* upon and creatively shaped by the activity of others.

What emerges from this understanding is a conception of God's relationship with the world very much analogous to Buber's concept of 'I and Thou', a point which has been explored by John Robinson in his book *Exploration into God*. He terms the eminent sociality of God a 'co-inherence', in which the intimacy between God and creation is characterized by a profound personal relationship. This awareness is integral, he says, to any God-statement made within the Judaeo-Christian tradition. This 'co-inherence' yields a dynamic tension between Creator and creation in which, particularly from the vantage point of the creation, there 'is the consciousness of being encountered, seized, held by a prevenient reality, undeniable in its objectivity, which seeks one out in grace and demand and under the constraint of which a man finds himself judged and accepted for what he truly is'.[58] This encounter is immanent in that it speaks to us from the deepest part of our being; yet it is also transcendent in that it is not ours to command. Conceiving life as a relationship of response and communication with this 'overmastering reality' is perhaps what Buber had in mind when he wrote that 'when he, too, who abhors the name, and believes himself to be godless, gives his whole being to addressing the thou of his life as a thou that cannot be limited by another, he addresses God'.[59]

To refer to God, therefore, is not to speak of an existence outside one's experience; neither is it a way of understanding the world. 'It is to acknowledge', says Robinson, 'a relationship, a confrontation at the heart of one's very constitution as a human being, of which one is compelled to say in existential terms, "this is it. This is the most real thing in the world, that which is ultimately and inescapably true".' This is to say, that 'God-statements are statements about the reality of this relationship'.[60] The concept of the eminent sociality of God means that we trust our lives and recognize meaning in the universe, not by belief in a sustaining Deity separate from ourselves, but at the level of an intimate relationship between God and ourselves so intensely personal as to be exemplified in the ability of Jesus to address his overwhelming reality as 'Abba'. To speak of the sociality of God is to say that 'personality is of ultimate significance in the constitution of the universe, that in personal relationships we touch the final meaning of existence as nowhere else'.[61] It is in this sense that I would agree with Feuerbach, that 'to predicate personality of God is nothing else than to declare personality as the absolute essence'.[62]

The meaning of God as love, then, is a belief that in pure personal relationship we encounter the deepest truth about reality. As

Robinson puts it, 'Belief in God is the trust, the well-nigh incredible trust, that to give ourselves to the uttermost in love is not to be confounded but to be accepted, that Love is the ground of our being, to which ultimately we "Come home".'[63] We testify to this personal encounter, not by asserting something ontologically separate about it, but by taking seriously our experience of God in our personal situation. Only from this personal perspective can we address reality as 'Abba' and know the meaning of God as *Summum Bonum*.

Like Hartshorne, Robinson makes it clear at this point that God, however intimate, is not to be subsumed into the created order. He again draws from Buber to make the point. However much the awareness of the encounter comes from within, he says, it confronts us with a profound otherness to which we can only respond: 'Thou'. 'We take the I-Thou character of the relationship most seriously when we recognize that of God we can only say "Thou", not "I".'[64] Quite simply, we can never put ourselves on the other side of the relationship.

Robinson offers another caution as well, stating that a personalization or hypostatization of God in terms of 'I-Thou' encounter is legitimate only as long as we recognize that it represents an understanding from experience: it is not the experience itself. 'All we can describe or designate,' he says,

> is the grace and claim of the 'Thou' from the side of the relationship in which we find ourselves held. In this reserve of utterance the believer is not being subjectivist in the sense of regarding God merely as a function of human existence. On the contrary, he knows that human existence is but a function of this utterly gracious, disturbing, all-encompassing reality to which his life is the response – or this reality cannot properly be given the name 'God' at all.[65]

To speak of the fact that God is social, then, is to recognize an intimate encounter between ourselves and the all-embracing reality of God, an encounter that connects the two sides into one overall dynamic of creative advance for both. It is an utterly personal relationship; indeed, one is only defined as 'I' within the response to the encounter with 'Thou'. Only in relationship to each other do either God or creation take definition and form. This is to say, that the universe is not understood as a purely immanent or static process but as a dynamic process 'called' into being and drawn forward to higher levels of relationship by mutual interaction between creation and Creator and by an evocative love that will not let the creative advance stop. Robinson reiterates that this position is fundamentally biblical: 'The Bible thinks of creation not in terms of emanation . . . as though it were being spun – or were spinning itself – out of the body of a spider, but in terms of evocation, of its responding to a call to ever higher life and freer relationship.'[66]

The above understanding of God and the creation as being mutually interconnected and interdependent in a dynamic relationship of encounter is the keystone to process panentheism and an important amplification of what I mean in referring to God as the *Summum Bonum*. Hartshorne considers these notions as essential components of his theory of dipolarity, although he uses several other terms, primarily 'panentheism' and 'surrelativism', a shortening of the term 'Supreme Relativism'. The terms are used interchangeably.

C. PANENTHEISM

It was Gustav Fechner in the last century who gave one of the first pantheistic definitions of God:

> . . . God, as the totality of being and acting, has no external environment, no beings outside himself; his is one and unique; all spirits move in the inner world of his spirit; all bodies in the inner world of his body; he exists purely within himself, he is determined by nothing external to him, his is a purely inner, self-determination, because he includes the determining grounds of all existence.[67]

The Divine is wholly Creator and wholly involved with the creation: proceeding from nothing, totally itself, and within itself creating creation. All things are produced from out of the divine potentiality and consequently find their actualization and completion within the same and singular Divinity. This conception of Fechner's is not pantheism, for the universe is not understood *as* God but *in* God. Perhaps a more modern way of putting it is to quote R. Gregor Smith, that 'God is not to be found in history but history in God'.[68]

The Oxford Dictionary of the Christian Church[69] defines panentheism as 'the belief that the Being of God includes and penetrates the whole universe, so that every part of it exists in him, but . . . that his Being is more than, and is not exhausted by, the universe'. John Robinson puts it another way:

> 'the world' is not simply something that can be joined to 'God' by

the word 'and', as in traditional theistic discourse, but that it is in God and God is in it in a way that perhaps enables one to talk of the 'divine field' as a physicist might talk of a magnetic field.

In this way of thinking, says Robinson, 'there is a coinherence between God and the universe which overcomes the duality without denying the diversity'.[70] Pittenger emphasizes this point, stating that

> For the panentheist, everything which is not in itself divine is yet believed to be 'in' God, in the sense that he is regarded as the circumambient reality operative in and through, while also more than, all that is not himself. . .[71]

Between the extremes of deism and pantheism, then, lies panentheism which Pittenger calls the 'mean' between them in that it 'attempts to preserve the relative independence of the world order, while at the same time it insists that God cannot be envisaged as totally separate from or alien to that order.'[72] It is God's dipolarity that allows this middle ground, argues Hartshorne, because it can express the perspective that

> God is, in one aspect of himself, the integral totality of all ordinary causes and effects, but that in another aspect, his essence, . . . he is conceivable in abstraction from any one or any group of particular contingent beings . . .[73]

It should be pointed out here that not all panentheists agree with the above description. W. A. Christian, for instance, while believing that panentheism is certainly more palatable than classical theism, feels that the notion of real independence for the creatures is made essentially pointless if they are literally *in* God. Rather, he suggests the following two propositions: first, that God is not the cosmos, nor does God include the cosmos in Hartshorne's sense; and second, that the divine activity is always conditioned though never determined by the cosmos.[74] His position is basically that of contingency without co-inherence. Peter Hamilton also has reservations about panentheism, that it overstresses the notion that all is in God; it would, he says, 'upset' the delicate balance articulated by Whitehead between God and the universe and between divine transcendence and immanence.[75]

These reservations, I think, are to a large extent based on a misapprehension of the term 'in God'. Cobb has an interesting amplification of panentheism, however, that might clear up some of the ambiguity. In *God and the World* he develops at some length a depiction of the spatial relationship of God and the universe which yields the following understanding:

> God's standpoint is all-inclusive, and so, in a sense, we are parts of God. But we are not parts of God in the sense that God is simply the sum total of the parts or that the parts are lacking in independence and self determination. God and the creatures interact as separate entities, while God includes the standpoints of all of them in his omnispatial standpoint. In this sense God is everywhere, but he is not everything.[76]

What Cobb is pointing to is that while panentheism is striving to overcome the classical duality that kept God and the world absolutely distinct and therefore in an ontological situation in which God could remain impassible, it is as strenuously attempting to maintain the diversity that allows genuine autonomy on both sides and consequently meaningful creative advance for both. It is important to recall that by their actions creaturely freedoms actually shape the actuality of God; but they have to be in contact with God in order for this actualization to take place. God must be every*where* in order to be able to incorporate into the Divine self creaturely activity, even if the Divine is not every*thing*. A baby in the womb is completely surrounded by the mother; but it is not the mother, neither is the mother the baby. Creaturely autonomy is real in panentheism, therefore, and so, it should be added, is God's autonomy and independence. Hartshorne is clear on this point, that God's abstract essence is forever distinct and consequently distinguishable from every particular instance within the Divine pleroma: 'Deity is in some real aspect distinguishable from and independent of any and all relative items, and yet, taken as an actual whole, includes all relative items.[77]

What is also important to point out is that God being everywhere does not mean a static presence; rather God's presence is dynamic. Process panentheism keeps the tension between God's omnipresence on the one hand and creaturely freedom on the other. The omnipresence of God, being ever sensitive to the needs and freedoms of the creatures, is ever fluid and malleable. It is an omnipresence that is continually changing in dimension and form and yet completely preserves each successive cosmic moment in perpetual memory. It is an omnipresence, moreover, that allows each occasion the amount of autonomy due to its point of development and maturity. From that point of knowing how creation anywhere and everywhere successfully deals with environmental challenges, God acts as the force bonding present actuality into a harmonious synchronicity that gives order and coherence to the creatures in their growth, each according to its degree of freedom. The totality of creation within God contemplates the next actuality from its myriad points of reference as it draws its subjective aim from the depths of divine potentiality. The movement forward is as infinitely diverse, given the multiplicity of creaturely degrees of freedom operative, as it is synchronistic, given the overall bonding of God, a bonding perceived by the creatures not as a deterministic fiat but a gentle lure, a subtle directing of aim. It is within this context that one can see the beauty of what both Whitehead and Hartshorne stress, that while God does indeed rule, the Divine does so in and through our freedom.

It is only within the vast and comprehensive totality of God, then, that our advances, limited to the confines of our finiteness, must be seen. Our significance is as minuscule as the significance of God is cosmic. It is God that sets the perimeters of human freedom, for the more impact God has upon humanity, the more important is the divine effect upon the possible human responses. God orders the world, therefore, and establishes the optimal limits for our free action by presenting the Divine as an essential object, so constituted as to instil within the possibilities of human response a desired direction. By presenting to us a new ideal or vision which our unselfconscious awareness takes as object, God exercises influential control over our entire activity, a point to be greatly expanded in the discussion of the Jungian notion of archetypes emerging from our unconscious to influence our conscious behaviour. To quote Hartshorne: 'Only he who changes himself can control the changes in us by inspiring us with novel ideals for novel occasions. We take our cues for this moment by seeing, that is, feeling, what God as of this moment desiderates.'[78]

Perhaps no more eloquent testimony to this depiction of God can be offered than that of Nikos Kazanzakis in *Report to Greco*, in which he states that 'blowing through heaven and earth, and in our hearts and the heart of every living thing, is a gigantic breath – a great Cry – which we call God . . .' Within the context of this, he says,

> . . . the human being is a centaur; his equine hoofs are planted in the ground, but his body from breast to head is worked on and tormented by the merciless Cry. He has been fighting, again for thousands of eons, to draw himself, like a sword, out of his

animalistic struggle – to draw himself out of this human scabbard. Man calls in despair, 'Where can I go? I have reached the pinnacle, beyond is the abyss.' And the Cry answers. 'I am beyond. Stand up!' All things are centaurs. If this were not the case, the world would rot into inertness and sterility.[79]

This 'Cry', like Teilhard's 'Omega point', is both immanent within life and transcendent beyond it; 'The call is of God and the response is of God.'[80] The divine presence is the 'beyond in the midst', at the heart of what we are, at the beginning of what we are, yet for ever ahead of us, beckoning us into an encounter that transforms our life into an evolving becoming. The constant evocation of God before us, coupled with the eternal response of God within us, is what makes life a process of creative advance for both God and humanity. This means that the perpetual change in nature seen long ago by Anaximander is not only harmonious, as Heraclitus later observed, but is dialectical as well, causing the motion ensuing from the interplay of the polarities – God evoking and creation responding – progressively to elevate the evocation/response to higher levels of creative synthesis. Each new creative synthesis yields a deeper co-inherence between God and humanity and a greater appreciation on the part of the creatures that only by grace are we saved.

Despite this overwhelming and all-encompassing presence of God around and within us, however, it must be remembered what Einstein observed, that 'God is subtle'. This means specifically within process panentheistic thought that there is definitely no room for divine 'intrusions' or indirect 'interventions' that interrupt the natural flow as classical theism believes. Pittenger stresses this point by noting that

> since nothing is 'outside' God and since he is the chief explanatory principle in and for all things, although the fact of creaturely freedom demonstrates that he is not the *only* one, it would be absurd to speak of his 'intruding' or 'intervening' in his world. He is always *there*, or else the world could not and would not be there either.[81]

God being 'always there', all actual entities intuit God's actual subjective aim for them, taking their cues for living in a particular moment by knowing what God at that moment desires. Says Hartshorne:

> God orders the universe, according to panentheism, by taking into his own life all the currents of feelings in existence. He is the

most irresistible of influences precisely because he is himself the most open to influence. In the depths of their hearts all creatures (even those able to 'rebel' against him) defer to God because they sense him as the one who alone is adequately moved by what moves them. He alone not only knows but feels (the only adequate knowledge where feeling is concerned) how they feel, and he finds his own joy in sharing their lives, lived according to their own free decisions not fully anticipated by any detailed plan of his own. Yet the extent to which they can be permitted to work out their own plan depends on the extent to which they can echo or imitate on their own level the divine sensitiveness or the needs and precious freedom of all. In this vision of a deity who is not a supreme autocrat, but a universal agent of 'persuasion', whose 'power' is the worship he 'inspires' (Whitehead), that is, flows from the intrinsic appeal of his infinitely sensitive and tolerant relativity, by which all things are kept moving in orderly togetherness, we may find help in facing our task today, the task of contributing to the democratic self-ordering of a world whose members not even the supreme orderer reduces to mere subjects with the sole function of obedience.[82]

What emerges from this quotation is a most profound amplification of process panentheism by Hartshorne. Not only are God and the world seen to be in a relation of co-inherence in which both operate according to their degrees of freedom and thereby co-create, but by virtue of the fact that God is directly affected by the choices made and the events actualized in God's consequent state, God emerges as the most vulnerable person in the universe. 'He is the most irresistible of influences precisely because he is himself the most open to influence.' God's power, therefore, is directly proportional to God's vulnerability; the divine influence is directly related to the divine ability to absorb creaturely actualization.

It is only within this context that panentheism offers an account of suffering, for in stark contrast to traditional theism's impassible God, panentheism depicts the suffering of God as a poignantly real aspect of divine experience. Through the Christian doctrine of the Cross, God is understood as wholly vulnerable rather than totally immune to creaturely error and pain. 'The dipolar view,' says Hartshorne, 'must hold not only that God contains suffering but that he suffers and that it is in his character to suffer, in accordance with the suffering of the world.'[83]

This understanding of a God who actually suffers with the creation makes Christianity 'truly a religion of tragic divinity', Hartshorne argues, and he points to the figure of Jesus himself to exemplify the claim. As the supreme symbol of Deity in our culture, Jesus made no attempt in his ministry to immunize himself from the suffering he witnessed around him; rather, he centred himself in the heart of human suffering, opening himself to its reality, and attempted to alleviate its crushing burden when and where the faith of those oppressed would permit. This suggests that God has absolute non-immunity to suffering, a being of complete openness and receptivity to the entire range of human experience. 'Jesus is the man,' says Hartshorne,

> who deliberately and effectively embodies in his life the conviction that it is nobler and more Godlike to share the sufferings of others . . . than to escape into mere private joy. The Cross is thus the symbol of sympathetic suffering divinity . . .[84]

What we shall see in later discussion is that Jesus' non-immunity to the suffering of the world was balanced by an equally radical non-immunity to the dark dimensions of God. I shall set forth Job as another example of this non-immunity to the antinomial character of God.

D. THE QUESTION OF EVIL

The question of suffering directly leads into the question of evil. First of all I shall examine Hartshorne's treatment of the problem; and then I shall articulate the general outlines of the theodicy for which I shall argue.

1. Hartshorne's treatment of evil

For Hartshorne, every actual entity and/or society of entities operates according to certain degrees of freedom that not even God can entirely control. This allowance of free will, no matter how minuscule, creates a division of powers and responsibilities in the universe that has tragic implications for both the universe and God alike. 'The minimal solution of the problem of evil', he maintains, 'is to affirm the necessity of a division of powers, hence of responsibilities, as binding even upon a maximal power'.[85] This is to say that in the schema of cosmic life God has ordered the limits of creaturely freedom, but that God does not compel certain decisions within the perimeters of the boundaries ordained. Inherent in the free decisions of the creatures are the possibilities of both good and evil. Each measure of free self-determination presents an irremovable risk of conflict as well as the potential for creative harmony. Because creaturely decisions and actions are part of the ongoing actualization of the potentiality of God, the Divine itself is vulnerable to what we choose to do in our continuing co-creation with God. 'The ground of good and evil,' Hartshorne asserts, 'is really the same, namely, from the realm of multiple freedom.'[86] As long as there is this element of freedom, which in process thought increases as the evolutionary process advances, every new phase of the cosmic process as it is experienced and built up within human space/time will afford more possibilities for evil as well as for good. Evil and suffering are co-terminous with freedom and therefore will never be totally eliminated from the universe nor from God's own experience. Moreover, evil is not to be dichotomized as distinct from good, with good being one army, as it were, and evil being another, each seeking the extinction of the other. 'Life is more than a battle,' comments Hartshorne, 'especially a battle between abstractions. It is an act of creation, with God the eminent but not sole creator.'[87]

The fact of evil, then, is a profound reality within the fabric of divine life as well as human life: as we suffer so does the very being of God; this, because it is integral to what it means to be autonomous. This is a reality that God can only mitigate, not eradicate. This means that there is 'chance and tragedy even for God'.[88] Because God experiences creaturely contingency and therefore must experience the quality of evil, God cannot remain immune to us. God must share perfectly with us our joy as well as our sorrow, preserving the entire spectrum of created experience within the everlasting memory of the Divine. Within the confines of human existence, therefore, God is radically dependent upon us for the actualization of divine happiness and/or divine suffering. Hartshorne's concept of God, then, while in abstraction and essence is blissful unity, is in actuality either joyful or sorrowing, depending upon what the creatures choose to share with God. Divine feeling concerning divine unity is predicated upon creaturely actualization. God is cosmic joy, God is cosmic sufferer, who, while not possessing a shadow dimension or committing evil, is vulnerable to both human evil and human suffering.

In essence, Hartshorne's theodicy places the locus of evil in creaturely freedom. This serves the purpose of making evil a genuine component of reality. In this sense, therefore, Hartshorne rejects the notion of the *privatio boni*. On the other hand, Hartshorne follows the arguments presented by those defending the traditional notion of God being the *Summum Bonum* without shadow. Indeed, as David Griffin summarizes the matter,

> the strategy of the traditional theodicies was to say that God is responsible for evil, but not indictable for it. They did this by maintaining that all evil is merely apparent so that there is no genuine evil. Process theology also says that God is in an important sense responsible for much of the world's evil but not indictable for it. But it does this without denying the reality of genuine evil.[89]

2. Evaluation

In evaluating this theodicy, I would like to recall D. M. Baillie's words in his book *God was in Christ*, that in speaking of the biblical God we must reckon with 'dialectical contradiction'. This means that

> We cannot know God by studying Him as an object, of which we can speak as third person . . . He eludes all our words and categories. We cannot objectify or conceptualize Him. When we try we fall immediately into contradiction.

The reason for a 'theology of paradox', he says, is that 'God cannot be comprehended in any human words or in any of the categories of our finite thought. God can be known only in a direct personal relationship.'[90]

This is an important point for two reasons: first, because it affirms Bulgakov's assertion concerning God being an antinomy; and secondly, it points to the fact that we cannot know God *qua* God but only as we experience God in direct personal relationship. Baillie affirms Kant's notion, therefore, that we cannot know the *Ding an sich* but only as it is mediated through our *a priori* categories of cognition. We cannot speak of Divinity in and of itself except in so far as we wish to make statements of faith which are deduced from and shaped by our experience.

With this in mind, I shall be arguing for a theodicy with the following general characteristics. First, I agree with process thinking that, because of creaturely freedom, God cannot be seen as an omnipotent divine monarch. However, I take Williams' criticism of Whitehead (and, by extension, of Hartshorne) that their notion of the divine lure within us is too passive or at least not adequately spelled out. I concur with the point that God cannot negate an entity's freedom ultimately to decide how it will respond to the divine lure, but this still leaves enormous room for an overpowering presence of God within us. The notion of divine lure I shall be articulating is one that is at times overwhelming, at times subtly suggestive, at times brutally violent. Human power is used in this way. Sometimes people war against one another; sometimes they bargain through negotiation; sometimes they whisper intimacies. Different degrees of pressure are appropriate to different occasions. One clear example of what I mean is in God's incarnation in Christ. God was working in that event in much more than a passive way. On the other hand, God came to Elijah in a 'still small voice'. God's freedom is infinite; therefore, the range of degrees of pressure God has is to be seen as infinite. How God uses this freedom of action can be known only as humanity experiences God in the encounter of a personal relationship. What emerges from the biblical witness of these encounters is that God is antinomial.

Secondly, I shall be arguing that God must be understood to be the chief instance of the freedom to commit good and evil. I have already referred to Hartshorne's assertion that God is one whose versatility of becoming is unlimited, whose potentialities of content embrace all possibilities. Moreover, he asserts that the 'ground of good and evil is really the same; namely from the realm of multiple freedom'.

We can only know how Divinity utilizes the infinite freedom at its disposal through our experience of it. I shall seek to establish, in particular through the experience of Job and Christ crucified, that human beings experience what they define as intrinsic evil at the hands of God. This is to say that the biblical witness gives evidence of God acting in such a manner as to cause destruction, chaos, suffering and unhappiness, as well as harmony, peace, happiness, and joy.

Thirdly, while God does commit what we define as intrinsic evil as well as what we define as intrinsic good, God, as infinitely free and powerful (though not omnipotent), can use those intrinsically evil and good acts committed by God and humanity alike instrumentally for a higher purpose. There is not a single instance in the biblical tradition where the intrinsic evil committed by God is not so used. This is how I am arguing that the notion of God being the *Summum Bonum* should be seen: not that God is without shadow, but that whatever the antinomial manifestation of God, God invariably brings out of whatever good and evil there is in a situation a higher co-inherence between God and humanity. To speak of God as the *Summum Bonum* therefore is to speak of the final benevolence of God's will; it is not to assert the unblemished 'goodness' of the divine nature. The paradox is an ultimate one. On the one hand, we experience the antinomial nature of God; on the other, we experience the reality that whatever the good and evil caused by God and humanity, God's will is benevolent, for God invariably weaves the intrinsic evil and good into a higher salvific unity.

It is of course impossible to speak of the Divine as it is in and of itself. God's reality is beyond concepts, which means from our side that anything we say about God must remain ambiguous and tentative at best and ultimately based upon our experience of God. In speaking about God being the *Summum Bonum*, therefore, I am painfully aware that I am trying to describe something beyond the frontiers of language. I have used terms like 'creative integration', 'salvific unity', 'co-inherence' to connote the meaning of *Summum Bonum* but these are not altogether satisfactory.

I could equally have used Teilhard's terms 'Christification' or 'Omega Point' or even the traditional refrain that God as *Summum Bonum* works in history for the 'salvation of the elect'. Perhaps Julian of Norwich sums up God as the *Summum Bonum* the best by stating simply: 'All shall be well, and all shall be well, and all manner of thing shall be well.' In all cases, however, we must remain content with describing our *experience* of God rather than to make metaphysical claims about the *nature* of God.

Beginning with Chapter V, I shall discuss further the question of evil, particularly with reference to God. First, I shall re-examine the biblical tradition, with emphasis on the wrath of God, the suffering of Job, and the crucifixion of Christ. Secondly, I shall examine the thought of several contemporary thinkers who understand God as an antinomy. Thirdly, I shall discuss the insights of Jung into the question of evil.

E. DIVINE ACTION

If I am to argue that God is revealed in the events of human history, then I need to show how observable historical happenings can be interpreted through a confession of the community of faith, which has a sustainable ontological grounding. In short, when we speak of the 'acts of God' what is our ontology of events?

In answering this question, I concur with Ogden in believing that 'the real issue is not *whether* the statement "God acts in history" makes sense, but *what* sense it makes'.[91] This is a subtle but important shift of emphasis and recalls the distinction raised by C.

A. van Peursen between ontological and functional categories of theological discourse.

With this in mind, I wish to make two points concerning divine action in history as it relates to the biblical witness. The first is that the scriptures tell us what *actually* happened, not just what *physically* happened, although many modern secularistic writers think that by learning what physically happened they have discerned what actually happened. By 'actual' I mean history as seen 'in God', and by 'physical' I mean history as seen scientifically and historically.

In describing the actual, scripture interweaves the confessional and historical strands together into a unique combination which we today can never undo, although there is considerable pressure to do so by the 'demythologizers' on the one hand, and the 'literalists' on the other. The paradox of the biblical theologians must remain a paradox, for to opt for either a purely scientific explanation or a literalistic approach is to sever the *complexio oppositorum* that makes the actual what it is. If our previous process panentheistic claim that history is 'in God' is a valid interpretation of the biblical witness, then we must stand 'in God' to understand history and hear the scriptures, for it is 'in God' that the mythic and the mundane strands of the actual are interwoven inextricably.

An example of this point can be taken from Exodus 15.21:

> Sing to the Lord, for he has triumphed gloriously;
> the horse and his rider he has thrown into the sea.

That the horse and his rider were thrown into the sea is the *historical* fact. That the Lord has thrown them into the sea is the *actual* fact; therefore, the confessional response, 'Sing to the Lord, for he has triumphed gloriously.' If one is to speak of the event purely scientifically, then all one could say is that the horse and rider were thrown into the sea. What makes the event revelatory, however, is the enigma of divine action in this otherwise apparently mundane event. God creates in the believing community the ability to 'see' the actual: that it is God who has thrown the horse and rider into the sea.

The modern hermeneutical challenge is to be concurrently so deeply-rooted both 'in God' and in the modern world as to create a relevant context of confessional witness; i.e., to interpret the hand of God in historical events in a way that touches modern humanity while remaining consistent with the ancient credo that history is 'in God' and that God acts decisively and centrally in certain historical events which shape the whole.

There are two aspects, then, which must be kept in a creative synthesis in order to grasp the actual happening of a divine event: the aspect of historical fact and the aspect of confessional response. That Jesus died on the cross is the historical fact. That 'Christ died for our sins in accordance with the Scriptures' is the confessional response. Both are necessary components of the actual occurrence. Only when historical facts and confessional discernment interpenetrate do we have history 'in God': *Heilsgeschichte*.

The second point I wish to make is that the intersection of the historical event with the confessional response yields a dialectic that gives a dynamic quality to the biblical concept of divine action. The confession is not made static within the recitation of cosmogonic myth nor is it solidified into a juridical system of doctrine; instead, divine action is an evolving development and made discernible within the continual interpenetration of new events with confessional heritage.

This can be seen in the prophecies of Deutero-Isaiah in Isaiah 40–55, particularly since they deal with the event we have just examined in Exodus 15.21, the exodus from Egypt.

The new event so revelatory for Second Isaiah included the cataclysmic events of 596–587 BC and the experience of the exile. All of these events were crystallized in prophecy by the campaign of Cyrus, reflected in Isaiah 41.2–3 and 45.1–3, in which Cyrus defeats King Croesus of Lydia in 546 BC and prepares to take Babylon in 539 BC. This web of circumstances set in motion by Cyrus' campaign was understood in Isaiah 42.13 as typologically a *new exodus*:

> The Lord goes forth like a mighty man,
> like a man of war he stirs up his fury;
> he cries aloud, he shouts aloud,
> he shows himself mighty against his foes.

Yahweh is seen here as re-enacting the exodus from Egypt, only this time it is from Babylon after the years of exile and the initiator is Cyrus rather than Moses. Again in captivity, the chosen people of God are being miraculously delivered by their sovereign and gracious Lord. The 'God of our Fathers' is again seen to be leading Israel out of bondage.

Indeed, the prophecy recites the all-inclusive power and understanding of Yahweh, the epistemological function of which is clear: to designate the new exodus event as profoundly universalized but as still entirely within the purposes of the one true God, who proclaims:

> I am the Lord, and there is no other,
> besides me there is no God;
> I gird you, though you do not know me,
> that men may know, from the rising of the sun
> and from the west, that there is none besides me;
> I am the Lord, and there is no other (Isa. 45.5,6).

The prophecy includes an awe-inspiring confession in which all things mundane and cosmic are relativized and subsumed under the one God who acts: 'I am the Lord and

> I form light and create darkness,
> I make weal and create woe,
> I am the Lord, who do all these things (Isa. 45.7).

(The word 'woe' here is a translation of the Hebrew word *ra'*, evil.)

In this last summary the traditions from antiquity are filled to bursting, for here even the Genesis account of creation is superseded by the vision of a Creator who creates the darkness as well as the light and who creates the weal and the woe of human existence.

This is an important point, particularly in the light of what Gerhard von Rad observes, that in expressing divine creation, the Hebrews utilized the verb *bārā'*, 'to create'.[92] This verb was retained exclusively to designate the creative activity of God; it means a creative activity which on principle is without analogy. The verb *bārā'* is never connected with any statement of the material and therefore clearly contains the idea of both complete effortlessness in creation and *creatio ex nihilo*. 'The hidden pathos of this statement,' comments von Rad, 'is that God is the Lord of the world.'[93] The fact that God as Lord of the world creates evil as well as good will require much further discussion.[94] I raise the point here, however, merely within the context of Deutero-Isaiah's development of ancient themes in the light of new events.

The model I am proposing implies a 'hermeneutic of engagement'.[95] It is thus described because through it the believing community engages simultaneously the two facets of divine activity in human affairs: heritage and event. In this way, the believing community brings the confessional heritage, through which the community perceives the purposeful movement of God through the historical process, into a living encounter with contemporary reality. In this engagement the heritage is amplified, and through it the believing community interprets the event as a further illumination of a pattern already witnessed and confessed to before as in some sense numinous. In the hermeneutic of engagement, therefore, the meaning and context of contemporary events will be clarified and given their religious depth by interpreting them in the light of the paradigmatic events of the community's past.

Because it is a hermeneutic based on the notion of revelation as dynamic and continual, it is a hermeneutic that is very much open-ended. Within this understanding the Bible becomes a confessional witness to those foundational and paradigmatic historical happenings which revealed to the believers the eschatological direction and universal dimensions of a creative, sustaining and redemptive God concerned with human response to the divine presence. Consequently, biblical authority does not lie in a literalistic description of the epic events through which God revealed the divine will and purpose 'once and for all'. Rather, the Bible gives a faithful account of the junctures at the beginning of our heritage which set in motion and established the trajectory of a divinely inspired process – within human history – that involved the whole of creation, meaning both God and humanity. The foundational authority with which the Bible speaks, therefore, flows from a living numinous awareness of the reality of the divine presence in human affairs. The hermeneutic of engagement challenges the believing community to interact as seriously and completely with the contemporary world as they do with their ancient confessional witness in order to discern divine activity in history.

While not offering believers a rock of ages to which they can cling and find the solace of unchanging dogmatic truth, this hermeneutic seeks to recapture the courage of biblical faith which accepts the challenges presented by new historical events and changing understandings of the world. It seizes the challenges, subjects them to the dynamism of a living though ancient confessional heritage, and then formulates a new confessional appreciation about the ever-changing circumstances of the constant relationship between the Divine and the human, reiterating in new language the perennial witness the community has given to a God who acts in human history.

F. SUMMARY

What emerges from the above discussion is a hermeneutic that is both comprehensive and mediating, one that has attempted to keep in mind what Whitehead says about philosophy, that it must not neglect the 'multifariousness of the world – the fairies dance, and Christ is nailed to the cross'. In the context of philosophical theology, this means an openness to a pluralism of methods in the conviction that if carried far enough one will discern a complementarity at work, a mutual illumination. Put negatively, this approach necessitates a resistance to any stance which claims to be the one and only perspective or vantage point from which to perceive reality.

This notion yields an important perspective in dealing with philosophical theology, for it means that neither philosophy nor theology can be laid as a normative grid upon the other; rather, what must be attempted is a tension that seeks a synthesis between them, a perspective which attempts to remain consistent with the modern scientific and philosophical world view on the one hand and with the distinctive claims of the Christian faith on the other. The result is a dialectic in which both aspects cohere in a living dynamic relationship, keeping their respective integrities, and yet producing a synthesis greater than either of the parts.

This has been my purpose thus far: to lay a foundational matrix, composed of a synthesis of the modern assertions of science and philosophy with the ancient confessions of the Judaeo-Christian heritage. This matrix is one that takes as a given the Christian claim that God acts through mighty deeds in our history to affect our salvation; simultaneously, the matrix takes as a given that this distinctive claim must be brought into creative tension with the structures of science and philosophy through which the contemporary world understands itself and God. What emerges from this synthesis is an ontology of 'the mighty acts of God' that is both ancient in its origins and modern in its amplifications. Although a complete ontology has not been attempted, I have set forth the following considerations which are germane to the subject at hand:

1. I have assumed as a given the distinctive Christian claim that God creatively acts in human history according to divine purpose.

2. I have rejected the traditional theistic notion of God in favour of a notion which I have termed process panentheism. Process panentheism is characterized by the following:

   a) God is dipolar, possessing both abstract and consequent aspects: i.e. God is both transcendent and immanent, both cosmic and historical.

   b) God and the world co-inhere panentheistically in relational encounter. God is the all-embracing reality within which history takes place.

   c) God is above all a social God, creatively shaping each occasion with a divine lure which is at times overwhelming, at times subtly suggestive, depending on the divine will for that particular event. However, God is not seen as omnipotent, in the traditional sense of an Absolute Monarch, because human freedom is taken seriously as an objectively real component of reality. Nevertheless, the power of God to work creatively with evil is ultimately sovereign.

d) God is creatively dependent upon the results of creaturely actions, assimilating the human actualization of the divine lure back into the divine pleroma.

e) The co-inherence of God and humanity is a relationship which brings both into a creative advance into novelty. Both God and the world are in a process of becoming, in which each is vulnerable to the activity of the other. The interface between the consequent aspect of God and human freedom is the co-creation of history.

f) God as experienced in history is antinomial, possessing light and dark dimensions. While antinomial, however, God is also experienced as the *Summum Bonum* because whatever the intrinsic evil or good committed by either God or humanity, God always creatively integrates the strands together according to a higher purpose.

Even as process panentheism asserts that God and humanity co-create the next creative advance which will affect them both, so the hermeneutic of engagement asserts that both the confessional heritage and the contemporary event are necessary in any ontology of divine action: both create the event as a 'mighty act of God', and both are mutually affected by it.

It is by way of this hermeneutic and the ontological considerations of process panentheism that I will proceed now into the particular divine/human encounter we are considering; namely, the atomic bombing of Hiroshima. I shall be designating it as the historical event. The aspect of our confessional heritage that this event directly affects and amplifies is apocalyptic; this is designated as the confessional heritage. Following a discussion of each separately, I will offer a synthesis which will give particular emphasis to the depth psychology of Jung.

IV

The Historical Event: The Atomic Bombing of Hiroshima

A. THE EVENT

On 24 July 1945, in an attempt to bring World War II to a close, President Truman ordered the atomic bombing of Japan.[1]

Nearly a year previously, on 1 September 1944, the 393rd Heavy Bombardment Squadron of the US air force, based in Nebraska, had been assigned to Lieutenant Colonel Paul Tibbets and directed to begin practice runs to prepare for dropping the bomb. By the time of the final days between Potsdam and 6 August, Tibbets and his crews were on stand-by on the Trinian Islands, southwest of Japan, from where the bombs were to be delivered.

Although Lieutenant General Leslie Groves, the Commanding Officer of the Manhattan Project which developed the bomb, wanted to bomb the city of Kyoto first, Secretary of War Henry Stimson overruled him, stating that while it was a military target of considerable importance, it had been the ancient capital of Japan and was therefore a shrine of Japanese culture and art. Instead, Stimson approved four other target sites, including Hiroshima and Nagasaki, stating that these were both 'active working parts of the Japanese war effort. Hiroshima was not only a major assembly and military storage point but was the headquarters of the Japanese army defending southern Japan. Nagasaki was a major seaport with several large industrial plants.'[2]

After several days' delay because of bad weather, the bombing mission finally took off from Trinian towards Japan at 2.47 a.m. on 6 August. The bomb was aboard the Enola Gay, commanded by Tibbets, and was accompanied by two observation planes carrying cameras, scientific instruments and trained observers. At 3.00 a.m. assembly of the bomb began; by 3.20 a.m. this was completed, making it a 'final bomb'.

Tibbets had been ordered to scrap the mission if Hiroshima was sealed in clouds. At 7.24 a.m., however, his weather plane radioed: 'Cloud cover less than 3/10ths at all altitudes. Advice: bomb primary.' This report, according to the official US air force history, 'sealed the city's doom'.[3]

To appreciate fully what happened next two things should be borne in mind. The first is the magnitude of what the Enola Gay was carrying. Most of the destruction that occurred during World War II was caused by bombs having the equivalent of about one ton of TNT. Towards the end of the war, new bombs were developed containing ten tons of TNT; they were termed 'blockbusters' because of their amazing capacity to devastate an entire city block. The very biggest of these blockbusters contained almost twelve tons of TNT, the largest one being the 'Grand Slam', made in Britain.

The bomb that was dropped on Hiroshima exploded with a force equivalent to 12,000 tons of TNT or *one thousand* times the force of the largest blockbuster. To appreciate the power of this, recall the fire-bombing of Dresden in 1944, perhaps the worst bombing event of the European theatre of the war. Over 60,000 people were killed in an attack composed of over fifteen hours of continuous saturation bombing by Allied planes. The Hiroshima bomb pulverized an entire city in one single blast.

The second thing to be kept in mind is that almost inversely proportional to the magnitude of the bomb was the city's unpreparedness for it. It was wartime, of course, and people had expected a conventional bombing raid to occur at some point, but though air raid alerts had been regularly sounded, only an occasional stray bomb had ever been dropped on Hiroshima. It is true that on 27 July American planes dropped leaflets warning Hiroshima residents that their city was going to be demolished if the Japanese did not surrender immediately and unconditionally, but research indicates that very few people ever saw these leaflets and those who did discounted them as enemy propaganda. In any case, the leaflets made no mention of an atomic bomb or any other kind of special weapon. This omission was a conscious one on the part of the American decision makers, as it was felt that any previous warning of a specifically nuclear attack 'would hinder rather than serve our wish to end the war at once'.[4]

There was a more immediate factor that contributed to the element of total surprise. The night previous to the bombing had witnessed two separate air-raid alerts during which no bombs had fallen. At 7.10 a.m. on 6 August a third alert sounded, following the spotting of Commander Tibbets' weather planes over southern Japan. Because of these three false alarms no additional alert was sounded when the actual bombing planes appeared over the city shortly after 8.00 a.m. The only warning was that of a radio announcement noting that the planes appeared to be on a reconnaissance mission.

Since people began their workdays early during the wartime summer, many were already at work or en route by 8.00 a.m. Housewives were completing after-breakfast chores with the charcoal still burning in their hibachis, the general atmosphere being that of early morning complacency. Hiroshima was quite simply as in the days of Noah before the flood: 'They were eating and drinking, marrying and giving in marriage, until the day when Noah entered the ark, and they did not know until the flood came and swept them all away . . .' (Matt. 24.38–39a). As one survivor later described it:

The sky was serene, the air was flooded with glittering morning light. My steps were slow along the dry, dusty road. I was in a state of absent-mindedness. The sirens and also the radio had just given the all-clear signal. I had reached the foot of the bridge, where I halted, and was turning my eyes toward the water . . .[5]

Precisely at 8.15.17 a.m. the bomb-bay doors of the Enola Gay snapped open. The plane lurched upwards nearly ten feet, suddenly 9,000 pounds lighter. Inside the bomb a timer tripped the first switch in the firing circuit, letting the electricity travel a measured distance towards the detonator. At 5,000 feet above the ground a barometric switch was triggered. At 1,890 feet the detonator was activated, the bomb exploding at 8.16, forty-three seconds after falling from the Enola Gay.

In the first milli-second after detonation, a pin-prick of purplish-red light expanded into a glowing fireball a half mile in diameter; the temperature at its core was 50,000,000 degrees fahrenheit. At Ground Zero, some two thousand feet directly underneath the explosion, temperatures reached several thousand degrees, melting the surface of granite 1,000 yards away. Nine hundred yards from the epicentre, several thousand soldiers, including one American prisoner of war, were doing their morning exercises in the courtyard of Hiroshima Castle: they were instantly incinerated, their charred bodies burnt into the ground.

Watching from below, one child remembered later the entire sequence leading up to this first milli-second:

I was watching the aeroplane the whole time . . . Suddenly a thing like a white parachute came falling. Five or six seconds later everything turned yellow in one instant. It felt the way it does when you get the sunlight straight into your eye . . .[6]

After this first blast of light, the fireball suddenly exploded into a mass of swirling flames and purple clouds out of which came a huge column of white smoke which rose to a level of 10,000 feet. At 10,000 feet, the column flattened outwards to form a mushroom-shaped cloud, then climbed upwards until it reached a height of 45,000–50,000 feet.

To those aboard the Enola Gay, observing the scene at an altitude of 29,000 feet eleven miles away, the scene was quite spectacular, as the tailgunner, Sergeant George Caron, recalls:

A column of smoke rising fast. It has a fiery red core. A bubbling mass purple-grey in colour, with that red core . . . It's all turbulent. Fires are springing up everywhere, like flames shooting out of a huge bed of coals . . . Here it comes, the mushroom shape . . . like a mass of bubbling molasses . . . It's very black, but there is a purplish tint to the cloud. The base of the mushroom looks like a heavy undercast that is shot through with flames. The city must be below that . . .[7]

It was, Caron remembered later, like 'a peep into hell'.

One person in the 'hell' Caron describes remembers things much more starkly, recalling only 'a sudden flash, a blast, and then a cataclysmic earthquake – all the representatives of disaster and death, each following the other.'[8] More eloquent is the recollection of another survivor who remembers it as being awesome and replete with diabolic beauty:

A blinding . . . flash cut sharply across the sky . . . I threw myself onto the ground . . . in a reflex movement. At the same moment as the flash, the skin over my body felt a burning heat . . . (then there was) a blank in time . . . dead silence . . . probably a few seconds . . . and then a . . . huge boom . . . like the rumbling of distant thunder. At the same time a violent rush of air pressed down my entire body . . . Again there were some moments of blackness . . . then a complicated series of shattering noises . . . I raised my head, facing the centre of Hiroshima to the west . . . (there I saw) an enormous mass of clouds . . . (which) spread and climbed rapidly . . . into the sky. Then its summit broke open and hung over horizontally. It took the shape of . . . a monstrous mushroom with the lower part as its stem – it would be more accurate to call it the tail of a tornado. Beneath it more and more boiling clouds erupted and unfolded sideways . . . the shape . . . the colour . . . the light . . . were continuously shifting and changing.[9]

The aiming point of the bomb was a central area of Hiroshima adjacent to an Army Headquarters with 60% of the population within 1.2 miles; the drop was accurate to within 200 yards of the aiming point. The explosion created an area of total destruction extending two miles in all directions in a flat city of homes and buildings made largely of wood. Within three miles of the epicentre 62,000 out of 90,000 buildings were destroyed. All utilities and transport services were demolished, and twenty-six out of thirty-three fire stations were destroyed, leaving only sixteen pieces of fire-fighting equipment to deal with a whole city on fire. Forty-two of the city's forty-five hospitals were devastated, killing 270 of the 298 doctors and 1,645 of the 1,780 nurses.

The number of deaths, both immediately and after a period of time, will never be known. They are variously estimated from 63,000 to 240,000. The official US estimate is 78,000, although the city of Hiroshima estimates 200,000. The reason for this enormous disparity is because of such things as differing techniques of calculation, varying estimates of the actual number of people in the city at the time, the manner in which military fatalities are included, and the census count on the basis of which the approximation was made. It is safe to say that of a city population variously estimated to be from 270,000 to 400,000, between 25% and 50% were killed by one solitary twelve kiloton atomic bomb.

It is also safe to say that the entire city became immediately involved in the atomic disaster. Within 1,500 feet of the epicentre, research has concluded there were 3,483 people; 88% died either instantly or that same day, only 53 survived beyond a few years. If a person survived within 1,000 yards, more than 90% of those around him or her were fatalities; at 2,000 yards, 80% of those unshielded were killed. Although mortality was lower if one was indoors, one had to be at least 2,200 yards (1.3 miles) from the epicentre to have even a 50% chance of surviving immediate death. The heaviest casualties were among the children.

So complete was the destruction that a history professor recalls that

I climbed Hijiyama Hill and looked down. I saw that Hiroshima

had disappeared . . . I was shocked by the sight . . . What I felt
then and feel now I just can't explain with words. Of course I saw
many dreadful scenes after that – but that experience, looking
down and finding nothing left of Hiroshima – was so shocking that
I simply can't express what I felt. I could see Koi (a suburb at the
opposite end of the city) and a few buildings standing . . . But
Hiroshima didn't exist – that was mainly what I saw – Hiroshima
just didn't exist.[10]

'Such a weapon,' he was to recall later, 'has the power to make
everything into nothing.'[11]

The press statement issued from Washington, DC, on the afternoon of 6 August announced that a bomb had been dropped on
Hiroshima with a yield of 20,000 tons of TNT. In simple and concise
language it stated:

It is an atomic bomb. It is a harnessing of the basic powers of the
universe. The force from which the sun draws its power has been
loosed against those who brought war to the Far East.[12]

Although the Japanese Emperor wanted to surrender at this
point, his generals remained in favour of the war effort, still arguing
that a decisive battle could be won that would ensure a negotiated
settlement. They further urged that the effects of the atomic bombing
be minimized. Without a large enough constituency supporting him,
the Emperor relented, and on the morning of 7 August Tokyo radios
reported that 'a small number of B-29s penetrated into Hiroshima
city a little after 8.00 a.m. yesterday morning and dropped a small
number of bombs. As a result a considerable number of homes were
reduced to ashes and fire broke out in various parts of the city.'[13]

On 8 August, while the US intensified its call for immediate
unconditional surrender, 'otherwise we shall resolutely employ this
bomb and all our superior weapons to promptly and forcefully end
the war',[14] the Japanese military continued to insist that the war be
carried on and the devastation of Hiroshima minimized. That
afternoon, with no Japanese surrender forthcoming, Top Secret
Field Order 17 was issued, naming Kokura as the primary target,
Nagasaki the secondary target, for the next atomic bombing.

At 10.58 a.m. on 9 August, as the Supreme War Council continued
to argue in Tokyo, Major Charles Sweeney, commander of the
second atomic bombing mission, began his final run over Nagasaki,
having been forced to relinquish Kokura because of weather con-

ditions. The bomb used against Hiroshima was of Uranium 235; the Nagasaki bomb was of Plutonium 239.

Like the Hiroshima bomb, the moment of detonation was an explosion of light exceeding 50,000,000 degrees fahrenheit. Frank Chinnock describes the impact of this first milli-second of heat:

> For some 1,000 yards, or three-fifths of a mile, in all directions from the epicentre . . . it was as if a malevolent god had suddenly focused a gigantic blowtorch on a small section of our planet. Within that perimeter, nearly all unprotected living organisms – birds, insects, horses, cats, chickens – perished instantly. Flowers, trees, grass, plants, all shrivelled and died. Wood burst into flames. Metal beams and galvanized iron roofs began to bubble, and the soft gooey masses twisted into grotesque shapes. Stones were pulverized, and for a second every last bit of air was burned away. The people exposed within that doomed section neither knew nor felt anything, and their blackened unrecognizable forms dropped silently where they stood.[15]

After this explosion of heat and light came the explosion of sound, travelling at a speed of 9,000 miles per hour. It destroyed every building within 800 yards, and of the 55,000 buildings throughout the city, 20,000 were demolished. More would have been damaged had it not been for the hilly topography of Nagasaki which kept much of the destruction confined to Urakami Valley in the northern sectors of the city.

Immediately after the explosion of sound came the third and final killer: radiation, probably the most frightening of all because it acted silently and invisibly and at the time was barely even known about, much less understood. At the moment of the explosion, various radiation rays were emitted: beta, gamma, alpha and X-rays and neutrons. The X-rays, gamma rays and neutrons were most injurious. In addition, fission products such as strontium-90, which attacks the white blood cells, causing leukaemia, and cesium-137, which is carcinogenic to muscle tissue and the ova of females, were scattered everywhere. These were later named by the survivors of both Hiroshima and Nagasaki the 'ashes of death', because they constituted the 'invisible contamination' which struck the people without warning and with no hope of cure.

The radiation released from both the Hiroshima and Nagasaki bombs was so massive that, even without the heat, blast or the explosion of sound, the number of deaths within 1,000 yards of the epicentre would have remained essentially the same. The primary difference would have been in the amount of time it took the victims to die. Those killed instantly would have lived instead for twenty-four to forty-eight hours, until the radiation destroyed their white blood cells and bone marrow, causing death from radiation sickness.

The overall estimate of casualties from the Nagasaki bombing, as at Hiroshima, varies greatly. The US official estimate is 40,000 killed; the Nagasaki estimate is 74,800 killed, 75,000 wounded. In all cases, what is certain is that Nagasaki, like Hiroshima, was immediately inundated by death and destruction on an unprecedented scale.

Even after this second cataclysm, however, the Japanese Supreme War Council wished to fight on. Finally, at 2.00 a.m. on 10 August, after a grim and protracted debate in which the War Minister, joined by the Chiefs of Army and Navy Staff, argued that Japan could get better terms than the Potsdam Ultimatum if she hung on, the Prime Minister, Suzuki, stepped forward and in an act unprecedented in modern Japanese history asked the Emperor to decide. An absolute command by the Emperor was known among the Japanese as the Voice of the Sacred Crane. When it was heard on this occasion, it called for immediate and unconditional surrender.

B. COMMENT

Henry Wieman, perhaps more incisively than anyone, describes the cataclysmic dimensions of the Hiroshima bombing:

> The bomb that fell on Hiroshima cut history in two like a knife. Before and after are two different worlds. That cut is more abrupt, decisive, and revolutionary than the cut made by the star over Bethlehem. It may not be more creative of human good than the star, but it is more swiftly transformative of human existence than anything else that has ever happened. The economic and political order fitted to the age before the parachute fell becomes suicidal in the age coming after. The same breach extends into education and religion.[16]

'More revolutionary than the cut made by the star over Bethlehem' is Wieman's description of the impact of the historical event of Hiroshima, a description which, hyperbole or not, indicates the depth of human experience with which Judaeo-Christian theology is being challenged to engage.

Hiroshima produced a qualitative leap in human capabilities to destroy that places us in a qualitatively different mode of being: we can now perform major surgical operations on the human body politic, if not destroy the collective human organism entirely.

The importance of this is brought out by Arthur Koestler:

> If I were asked to name the most important date in the history of the human race, I would answer without hesitation, 6th August, 1945. From the dawn of consciousness until 6th August, 1945, man had to live with the prospect of his death as an individual; since the day when the first atomic bomb outshone the sun over Hiroshima, he has had to live with the prospect of his extinction as a species.[17]

It is ironic that 6 August is also the day each year when Christians celebrate the Feast of the Transfiguration, when Jesus went to the top of a mountain with his disciples Peter, James and John and was transfigured before them.

The Hiroshima experience, as that of Nagasaki three days later, was a transfiguration as well, shining 'brighter than a thousand suns', but its transfiguration was the opposite of the healing and redemptive light of Christ. Two cities of several hundred thousand people were instantly pulverized without warning in a raw display of power that shocked the world.

The Japanese in Hiroshima and Nagasaki who survived are known as *hibakusha*, a coined work that means 'explosion-affected person'.

The phrase used repeatedly by many *hibakusha* is 'mugamuchu', literally meaning 'without self, without centre'. As the *hibakusha* recall it, the atomic attack quite simply exploded the boundaries of the self. What the *hibakusha* found themselves thrust into, therefore, in terms of the immediate impact of the bomb as well as of the longer-term physical and psychological consequences, was, to quote Robert J. Lifton, author of the definitive study on the *hibakusha*, *Death in Life*, 'a vast breakdown of faith in the larger human matrix supporting each individual life, and therefore a loss of faith (of trust) in the structure of human existence'.[18]

This 'vast breakdown' was due primarily to what Lifton terms the 'indelible imprint of death immersion'. This immersion involves a complex of many factors: the fear of annihilation of both self and individual identity after having virtually experienced that annihilation; the destruction of the ecological environment; the devastation of the field of one's normal existence and hence of one's general sense of 'being-in-the-world'; and finally and most importantly, what Lifton calls the *'replacement of the natural order of living and dying with an unnatural order of death-dominated life'*.[19]

The key to understanding the Hiroshima experience, then, in terms both of its immediate devastation and of its impact on the psyche of the survivors, is by way of the overwhelming imprint of death on both environment and people. It is an imprint that permanently 'engraved' in their minds the imagery of death. This imprint has been a lasting one in the life of the *hibakusha* for two reasons: (a) the long-term effects of radiation upon the body, affecting even future generations; and (b) the lasting impact of the bombing event upon the psyche of the *hibakusha*.

What needs to be stressed is that the death immersion experienced by the *hibakusha* is not limited to them.

Just as Lifton observed that all Japanese, whether officially *hibakusha* or not, suffered the impact of the atomic bomb experience, particularly the youth, so all of us are in some degree affected as well; that is to say, that the psychological occurrences in Hiroshima and Nagasaki have an important bearing on all of human existence. What happened then can happen again to all of us. As Lifton puts it: 'We are all survivors of Hiroshima and, in our imaginations, of future nuclear holocaust.'[20] This is a link which is not metaphorical but real. This is because of the omnipresent spectre of this holocaust in fact happening again, and it is also because the specific psychological components of the Hiroshima *hibakusha* can be explored in relation to the general psychology of the 'survivor', a category in which, since 6 August 1945, the rest of humanity can be placed.

That we are all survivors can be seen from the definition of survivor Lifton offers, namely 'one who has come into contact with death in some bodily or *psychic* fashion and has himself remained alive'.[21] I have emphasized psychic because that is the category in which all non-official *hibakusha* fall. It is the category, therefore, which must be thoroughly explored in order to comprehend the magnitude of the impact of the Hiroshima experience upon human history and psychic life.

Perhaps this psychic dimension has been most eloquently described by one particular *hibakusha*, Pedro Arrupe, a Jesuit priest who was later to become Father General of the Society of Jesus. He was near Hiroshima when the bomb was dropped, and therefore fits into the category of *hibakusha* since he was a doctor and spent weeks in the city caring for the victims. He details his impression as a witness to that event by what the initial blast did to his wall clock: it stopped it. The Hiroshima event, he says, did precisely that to the traditional historical process: it stopped it. 'For me', he writes in his book, *A Planet to Heal*, that silent and motionless clock has become a symbol. The explosion of the first atomic bomb has become a para-historical phenomenon. It is not a memory, it is a perpetual experience, outside history, which does not pass with the ticking of the clock. The pendulum stopped and Hiroshima has remained engraved on my mind. It has no relation to time. It belongs to motionless eternity.[22]

By exploding the normal cyclic patterns through which the human family is accustomed to live and to die, the atom bomb placed us all in an altered state of space/time, revolutionizing crime and punishment and demanding a corresponding transformation in our conception of world justice to balance our new-found powers to mete out destruction. Quite literally, Arrupe recalls his consciousness being seared by the atomic bomb, cutting him off from his past and placing him within the perpetual context of death immersion. His experience is similar to the *hibakusha* Lifton studied, people who were all caught up in 'the sense of a sudden and absolute shift from normal experience to an overwhelming encounter with death'.[23]

In an examination of the *hibakusha*, what emerges are the themes of death imprintation, death guilt, psychic numbing, counterfeit nurturance and contagion, and re-integration. These are all universal psychological tendencies, ones in which all of us to some degree participate as we try to reconcile the omnipresent possibility of nuclear holocaust with our personal lives, and as we attempt to put time back in motion, and space back in order, after the Hiroshima bomb exploded all our known categories. We are all survivors of Hiroshima; we are all potential victims of its re-enactment.

In order to understand the full impact of Hiroshima, detached intellectual appreciation is not enough. The demand is that the 'observer' realize that she or he is part of that experience, that the same psychological reactions and formulations occurring then and there are playing a role in each of us here and now. Our connection, therefore, must be seen as *organic*; organic because Hiroshima has deeply affected our very psyche. With Arrupe we must realize that Hiroshima has remained 'engraved' on the human mind since 6 August 1945. Therefore, it is fundamental to realize that the experience of the *hibakusha* is paradigmatic for all of us: 'the survivor becomes every man'.[24]

C. THE PLUTONIUM CULTURE

I shall have much more to say about the psychic reality of the Hiroshima event in our present historical situation. What needs to be stressed here is that our organic connection with Hiroshima is more than psychic; it is a corporeal reality which directly affects our everyday lives. This is due to two factors: the first is the connection between nuclear weapons and the rest of nuclear technology; the second is the relationship between nuclear technology and the technotronic society in which we live. In discussing these points what shall emerge is the realization that Hiroshima was not an event that happened once and for all in 1945; rather, 6 August 1945 signalled the beginning of a new age in human history. The mentality and technology that produced the nuclear annihilations of Hiroshima and Nagasaki shaped the 'peace' that followed the Second World War and have permeated decisions concerning foreign policy, energy and economics ever since. In this way what happened in 1945 to two cities in Japan has come to touch us all.

1. Nuclear technology and nuclear weapons

The first point mentioned, that of the connection between nuclear weapons and the rest of nuclear technology, is of utmost importance. While none of us experienced the bombing of Hiroshima, virtually all of us have seen nuclear reactors, plutonium reprocessing centres, or uranium enrichment plants. These are the children of Hiroshima. A little history illustrates the point.

During the 1930s, growing understanding of the structure of the atom and the properties of radiation led physicist Wolfgang Pauli to suggest that large amounts of energy could be derived from both nuclear fission and fusion. At about the same time the postulate was made in another field of research that the photovoltaic conversion of light was also a possible source of large amounts of energy. By the outbreak of the Second World War, the potentials of both nuclear energy and solar energy were known and were the focus of research. Investment in both areas by government and scientific institutions was balanced, and research was largely theoretical. When the Americans, Canadians and British set up the Manhattan Project in their attempt to create an atomic bomb, however, investment ceased to be balanced, and theoretical research became practical. Military priorities, and the deep-seated fear on the part of many scientists that Hitler might get the Bomb first, resulted in the most massive capital investment and coordinated scientific research ever attempted by humankind. The consequence was the atomic bombing of Hiroshima on 6 August 1945, and the plutonium bombing of Nagasaki on 9 August 1945. In many ways, this development of the Bomb was an inevitable result of the scientific knowledge of the time and the magnitude of the Nazi threat.

What was not inevitable was the way the imbalance created by the war became institutionalized in the peace that followed. By the 1950s, the same criteria which had selected the energy for weapons selected the energy for peace: massive investments were poured into nuclear reactor research and development with the same single-mindedness that had produced the Bomb. Completely ignored were the solar energy possibilities that had looked equally promising in the 1930s. This has caused such a disruption in the post-war world that Anthony Tucker, science editor of *The Guardian*, has asserted that 'when historians look back from next century, if there are any in the next century, they may well see this as the greatest error of technical, social and political judgment ever made by mankind'.[25]

Nuclear power was born within the context of nuclear weapons; indeed, the first uranium enrichment plants, nuclear reactors and plutonium reprocessing facilities ever built were operated for the express purpose of producing either the enriched uranium or plutonium necessary for nuclear bombs. For example, when in January 1947 the British government decided to develop an 'independent' nuclear arsenal, enrichment and reprocessing facilities were built at Capenhurst and Windscale. These facilities enabled Britain to detonate its first atomic bomb in 1952. Britain's first nuclear reactors, at Calder Hall (1956) and Chapelcross (1958), provided plutonium for Britain's expanding nuclear arsenal. It was only after serving a military purpose that the Capenhurst uranium enrichment plant, the Windscale reprocessing centre and the nuclear reactors were used for civil purposes. This same pattern can be seen in every other country which has become a nuclear weapons state: the US, USSR, China, France. In 1974, India exploded a nuclear device after diverting plutonium from an 'experimental' reactor, although it has yet to demonstrate actual nuclear weapons capability. According to the CIA, Israel also has nuclear weapons, but it is unclear how it obtained the material. Suggestions range from theft to secret agreement with the Americans to provide the material. Other countries are on the verge of nuclear weapons status by virtue of their possession and utilization of various other aspects of civil nuclear power. These include: Argentina, Brazil, South Africa, Pakistan, Taiwan, South Korea and Iraq. Indeed, so close was Iraq to gaining nuclear weapons capability from its 'civil' nuclear programme that Israel found it necessary in June 1981 to launch a secret raid that completely demolished the 70 megawatt Osirak nuclear reactor the Iraqis had built near Baghdad. Prime Minister Begin defended Israel's 'pre-emptive strike' by saying that Israeli intelligence had data indicating that the Iraqis intended to build nuclear bombs from that particular reactor which were intended for use against Israel.

The Iraqi incident highlights the point being made, for it not only brings into dramatic focus the inseparable link between nuclear power and nuclear weapons, but it also offers an example of the international intrigues and high tensions which surround nuclear technology generally.

Iraq first entered the nuclear field in 1959 with an agreement with the Soviet Union to build a small nuclear reactor outside Baghdad. During the 1970s, however, Iraqi President Saddam Hussein sought to make Iraq the leading Arab power in the Middle East. He turned to France and Italy, two of Iraq's major oil customers, for sophisticated nuclear technology, including a research reactor and a plutonium separating facility capable of producing nuclear weapons-grade fuel.

Israel's intelligence agency, Mossad, began to become alarmed in 1976 when the budget for Iraq's Atomic Energy Commission went from $5 million to $70 million. President Hussein contracted with Italy to buy a 'hot cell' – processing equipment capable of producing weapons-grade plutonium. Iraq also signed a contract with France to build the $275 million Osirak 'research' reactor, to be operational by 1981. Iraqi delegations also began touring nuclear installations in France, West Germany, Sweden, and Italy.

Israel's counter-measures were initially modest. Israeli diplomats urged France and Italy to use greater caution in dealing with Iraq. France pointed out in reply that unlike Israel, Iraq had signed the Nuclear Non-proliferation Treaty and that the Osirak project contained safeguards against diversion for military purposes.

With diplomatic results not forthcoming, Mossad turned to more underhand methods. The French-Iraqi nuclear project suddenly became plagued by sabotage and mysterious deaths. In April 1979, saboteurs attempted to blow up the French reactor shortly before it was to be shipped from a warehouse in La Seyne-sur-Mer to Iraq. Only minor damage resulted. In 1980, Yahia El Meshad, the head of the Iraqi nuclear programme, was found bludgeoned to death in his hotel room in Paris. Several weeks later a French prostitute named Marie-Claude Magal who was reported to have been a witness to Meshad's murder, was herself killed in Paris by a hit-and-run driver. Following this incident, bombs wrecked the Rome offices of the Italian nuclear company working in Iraq, SNIA Technit. There was also an unsuccessful assassination attempt on a French scientist working on the Osirak project.

Undaunted, the Osirak project continued. In early 1980 Iraq signed an agreement with Brazil – another country refusing to sign the Non-Proliferation Treaty – for exchange of nuclear technology and supplies of uranium. Iraq also began buying both legal and black market uranium from Italy, Portugal and Niger; and it began to carry out exchanges of information with Pakistan within the International Atomic Energy Agency.

Iraqi intentions became so obvious that in the spring of 1980, US President Carter asked that both the French and Italian governments halt the project. Specifically, Carter asked the French not to ship their first twelve-kilogramme load of weapons-grade enriched uranium to Iraq. The US request was turned down by both governments.

Late in 1980, French Prime Minister Raymond Barre, in a trip to Iraq, tried to persuade the Iraqis to accept a different design for their project. Barre proposed that they use 'caramel' fuel, a low-grade French uranium that cannot be used for weapons purposes. Hussein refused. He threatened to cancel the rest of the 1976 agreement with France, which besides committing the French to build the Osirak reactor, provided the export of 10 million tons of Iraqi oil to France and $1.6 billion worth of French helicopters, missiles and other weapons to Iraq. Faced with this threat, the French backed down.

On 30 September 1980, during the early period of the Iraqi-Iranian war, two Phantom jets swooped down on the Osirak complex and dropped bombs which damaged the facility but did not knock it out. Whether these were Iranian or Israeli jets is unclear. Following the raid, President Hussein declared that Iran had nothing to fear from Iraq's nuclear capability. Any of its weapons, he said, would be used 'against the Zionist enemy'.

The 'Zionist enemy' was not asleep. In the spring of 1980, Israel received its first F-16 fighter bombers from the US. The Osirak project was now within range of the Israeli Air Force. In the summer of 1980 Israel again tried diplomatic pressure on the French to get them to desist from giving Iraq weapons-grade fuel. When this failed Israeli Prime Minister Menachem Begin summoned General David Ivri, the chief of the Israeli Air Force, and directed him to start planning an air strike. Ivri's reply was Operation Babylon, which on 14 June 1981 completely demolished the Osirak complex with fifteen tons of air-dropped TNT.

What emerges with stark clarity from the Osirak raid is the interrelationship between civil nuclear power and nuclear weapons, for although civil nuclear power appears peaceful enough, quietly providing work for research laboratories or producing electricity, it can be used to make bombs. This is why the Israelis sent their Air Force to Baghdad.

Whether for bombs or fuel, the basic ingredient is uranium. Uranium comes from the ground and must first be mined, milled and enriched before it is usable for either reactors or weapons. Uranium contains two isotopes: U–235 and U–238. U–235 fissions more quickly than U–238 but it makes up less than 1% of the natural uranium. Thus the uranium has to be 'enriched' – reactor fuel to 3–5% U–235 and research reactors to 90% U–235 optimally. Since atomic bombs must use at least 50% U–235, reactor fuel will not work; but fuel for a research reactor such as Iraq's would.

A more efficient way to build a bomb is to 'breed' plutonium from the more common U–238. This happens as a matter of course in a power reactor, where the neutrons bombarding the uranium gradually turn much of the U–238 into plutonium–239. In a research reactor, the target of the neutrons is generally cobalt or something equally harmless. If the intent is for weapons, however, the operators can just as easily aim their neutrons at a pile of uranium. A reactor like Osirak could produce enough plutonium for a bomb every two years.

Although in 1973 the US Atomic Energy Commission exploded a plutonium device in Nevada, using plutonium straight from a reactor, i.e. plutonium that was not reprocessed, the usual procedure is to separate the plutonium-uranium mixture. Doing this from a research reactor is easier than from a regular power reactor because in a power reactor, the plutonium sits in the core for long periods, up to seven years, and so gathers impurities. In a research reactor, the plutonium can be extracted before impurities have time to settle in. Technicians simply add an acid and beads of resin that pull the metal out of its solution. Any country with a modest chemicals industry has the capacity to purify enough plutonium to build bombs.

Once this is done, it is a question of which kind of nuclear device is wanted. The atomic bomb dropped on Hiroshima was of the 'gun' design: conventional explosives drove two pieces of uranium together to form a critical mass, triggering the nuclear explosion. In

Nagasaki the 'implosion-type' design was used: a core of plutonium was surrounded by conventional explosives. When the explosives detonated, the plutonium was crushed into a critical mass, which in turn exploded.

What the situation boils down to is that if a country has a civil nuclear enrichment or reactor programme, it has both the necessary ingredients and the basic technology for developing a nuclear weapons capability. I stress that this is how Britain, the US, USSR, France and China got the Bomb. What is there to stop other countries from doing so? There are over fifty countries now with nuclear programmes, eighteen of which already have plutonium stockpiles. Each country will make its own political judgment as to whether or not it will go nuclear. The only way to stop nuclear weapons is to stop the proliferation of nuclear technology. Being inseparable, the two will rise and fall together.

Unless one insists on dichotomizing one's thinking, therefore, one cannot be opposed to nuclear weapons and then be in favour of the technology that produces the uranium and plutonium necessary for these weapons. Rather, one must be willing to realize that Oppenheimer was right in saying after Hiroshima that 'physicists have known sin'. Nuclear reactors are merely the extension of the nuclear weapons programme into the civil sector, and in many cases are the cover under which military intentions are hidden, until such time as the nuclear devices secretly built can be publicly exploded, as in India in 1974.

Two objections are generally raised by those supporting nuclear power against the interconnection I am describing between nuclear power and nuclear weapons. The first is that there are other methods of obtaining bomb grade material than from reactors, and therefore reactors *per se* are not the problem. Terrorist groups would find it extremely difficult, for instance, to penetrate into a reactor compound and steal enough plutonium. This objection has some merit. As I have argued, weapons-grade material can be obtained from the enrichment stage of the uranium fuel cycle. Nor is this technology very complex; indeed, Amory Lovins has pointed out that one unirradiated fuel bundle from a Light Water Reactor (it takes about a hundred fuel bundles to make up the reactor core) can be made into a bomb's worth of plutonium in one year by one technician with about £800 million of materials that are available over the counter. Clearly this route would be much easier for terrorist organizations than using reactor waste. However, what is being exported to *countries* is not so much enrichment technology as reactor technology and therefore this is the route they will most likely use. Worldwide production of plutonium from reactors is currently estimated to be at 30 tons – 10,000 nuclear bombs' worth. One third of this is being produced by non-weapons states. 'Research' reactors capable of producing bomb-grade plutonium are in thirty countries. Argentina is an example of a country currently on the verge of nuclear weapons status because, following India's example, it is diverting plutonium from its nuclear reactors for military purposes.

The second objection stems from the example of Canada announcing at the 1979 UN Special Session on Disarmament that it would refuse to site nuclear weapons on its soil but would continue with its civil nuclear power programme. Nuclear advocates argue from this that it is possible to separate the two. I agree it is possible – but probable? It is important to note that when Prime Minister Trudeau made this announcement, he admitted that Canada was under the US nuclear umbrella no matter what it did. Geographic proximity and the US Monroe Doctrine make this a certainty. But what about countries not under the US or Soviet umbrellas, like Iraq or South Africa or Pakistan? In an era where political power is too often equated with the strength of one's military industrial complex and where ultimate military power is symbolized by the nuclear bomb, it is unlikely that many countries will follow Canada's lead.

Even if this were the case, however, nuclear reactor technology is extremely dangerous in its own right. Each large reactor has about a thousand times the radiation in its core as that produced by the Hiroshima bomb. In 1964, the US Atomic Energy Commission did a study which concluded that if only 50% of this radioactivity was released in an accident in a reactor, thirty miles from a city of one million people, 45,000 immediate deaths and over 100,000 injuries would result. Permanent contamination would result over an area the size of Pennsylvania. Without an accident, the reality of nuclear reactors is still grim: scientists are discovering that the effect of low levels of ionizing radiation – and all nuclear facilities are legally allowed to release certain amounts into the surrounding air and water – is dangerous.

This point is often overlooked in the nuclear debate. Yet what the accumulated evidence of scientific research is indicating is that low dosages of radiation such as are routinely emitted from nuclear reactors are in many ways as dangerous as high dosages such as those which come from a nuclear bomb blast.

Radiation harms us by ionizing the atoms and molecules comprising our body cells, i.e. by altering their electrical charge. Whether the effects of this damage are observable in hours, days or years depends on the amount of exposure. We know from Hiroshima and Nagasaki what the effects of large dosages can be. Yet if we receive separate small amounts of radiation over a period of time, the long term biological effects – cancer, hardening of the arteries, genetic mutations, cataracts, heart disease, leukaemia – may be similar to receiving a large dose all at once.

This may seem surprising, but it makes sense when it is realized that it only takes one mutated cell to cause cancer. If our bodies are irradiated by gamma rays, for instance, or if we inhale a particle of radioactive matter into our lungs and one of its atoms emits an alpha or beta particle, this radiation can collide with any one of the body's thousands of millions of cells and chemically damage it. The cell might die or might recover, but with a damaged nucleus. The damaged cell might multiply normally for years until one day, after the latency period of carcinogenesis is over, it goes beserk and instead of dividing to produce two new cells, manufactures thousands of millions of identically damaged cells. This uncontrolled growth, which leads to the formation of a tumour, is called cancer.

It is true of course that we are constantly exposed to natural background radiation. This comes from outer space and from natural sources on earth such as radium, radon, potassium–40, and carbon–14. This radiation has been responsible for many of the genetic mutations of our evolutionary past. Although most genetic mutations have been detrimental and caused disease and deformity, there have been infrequent beneficial mutations, and the evolutionary process has ensured that the stronger strains have prevailed. Background radiation continues to affect us, although the earth's ozone layer filters out the most harmful rays coming to the earth from outer space.

The radiation coming from nuclear facilities is adding massive amounts of radioactivity to the environment, and we have no equivalent to the ozone layer to protect us. What is significant about this nuclear radiation is that much of it is rarely found in the natural background radiation, and much of it remains lethal for extremely long periods of time. The dangers of radiation emitted by nuclear facilities can be illustrated by examining four of the approximately 300 radioactive effluents that are emitted in the routine operation of a nuclear reactor: strontium–90, cesium–137, iodine–131, and plutonium–239.

Strontium–90 and cesium–137 are both found within the reactor fuel rods under normal operation conditions. Both emit penetrating radiation and large amounts of heat and are so toxic that they must be isolated from the environment for more than a century. Strontium–90 is a bone-seeking isotope, meaning that if taken into the human body it will accumulate in bone marrow. Yet it is so lethal that to dilute one gallon of liquid containing 100 curies of strontium–90 down to legal levels would require from 500,000,000,000 to 1,000,000,000,000 gallons of water. Strontium–90 can cause leukaemia (cancer of the tissues forming the blood-cells in the bone).

Cesium–137, like strontium–90, remains radioactive for centuries and is equally lethal. It emits gamma rays and concentrates itself in the muscle tissue and in the ova of females, and can cause cancer.

Iodine–131, while as toxic as both strontium–90 and cesium–137, has a half-life of only eight days. If ingested, however, it concentrates in the thyroid gland, and can cause cancer.

Plutonium–239 is the most lethal of all the radioactive elements produced during the normal fission process in nuclear reactors. As discussed, it can be used in the construction of nuclear bombs. In terms of its effect on the human body, plutonium is one of the most potent carcinogens known.

Single particles weighing one millionth of a gram, so small that they can only be seen under microscopes, can cause cancer of the lung if inhaled. The toxicity of plutonium can only be understood by comparison. Potassium cyanide, pellets of which are used in gas chambers to kill convicted criminals within minutes, is generally thought of as being one of the most toxic substances available for use in capital punishment.

The single particle of plutonium just described, however, is 20,000 times deadlier than a pellet of potassium cyanide. Ten pounds of plutonium, evenly distributed amongst every person in the world, would give them all a high probability of dying from cancer. And yet each operating nuclear reactor produces between 400 and 600 pounds of plutonium each year in its normal operations.

Plutonium–239 also lasts much longer than most other radioactive agents: its half-life is 24,400 years, meaning that it remains potentially dangerous to life for nearly a quarter of a million years. Moreover, plutonium does not disperse itself evenly throughout the environment but tends to concentrate in the organic life in the environment and in the food chain. This is true for other radioactive agents.

If, for example, cesium–137 were released into a river, the fish in that river would absorb the cesium to 1,000 times the levels found in the river as a whole. If strontium–90 were released into a pasture, the cows and their milk would have a much higher concentration of the strontium than the grass or the ground would. This concentrated radioactivity is then passed on to anyone eating the fish or drinking the milk.

Additionally, radioactivity attacks that part of life which is the most vulnerable: the old and the young. Children are much more susceptible than adults, and infants and the unborn are the most susceptible of all, with their rapidly dividing cells and their immature bodily defence systems.

Another crucial fact concerning ionizing radiation is that its impact is cumulative. This means that successive doses of radiation add to the damage done by the previous dose. For the nuclear industry to say that an atomic worker can receive 5 rems per year without undue risk is fallacious. The worker does not begin each new year with a clean slate; rather, the dose received this year adds on to the dose received last year.

Finally, quite apart from the effects of low-level ionizing radiation upon both workers and members of the public in terms of increased cancer and leukaemia rates, there is a growing body of evidence indicating that radiation produces a generalized ageing effect on the body. This is the conclusion of the study of Dr Rosalie Bertell of the Roswell Park Memorial Institute after nine years of research examining a population-base of 16 million people. Called the Tri-state study, it is the most massive leukaemia study ever done. The conclusion that Dr Bertell has drawn is that the health effects connected with radiation seem to be a secondary phenomenon, the primary one being the acceleration of the breakdown of the body, which is the ageing process. Dr Bertell's data indicate that the exposure to 1 rem (the amount of radiation one receives from a heavy abdominal or spinal X-ray) is the equivalent, roughly, to one year of ageing.

This is not to say that exposure to 1 rem literally shortens one's life by one year; rather, the effect of the radiation is to break down the body processes, particularly the system which enables the body to withstand diseases. This means that nuclear workers and populations around nuclear facilities receiving radiation dosages would come down with death diseases at earlier ages. So, for example, if a worker receives 5 rems exposure to his or her body, the worker would 'age' five years as a result; i.e. while his or her chronological age may be thirty, his or her *body* age would increase to thirty-five, and therefore be that much more susceptible to disease. Consequently, what is affected by radiation is more the quality of life than its duration.

What is important to realize about the radiation releases from nuclear facilities is that, according to existing standards, the general public can receive legally the equivalent of seventeen chest X-rays per year without the nuclear facilities going over 'acceptable' limits. (An X-ray gives about 0.29 rem whole body dose.) Workers can legally receive the equivalent of several hundred.

What this has meant is dramatic increases in the cancer and leukaemia rates of nuclear workers and populations down wind and downstream from nuclear facilities. A number of studies by Dr Ernest J. Sternglass, Professor of Radiological Physics at the University of Pittsburgh, have indicated high levels of radioactive elements in the water and food in areas surrounding nuclear reactors and correspondingly higher incidences of leukaemia and cancer.[26] Around the Shippingport reactor in Pennsylvania, leukaemia and cancer of lymphatic and blood-forming systems of the body rose nearly 70% in the ten years following the opening of the plant. By 1968, cancers of all types were 30% higher than before the reactor started, while throughout the state as a whole the cancer rate had risen only 9%. Milk from irradiated pasture contained 50% more strontium–90 than elsewhere, and the incidence of childhood leukaemia had risen 50% by 1972. At the Millstone reactors in Connecticut, similar increases in radioactivity were found around the plant, and corresponding increases in cancer and leukaemia rates.

Studies by other scientists have confirmed the general trend of these findings. For example, around the Big Rock Point reactor on Lake Michigan, child leukaemia rates were found to be four times greater than for the rest of Michigan State.[27] A study by the Bremen Institute for Biological Safety on the population around the Lingen reactor in West Germany found that ten years prior to the operation of the plant there were 30 leukaemia deaths; in the ten years after nuclear operations began (1968–78), the same population suffered 230 deaths from leukaemia; 170 of these were children under fifteen.[28]

Perhaps the most extensive study yet undertaken was that of Dr Thomas Mancuso of the University of Pittsburg at the Hanford Atomic Works in the USA.[29] This study involved a working population of some 25,000 men and women over a period of 29 years. The results were astonishing. At doses well below the 5 rems per year recommended limit for nuclear workers, there was a doubling of the risk of bone-marrow cancer, and the risk of lung cancer was also much greater than expected. All cancers were increased, especially cancers of the lymph glands and bone marrow. For women the death rates were higher than for men (31% of the women who died by 1973 had died of cancer: the national average was 18%). Older men were found to be more susceptible than younger men to cancer risks (though the younger workers would carry the main genetic burden). Dr Mancuso concluded that the dose required to *double* a person's risk of contracting cancer is less than half the internationally accepted limit.

Supporting the conclusions of the study on atomic industry workers by Dr Mancuso, there is also the work of Dr Najarian.[30] He became interested in the high incidence of blood-related diseases among relatively young workers in the Portsmouth Naval Shipyard, USA, where atomic submarines were being maintained. The Navy refused access to its medical records but, using death certificates, he discovered that 38% of those who had died after working in the shipyards had died of cancer (twice the national average) and that those workers who had been exposed to accidental spills of radiation had leukaemia rates four and a half times the national average. Amongst older workers exposed to spills, 60% had died of cancer. Following publication of this preliminary finding, the Navy agreed to provide data for a full scale study. Dr Radford, Chairman of the influential Biological Effects of Ionizing Radiation Committee in the USA, has also assessed the present levels as being ten times too high and likely to double the chances of a worker getting cancer.[31]

There are similar problems with other aspects of the nuclear fuel cycle. After a time the fuel in the reactor is 'spent', and the fuel rods have to be removed and either buried as waste or 'reprocessed' to extract unused uranium and most of the plutonium created in the fission process. The original reason for reprocessing was to extract plutonium for the nuclear weapons programme. Two of the largest reprocessing plants operating are at Windscale in Britain and at Cap de La Hague in France. While the authorities maintain that technical failures at these plants are rare, the truth is very different. In any case, there are 'internationally accepted limits' for radiation exposure. At Windscale 952 workers had received 1.5 to 5 rems as of 1975, and 36 had received more than 5 rems. During the Windscale inquiry, in 1978, it was revealed that there was a significant increase in the number of myelomas (bone marrow cancers) among the workforce, and this despite a reluctance to follow up those workers who had left or retired. Moreover, numerous workers have been dying of leukaemia. Their widows have received compensation from the industry of £30,000 to £67,000.

Besides radioactive contamination of workers, these plants also release considerable quantities of radioactive material into the environment. It is common practice to dump waste, some with long radioactive hazard periods, into the Irish Sea: up to 6000 curies of plutonium may legally be dumped there each year. As a result of these emissions, the levels of radiation in the Irish Sea show a ten-fold increase, while around Cap de La Hague tests by the French AEC have shown the level to be five times higher than normal. The radioactive emissions from Windscale are also detectable off Norwegian coasts.

A study undertaken at Manchester University showed that the leukaemia rates in towns down wind from Windscale in Lancashire had doubled in the ten-year period up to 1975.

Even more devastating is the evidence of Dr Carl Johnson, former Director of Health in Jefferson County, Colarado, USA. He found a 10 to 25% increase in cancers among people living down wind from the Rocky Flats plutonium plant in Denver, with an increase in testicular cancer nearly two and a half times the normal. An official study in 1977 predicted one extra case of cancer and one genetic defect as a result of emissions from the plant; Dr Johnson has already found an extra five hundred.

The conclusions from these studies is clear: a very small increase in the amount of radiation over natural background levels will have a significant adverse effect on public health.

Besides the problems associated with the biological effects of low levels of radiation, however, there is also the problem of disposing of the radioactive wastes. Cesium–127 and strontium–90 are lethal for centuries, plutonium–239 for tens of thousands of years. There has yet to be found either a technology sophisticated enough or a geological site stable enough to contain the longer-lived isotopes such as plutonium for the time required. If the Romans had built a reactor at the time of Jesus, we would still be guarding their waste. With all the chaos of history, what guarantee is there of the social stability necessary for long-term waste maintenance and control?

Finally, there is the problem of decommissioning nuclear reactors. After only thirty years of service, the reactor is so irradiated that the entire complex must be either dismantled and buried as waste or entombed. Although only a few reactors have been decommissioned, entombment seems to be the 'cheapest' way, costing about what it took to build the plant initially. The entire complex is cased with concrete and left to stand for the one hundred years or more it takes for the more lethal radioactive isotopes to 'cool' enough to allow workers to dismantle the reactor and attempt to restore the area to its natural beauty. After the incident at Three Mile Island, residents were told that if the damaged reactor had to be entombed, they could not go near the site until the year 2210.

The primary point here is that nuclear weapons, particularly as symbolized by the Hiroshima event, are not something separate from us. Nuclear weapons technology spawned nuclear power technology, and both have become so pervasive around the world as to have brought history into the era of the plutonium culture. The civil side of this culture is no less dangerous than its military side.

It is interesting to note that during the Manhattan Project which produced the original atomic bomb, the scientists involved were amazed and deeply troubled by the characteristics of the waste product produced when the uranium was fissioned in their small reactors. At first the scientists termed this ingredient the 'K factor'; then the 'great god k'. The more they learned of its properties, the more diabolical it appeared until they officially named it 'plutonium', after Pluto, the ancient Greek god of hell.

To endorse its use, whether for weapons or reactors, is to make a Faustian pact with the devil. Like Faust, we can of course delude ourselves over the short run that our plutonium culture is necessary to keep us 'safe' from the Russians and in plentiful electricity supply. If not rejected categorically, however, as something humans know about but in wisdom choose not to pursue, plutonium will come back to haunt us, through the perils of nuclear war or a nuclear reactor meltdown, from the effects of low level ionizing radiation or through the hazards inherent in the long-term storage of plutonium in the bowels of the earth.

In the face of this, Christians above all should pause and reflect whether they will accept this latest round of scientific progress or should reject nuclear technology as something born in sin and which must be banned if our species is to survive.

We must realize that we must make a distinction between knowledge and application. To know something does not mean you have to do it. We know how to make gas chambers – Hitler showed us how – but in wisdom we have chosen not to pursue their application. Christians can be a light to the world by helping society to choose which aspects of its burgeoning knowledge it should pursue and apply as technology. Nuclear technology, with the possible exception of its medical application, is not one which can be applied without damaging those who apply it.

2. *Nuclear technology and the technotronic society*

The tragedy of the post-war era is that nuclear technology has become indelibly interwoven with contemporary culture, a fact which leads to the second way in which we can discern our organic connection with the Hiroshima event. I have used the term 'plutonium culture' to signify the pervasive influence of nuclear technology. But why is it that our culture is so susceptible to a technology so dangerous? Part of the answer lies in the fact that modern society has developed into what Zbigniew Brezizinski, former National Security Advisor to President Carter, calls the 'technotronic' society. By this term he means a society which interlocks people into the reality of instantaneous communications systems around the globe. These communication systems are themselves interconnected with an instant access to information through computer technology. It is a society which determines human worth by the measure of silicon chips, a society which, while certainly pulling all of humanity into one common historical stream, has done so through the wrenching dislocation of imperialism, colonialism and the ruthless destruction of traditional societies.

This has caused what L. L. Whyte calls a 'fundamental division between deliberate activity organized by static concepts and the instinctive and spontaneous life.'[32] This 'fundamental division' has reached such an extent that the 'static concepts' of the technotronic age have taken on a life all their own and are currently drawing humanity along behind them. This is causing 'behaviour patterns unrelated to organic needs' and an 'uncontrolled industrialism and excess of analytic thought' that has been completely detached from the 'catharsis of rhythmic relaxation or satisfying achievement' that each human being needs to maintain inner balance and a sense of rootedness.

Viewing this phenomenon from India, Ananda Coomaraswamy was right in observing that 'we are at war with ourselves and therefore at war with one another . . . Man is unbalanced, and the question, Can he recover himself? is a real one.'[33]

Thomas Merton puts the matter even more starkly by stating that what twentieth-century humanity is confronted with

is a crisis of *sanity* first of all. The problems of the nations are the problems of mentally deranged people, but magnified a thousand times because they have the full, straight-faced approbation of a schizoid society, schizoid national structures, schizoid military and business complexes . . . and schizoid religious sects.[34]

This 'crisis of sanity' is not merely the result of a technotronic society gone amok; it is as much the result of an explosion of knowledge that has outpaced the individual's ability to integrate it. Alvin Toffler calls this 'future shock', a psychological dislocation produced when the knowledge and technology that are outpacing our ability to integrate them explode our present from the vantage point of the future. And yet, the shattering stress and disorientation that we induce in individuals by subjecting them to too much change in too short a time is not a future possibility but a present psycho-biological condition which Toffler calls 'the disease of change'.

Toffler offers a further important insight: that 'the *rate* of change has implications quite apart from, and sometimes more important than, the *direction* of change.'[35]

At base, therefore, what future shock consists of is a time phenomenon which Toffler exemplifies in the following way:

It has been observed that if the last 50,000 years of man's existence were to be divided into lifetimes of approximately 62 years each, there have been about 800 such lifetimes. Of these 800, fully 650 were spent in caves. Only during the last 70 lifetimes has it been possible to communicate effectively from one lifetime to another – as writing made it possible to do. Only during the last six lifetimes did masses of men ever see a printed word. Only during the last four has it been possible to measure time with any precision. Only in the last two has anyone anywhere used an electric motor. And the overwhelming majority of all the material goods we use in daily life today have been developed within the present, the 800th, lifetime.[36]

Commenting on this phenomenon, Hans Küng states that

The upheaval of our lifetime . . . must be regarded as the second great break in the history of mankind, the first being the invention of agriculture in neolithic times, and the transition from barbarism to civilization. Now, in our times, agriculture, which constitutes the basis of civilization for thousands of years, has lost its dominance in one country after another. And at the same time the industrial age, begun two centuries ago, is passing. As a result of automation in the progressive countries, manual workers are also rapidly becoming a minority and a superindustrial culture appears on the horizon, perceptible only in outline.[37]

The technology for Utopia is present amongst us but 'something is wrong in this fantastic quantitative and qualitative progress', says Küng. It is a progress whose rate of change has caused future shock; and it is a progress whose direction of change has led the world into the Age of Overkill. By 1958, there had been detonated by both the US and the Soviet Union in their respective nuclear programmes more than a hundred times as much explosive power as that dropped on Germany in all the years of World War II, the megatonnage being equivalent to the total body weight of the entire human population.

In 1960, John Kennedy observed that 'the world's nuclear stockpile contains, it is estimated the equivalent of 30 billion tons of TNT – about ten tons for every human being on the globe'.

And still the pace continued, incorporating more money, more scientists, more commitment on the part of the nations involved. By 1978, the US had enough nuclear explosive power to be able to destroy completely every Soviet city above 100,000 in population forty-one times over; the Soviet's could do the same to American cities above 100,000 twenty-three times over. And still the spiral continues, until the multiplicity of weapons systems, delivery systems and satellite systems co-ordinating the entire complex of nuclear 'preparedness' has become truly staggering. The Stockholm International Peace Research Institute 1978 Yearbook, *World Armaments and Disarmaments*, lists five different nuclear weapons categories, twenty-one different nuclear weapons types, with thirty-seven different maximum ranges and thirty-four different kiloton/megaton yields, just for the nuclear weapons deployed in Europe by the North Atlantic Treaty Organization (NATO) and the Warsaw Treaty Organization (WTO). By 1982, the explosive power of the world's nuclear stockpile equalled more than two million Hiroshima bombs.

Through these nuclear weapons, according to Max Lerner,

> we have created a world of buttons existing to be pressed at need, with the underlying premise that they will not have to be pressed if one threatens clearly enough to press them; a world of peace to be achieved through the promise of nuclear terror; a world bedecked with the new vocabulary of 'credible first-strike capability', 'second-strike (retaliatory) capability', 'escalation', 'reciprocal fear of surprise attack', 'calculated pre-emption', and

even 'striking second-first'; a world in which chance has all but been squeezed out, through 'fail-safe' built-in controls of the weapons systems, with crucial decisions reserved for a few men at the top; a world of constant wariness and suspicion, of a death's-head game in which each side is bent on convincing the other that it has the means and the will to destroy him utterly before it is itself utterly destroyed, that it is powerful enough to instil terror, yet prepared enough to feel none. Only thus, it is argued, will the weapons so arduously conceived, placed on the drawing board and brought into the stockpiles, remain unused. Out of this nettle, deterrence, we presumably pluck this flower, safety.[38]

While the world arms itself to death, much of the world is being starved to death. It is estimated that during each twenty-four hour period the total world expenditure for armaments averages $1.26 billion; it is also estimated that during each twenty-four hour period 50,000 people starve to death or die of some hunger-related disease. Each year 15 million children under the age of fifteen die of hunger, while 800 million to 1,000 million people live in total want, meaning they are barely staying alive – this amounts to almost one-fifth of the entire human population. Over half the human population lives in shanty towns, mud huts, or slums, without running water, electricity, sanitation, or insulation against the heat or the cold. Living in poverty means living with little or no hope. The world's poor are also the world's illiterate. There are over 400 million children for whom there are no schools.

If the $560 billion that is being spent every year on nuclear and conventional arms was reallocated for human needs, what could be done? It would cost about $20 billion properly to house, clothe, and feed everyone in the world. This amount is spent every two weeks on weapons. The World Health Organization estimates that with a budget of $10 million it could eliminate malaria. This amounts to just twelve minutes of arms expenditures. The cost of only one modern jet fighter would pay for 40,000 village pharmacies.

According to the Brandt Commission, which completed a study on world poverty in 1980,

> History has taught us that wars produce hunger, but we are less aware that mass poverty can lead to war or end in chaos. While hunger rules, peace cannot prevail. He who wants to ban war must also ban mass poverty. Morally it makes no difference whether a human being is killed in war or is condemned to starve to death because of the indifference of others.[39]

We are living in a world gripped by a plutonium culture polluting the planet with radioactive wastes; by a technotronic society which dehumanizes our dignity by forcing us to interlock with technologies over which we have less and less control; by a permanent war economy that employs 40% of the world's scientists and consumes vast amounts of material and human resources; and by the cries of those who are poor, who are hungry, who are illiterate, and who are diseased. The tragedy is that this is not a world that has been forced on us; it is a world we have built up of our own accord. We are so out of touch with not only ourselves but also the natural order that it is estimated that between 1980 and the end of the century our pollution and ruthless exploitation of the planet will be responsible for the extermination of over 500,000 other plant and animal species – that is one more species made extinct every hour until 1 January, 2000.

The planet is indeed witnessing 'the second great break in the history of mankind', and the anxiety of the transition is causing entrenchment and fortification on the part of the established élites rather than a joyful embrace of the future, to the point of even risking collective suicide before releasing the fading security of the past.

Nuclear technology starkly dramatizes the anxiety involved in the transitions that have been occurring and starkly symbolizes the alienation from the very life that human hands have built. It may well usher in, therefore, the final consummation of a dying civilization and a species who could not creatively transform its aggressiveness into peaceful competition.

The atomic bomb, therefore, has become a new symbol in human relations, giving to human life a new meaning with portents of dread and possible extinction. This is not because of its economic or political impact, although it surely includes these dimensions, but because of the suddenness with which it presented to human consciousness alternative destinies never before considered. This is why Hiroshima divides history: it challenges us to redirect radically the course we have set or else face planetary cataclysm.

It is clear that we can no longer live by the norms of previous ages but must reckon with the fact that some generations find themselves at a juncture in time when many previous potentialities and possibilities are synchronistically reaching fruition and are thereby turning to challenge what has gone on before. Such was the case of the Christ event. The fulfilment of the law and the prophets paradoxically filled the old skins with new wine, bursting them asunder. In the case of Hiroshima, the created threatens to devour its creator by the very dynamic of fulfilling the creator's visions. In this interplay, continuity becomes metamorphosis, the larva becomes the butterfly. Hiroshima has placed humanity at such a crossroads by being, as Lifton puts it, 'both a direct continuation of the long and checkered history of human struggle, and at the same time a plunge into a new and tragic dimension.'[40]

The paradox is an ultimate one: the existence of weapons that can annihilate man and his history could also, however indirectly, be a stimulus toward a deeper and more humane grasp of the same. Hiroshima was the prelude to all this – an expression of technological evil and madness which could, but will not necessarily, be a path to wisdom.[41]

V

The Confessional Heritage: Apocalyptic and the Wrath of God

A. INTRODUCTION

If there is any single point which emerges from the preceding discussion of Hiroshima and the advent of the nuclear age, it is that it is now possible to terminate human history completely and irrevocably, a possibility never before conceivable by, much less in the power of, humankind. We have ushered in the plutonium culture and the Age of Overkill, and in so doing we have brought ourselves face to face with challenges to our self-understanding which, before Hiroshima, could be largely ignored.

In Chapter III, Section E, I set forth the hermeneutic of engagement as the one I shall follow in attempting to understand our new situation. Hiroshima is the historical event; it is the new historical *Sitz im Leben* in which the confessional community of Christians living in the late twentieth century finds itself. Because Hiroshima symbolizes the possibility of the cataclysmic termination of history, the category within our tradition which it evokes for its interpretation is that of apocalyptic, which also focussed attention on the termination of history. With the hermeneutic of engagement, we can use our ancient confessional understanding of apocalyptic to understand Hiroshima in theological terms, while simultaneously allowing the new reality with which Hiroshima confronts us to amplify and expand our ancient category. It is within this dynamic tension between ancient heritage and new event that the confessing community is given a frame of reference within which it can understand the present, and an impetus whereby it can grow into the future, while remaining firmly rooted in a confessional heritage which has spoken of this theme for millennia.

Like Deutero-Isaiah who interpreted the return from Babylon as a new Exodus, we, too, must now reflect upon our new historical situation of having collectively entered into the Age of Overkill in terms of a 'new apocalyptic'. The following two chapters, therefore, will cover two aspects. The first will seek to delineate the ancient confessional witness of the apocalyptists themselves as they in their times of anomie tried to come to grips with the wrath of God and the impending end of the world. With this clearly understood, particularly those aspects relevant to the contemporary situation, in the following chapter I shall discuss the interface between the ancient witness and the historical situation Hiroshima represents. My purpose in this chapter on apocalyptic and the wrath of God is to begin the exposition of God's antinomial character. This will in turn help clarify the later discussion of Christ crucified as the fundamental event which illumines and potentially transforms our present situation.

B. CLASSICAL APOCALYPTIC

S. B. Frost makes the point that apocalyptic is essentially a 'protest literature', expressive of a 'persecution complex' arising out of historical times of deep despair when, wherever one looks for justice or deliverance within one's historical reality, none seems forthcoming.[1] Apocalyptic thinking stems from a time in which darkness reigns, and all light seems to have been eclipsed. W. Schmithals agrees, stating that the despair giving rise to apocalyptic runs so deep that it is ultimately 'rooted in the doubt whether there is any *meaning in history at all*'.[2]

The first radical expression of this doubt arose in the post-exilic experience of the Hebrew people when, upon returning home to Jerusalem after the exile in Babylon, they were confronted by hostile forces and by the loss of ancient institutions. This produced the peculiar confluence of uprootedness, confusion, and anomie that inevitably gave rise to the germination and flowering of apocalyptic thought.

During the exile they had been encouraged by the prophecies of Deutero-Isaiah which had told them that their sins had been forgiven and that Yahweh was going to restore to them glories beyond anything pre-exilic Israel had known.[3] However, when Cyrus captured Babylon and the Hebrew people were allowed to return to Jerusalem to rebuild the Temple, they discovered that the Second Exodus from captivity, which Deutero-Isaiah had described in such glowing terms, was leading to anything but a promised land. Their return was not a release from captivity but merely a mitigation of it, for they were still part of the Persian empire; moreover, they were confronted by indigenous populations who resented and actively opposed the Hebrew efforts to rebuild their cities and their Temple. Perhaps most critical of all, as Otto Plöger points out, is the fact that the Hebrews returned from exile deprived of the institutions of kingship and nationhood to which they had grown accustomed over the six hundred years since the days of the Judges.[4]

This confrontation by hostile forces in their own homeland, combined with the loss of those institutions with which they were accustomed to fight these forces, produced a radical transformation of Jewish life and a corresponding radicalization in their self-consciousness and religious reflection. As Schmithals explains it,

> at the beginning of the Persian period Israel changed from a people to a community, from a nation to a theocracy. Israel ceased to understand herself as a political entity and conceived of herself as God's people, assembled around temple-cult and law. Israel became a churchlike divine foundation.[5]

Israel was unable to adapt to this new situation and new self-definition, however, and fell into what Frost calls a 'strange lethargy'.[6] The Jewish people lost interest in keeping records of their history, and prophecy, which had grown up co-terminous with and dialectically connected with kingship, faltered now that kingship was gone. Indeed, so lethargic and depressed were the Jews during this period that no time during their entire history is as obscure as the two centuries following the exile. Frost observes that, with the exception of the deeds of Ezra and Nehemiah, 'no history was written because none was made'.[7]

With the spectacular victories of Alexander the Great, however, the Persian empire crumbled and the Hebrew people were caught up in the maelstrom of Hellenization. This culminated in the attempt by Antiochus IV Epiphanes to destroy Judaism by forbidding the observance of the Sabbath, the rite of circumcision and sacrificial temple worship. He also ordered that all copies of the Torah be burned and that an altar to Zeus Olympios be erected in the Jerusalem Temple.

'This persecution,' says Frost, 'was the salvation of Jewry',[8] igniting the long dormant fires of nationalism and sparking the Maccabaean revolt. In 162 BC, Jewish religious liberties were restored by treaty, and to many it seemed as if the glories long promised them were at hand. But again Jewish hopes were deprived of historical fulfilment as the successors to Judas Maccabaeus became politicized and degenerate until, under the reign of Alexander Jannaeus, domestic discontent grew to open revolt, and the reigning Maccabaean was drawn into a war with his own people.[9] In 64 BC, the Romans marched in to 'restore order' and in doing so ended up by replacing the forces of Hellenization with a Roman yoke. So again the Jews came under foreign domination until in AD 70, after sporadic outbursts, the entire nation rebelled. In retaliation, the Romans destroyed the Temple. In AD 135, after yet another uprising, Jerusalem was destroyed, rebuilt and renamed Aelia Capitolina, into which no Jew was allowed.

It is within this milieu that Jewish apocalypticism grew up: a milieu characterized by social upheaval and foreign domination, by the radicalization of self-perception arising from the loss of ancient institutions and by an utter lack of faith and hope in any deliverance from within the boundaries of the historical present. 'Conditions were so grim,' says Paul Hanson, 'that the situation could not be righted by a change within human hearts alone, not even by a universal assize dividing the righteous from the wicked. The corruption had permeated the natural order itself.'[10] Any salvation could only come through the complete destruction of the existing order by God alone and its replacement by an entirely new creation, again designed and enacted by God alone.

Apocalyptic, therefore, is the religious expression of a people who are crying out for justice in a world perverted to its very roots with injustice, who are seeking retribution and vengeance upon their enemies yet are powerless to bring them about, and who are desperate to be delivered from their plight but who see no deliverer in sight. They were a people who seemed to have gone beyond the realm of paradox into the anomie of the absurd: those of them who clung to the Mosaic covenant were not blessed but persecuted and killed; those who apostasized were materially blessed and given status and honour; but both those cursed and those blessed were given their reward or punishment by Greeks or Romans only – the 'God of our Fathers' seemed nowhere in sight. For the faithful, therefore, history had entered into the realm of the eschaton and the *end of time*, for the outpouring of evil around them had become so great that only a complete termination of history itself would suffice to eradicate the injustices they faced and bring them their long due rewards.

While the prophetic tradition, even prophetic eschatology, could focus its pronouncements upon the nation state of Israel, upon the

king and upon the ruling élite, translating the divine plan into
concrete history, real politics and human instrumentality, apocalyptic eschatology could not. The focus could only be upon the cosmic
vision of Yahweh's sovereignty which alone could destroy the
historical order and rebuild a new creation. The concrete history,
plain politics and participation of human instrumentality formerly
utilized by the prophets were now transcended. History had fallen
to such depths that only the God of the Universe would be sufficient
for the deliverance so desperately sought. As Hanson explains it,

> the Prophets, affirming the historical realm as a suitable context
> for divine activity, understood it as their task to translate the
> vision of divine activity from the cosmic level to the level of the
> politico-historical realm of everyday life.[11]

The apocalyptists, however,

> disillusioned with the historical realm, disclosed their vision in a
> manner of growing indifference to and independence from the
> contingencies of the politico-historical realm, thereby leaving the
> language increasingly in the idiom of the cosmic realm of the
> divine warrior and his council.

While prophetic eschatology could speak of an eschaton within
history, therefore, apocalyptic eschatology could only speak of the
eschaton of history itself.

In essence, says Hanson, apocalyptic 'bespeaks total loss of
control over existing structures . . .' Dominating the outlook of the
apocalyptists

> is a vision of restoration which loses all specificity, both in relation
> to the oppressors and the brethren, and dwells on the gruesome
> details of the final conflict issuing forth in the extermination of the
> enemy and the restoration of a brilliant paradise.[12]

It is a vision in which

> the nations of the world, the ravished women, the exiled people,
> and the escaping remnant are mentioned, but they are passive
> objects in a drama acted out exclusively by the Cosmic Warrior,
> Yahweh.

After 587 BC, then, with Israel's political identity as a nation
terminated, with the office of kingship and prophet vacant, with a
proud people suppressed by foreign cultural and religious norms
alien to their own, and with an oppression by successive tyrannies

which was to culminate in the razing of their sacred Temple and holy city and in the martyrdom of Masada, the Jewish visionaries began increasingly to abdicate their responsibility to translate the will of God into historical events as the prophets had done; rather, history was replaced by myth as God and God alone was recognized as the only referent for justice and deliverance.

It was the replacement of history with the images of myth which, when wedded to eschatology, produced apocalyptic. 'In fact', asserts Frost, 'we may define *apocalyptic* as the mythologizing of eschatology.'[13] This is so, he says, because in the pre-exilic days of nation-state, kingship and temple cult, the 'Day of Yahweh', when God would dispense justice and effect deliverance to the oppressed, was proclaimed and accepted as a present and cyclically re-occurring reality; with the disintegration of the nation, kingship and cult, the 'Day of Yahweh' 'came to be projected more and more into the future, and so eschatological thinking as opposed to cultic thinking was born.'[14]

To say that apocalyptic eschatology resided in the realm of myth while prophetic eschatology remained in the realm of the historical is not to say that they were completely disconnected. While there were certainly the distinctions already discussed, there were also clear similarities. Apocalyptic stayed true to themes deeply embedded in the very fabric of Israelite religious belief, themes so deep that even apocalyptic pessimism was kept from degenerating into nihilistic despair. As Rudolf Otto puts the matter:

> The new motives which are active in the eschatology of late Jewish apocalyptic are far from being absolutely and radically alien to ancient Israelite religious feeling, for in that case we should have had to do with a syncretism in the sense of mechanical addition, and the eschatology of late Judaism would then be simply and solely an alien phenomenon, which is not the case. Rather they work upon germinal ideas found even in ancient Israel.[15]

D. S. Russell amplifies this by pointing to the fact that while the apocalyptists did indeed believe that the world was 'past redemption', they nevertheless clung throughout their despair to the cornerstone of the Jewish faith: that their God was a God who acted in history for their salvation. In the midst of anomie, they were persons

> of faith who could see within history, through history, and beyond history the working out of God's triumphant purpose, not only

for themselves as a nation, but also for men of every nation who were prepared to follow the way of righteousness.[16]

In the face of oppression by their Greek and Roman overlords, therefore, they believed in the ultimate victory of God; and in the midst of the despair of seeing apostasy rewarded and orthodoxy persecuted, they asserted the hope that divine justice would finally prevail at that point where God would break the bonds of history and work the divine will. In essence, says Russell, 'They believed that "man's extremity is God's opportunity" ', that at the nadir point of human sinfulness, the apogee of divine love would save the day: 'the great *denouement* of history was close at hand. In it God would take the initiative as He had done from the very beginning of time.'[17]

Fundamental to the understanding of the hopes and fears to which apocalyptic bears witness, then, is the historical situation in which apocalyptic arose, for while apocalyptic consistently appealed to a point of reference *outside* history, it was very much produced and conditioned by conflicts and forces *inside* history. Indeed, as Russell observes, 'their writings, like boiling lava from a volcano, were thrown up out of explosive historical circumstances over which they themselves had no control'.[18]

It can be seen from this that apocalyptic consists above all in a religious *mood* rather than in clearly defined dogmas or delineations. It is an expression of pent-up rage against the existing order, an outpouring of emotion which the writers believed would find no listener until it reached the ears of God. This mood has many characteristics, by no means present in each book or tradition. J. Lindblom suggests the following list: transcendentalism, mythology, cosmological survey, pessimistic historical surveys, dualism, division of time into periods, teaching of two Ages, numerology, pseudo-ecstasy, artificial claims to inspiration, pseudonymity, and esotericism.[19] To this list Russell adds the notions of the unity of history and the conception of cosmic history, including heaven and earth; the notion of primordiality with its revelations concerning the creation, fall and judgment of humankind and angels; the source of and solution to the problem of evil: the conflict between light and darkness, between good and evil, God and Satan; the emergence of the transcendent yet immanent 'Son of Man' and other messianic figures; the development of belief in life after death with its various component aspects of Hades, Gehenna, paradise and heaven; and the increasing significance of the individual in the resurrection, judgment and new world to come.[20]

E. Stauffer suggests four primary presuppositions for apocalyptic: primordiality, conflict, eschatology and universalism.[21] In commenting on these, Russell suggests a further two: determinism and supernaturalism; history as interpreted not only in terms of its foreordained End but in terms of the transcendent God above history.[22]

The above characteristics and presuppositions indicate the immense complexities one faces in attempting to understand apocalyptic. The challenge becomes more daunting when one recalls that they are all component parts of an attempt to discern meaning in what had become meaningless; somehow to find a rock of salvation in a historical situation that had blasted away the rocks to which the believers had formerly clung. Finally, it must be borne in mind that the above characteristics and presuppositions are both the result of, and conditioned by the apocalyptists' experience of, the outpouring of evil on an absolutely unprecedented scale, so much so in fact that all the old categories by which they had previously understood not only evil but God, humanity and the world were completely shattered. Indeed, the whole of apocalyptic can be seen as an attempt to come to terms with a historical situation in which the manifestation of darkness, suffering and sin was the dominant if not exclusive component. The question asked by Job concerning a reality in which good was not only being repaid with evil but with an overabundance of evil, was asked by countless thousands in the apocalyptic times after the exile. As with Job, the answer emerged from the cosmic myths themselves – from the whirlwind of God.

There are two particular aspects of apocalyptic on which I wish to focus: first, to discuss briefly the forces of evil which the apocalyptists believed to be responsible for the conditions they were in; and secondly, to discuss in greater depth the wrath of God which they believed would wipe this evil away.

C. THE EVIL FORCES IN THE WORLD

In keeping with the underlying theme of this thesis, that of the 'mighty acts of God' in human history, it is important to bear in mind that above all this is what the apocalyptists sought to know and describe. For them the final meaning and consummation of history were found in discerning the signs and patterns of the divine purpose; hence the term 'apocalyptic', which in the Greek meant 'revelation'.

The visionaries sought to have 'revealed' to them both the timing and the manner in which the mighty acts of God would terminate history and recreate a new world for the elect.

It is to a particular moment of history, then, and to a specific aspect of divine activity that the apocalyptists directed their interest. For them it was not an academic question but one they were compelled to ask, since they lived in a situation in which the God who had acted so decisively for their salvation before had seemingly forsaken them. They were forced to attempt a reconciliation between their actual *existence* of being buffeted by the forces of evil, apparently without historical deliverance, and their *concept* of a good God, faithful in keeping the covenant and consistent in the dispensation of justice.

The answer given by the apocalyptists to this contradiction was that the evil they were being plagued with came from two sources: angelic disruption and human nature itself.

Basic to apocalyptic cosmology was the notion of an intricate hierarchy of beings between humanity and God. These angelic beings were originally seen as messengers and enactors of God's will, but at a certain point one of the high angelic figures, called Satan, Satanael, Beliar or Mastema, leads a rebellion in heaven, thus initiating evil and sin in the universe. Innumerable lesser angels join Satan in his rebellion, bring the rebellion to earth, and cause humanity to sin. In the final battle against God, Satan and his hosts are vanquished along with all those human beings who do not repent of their sins; all are thrown into the bottomless pit of fire and eternal torment.

One passage which is particularly interesting in this regard comes from the Book of Jubilees. Here the evil spirits in rebellion against the Almighty are ruled by an angel called Mastema, whose sole purpose is 'to do all manner of wrong and sin, and all manner of transgression, to corrupt and destroy, and to shed blood upon the earth' (11.5). After he and his angelic forces lead humanity into sin, God decides to send the Flood. When the Flood is approaching, however, and the angels of darkness are being imprisoned, Mastema appeals to God to spare one tenth of his hosts, in order that they might be free to roam the earth *after* the Flood. God grants this request, fully aware that 'they would not walk in uprightness, nor strive in righteousness' (10.11). God spares evil knowing that it will infect the creation again.

This strange tolerance for evil on the part of the Most High is a subject that will require much further discussion. I raise the issue now merely to indicate the control God has over the evil, in terms both of its extent and of its degree of penetration of the created order. It exemplifies the apocalyptic insistence in attributing evil to a source other than God yet nevertheless maintaining God's sovereignty over it, even to the point of mercifully sparing it. The Book of Jubilees sets forth a parallelism, therefore, between the sparing of a small percentage of humanity to endure the coming cataclysm of the Flood and a small percentage of evil angels to continue plaguing humankind after the Flood. God sends the Flood to wipe out evil but then allows enough of it to persist so that another apocalypse will in time be necessary.

A further point of importance is that while in apocalyptic Satan is certainly described in mythic terms, he is also depicted as an historical being who is capable of taking human form. Schmithals emphasizes this point:

> This Satan can be presented in mythical fashion as a monster, so that the final struggle of the old age is waged as a struggle against the dragon. But Satan can also assume historical contours and appear in the form of feared rulers such as Antiochus IV Epiphanes, Herod the Great, or Nero, in whom Satan appears masked, the tyrant in the end-time of the old age.[23]

When historicized, however, Satan is often represented by another epitomization of evil: the Antichrist.

The book of Revelation exemplifies a fairly clear pattern concerning the Antichrist, a pattern not always present in all details in all the texts and certainly presented with numerous variations, but a pattern nevertheless. The pattern can be stated as follows: first, the Antichrist is identified as the arch-enemy of God, as the epitome of the forces of evil, and is symbolized most frequently by a monster or dragon; secondly, the Antichrist is initially victorious owing to supernatural powers, by the ability to work wonders and, in several Christian writings, by an ability to imitate the light of Christ; thirdly, the Antichrist generally establishes rulership over the world for a specific period of time, the marks of his rule being drought and famine and the persecution of the elect; fourthly, those remaining faithful to God are forced to flee into the wilderness; fifthly, the Antichrist marshals his forces and engages in a final eschatological battle with the forces of light that consumes not only the earth but the whole universe; and lastly, the Antichrist is defeated by the Messiah and either killed or banished for ever to a place of torment while the elect are given a new heaven and a new earth to enjoy eternally.

The ongoing interplay of chaos and order has meant that the image of Antichrist, given its extreme adaptability, has remained very much alive in the Christian tradition. It has been applied in times of extreme political and/or social chaos and has been identified with different Roman emperors, different popes and different blasphemers such as Hitler and Stalin. As H. H. Rowley observes,

> times of evil and of persecution have been renewed again and again in the world, and neither Antiochus Epiphanes nor Nero has proved the last cruel oppressor to have a mouth speaking great things and blasphemies, or to measure himself against the Most High and claim divine honours.[24]

The demonic Antichrist, then, 'stands for a persistent force of evil, not in any one man alone, but behind all evil men, incarnate in them in varying degrees'.

When chaos and evil reach certain proportions, humans are reminded of the power of Satan, of the strength of Antichrist, and the good tremble and pray for guidance and deliverance. In all apocalyptic writings, however, it is observed that while evil is always cast as the 'enemy', the great majority of humanity welcomes its rule. The tragedy apocalyptic records is that most people whore after the beast and the dragon, seeking to enthrone them, even while being warned that they will soon manifest their true characteristics and bring famine and drought and persecution. Nevertheless, evil gains sway over human loyalty, and soon the Antichrist appears to gather together all the forces of darkness to do final battle with God Almighty. Without the beast and the human obeisance to the evil he evokes, there could be no Antichrist, for what Rowley observes is true, that 'Antichrist is thrown up by the age that worships Beliar'.[25]

The apocalyptists, therefore, while positing evil in an angelic hierarchy above the earth, were also troubled by the apparent human receptivity to this evil.

Many passages assert that Adam and Eve were responsible for the admittance of evil into the world, even as the fallen angels were responsible for the temptation to do evil.

What emerges from the texts is a description of human nature that, while attempting to preserve free moral choice on the one hand and on the other positing the origin of evil in an angelic rebellion in heaven, nevertheless understood humanity to be in some sense 'fallen'; i.e., imbued with an 'evil inclination' that was producing in their day a wickedness far in excess of any good.

The apocalyptists, then, lived in a world dominated by a deep consciousness of the reality of evil. They were in a world permeated with corruption; a world from which they could not escape; a world in which their only way of coping was to praise God and await the final consummation of the divine will for history. This would come, they believed, when God, seeing the extent of human evil and the arrogance of the Antichrist, would do battle with the forces of evil and allow the divine wrath to wipe the world away.

D. THE WRATH OF GOD

What the apocalyptists perceived as happening within history, no matter how much they might seek to explain it in terms of Satanic influence or human sinfulness, was always understood as happening within the context of an all-controlling God.

This point is brought out perhaps most clearly by Abraham Heschel, who asserts that the Old Testament writers

> had no theory or 'idea' of God. What they had was an *understanding* . . . God was overwhelmingly real and shatteringly present. They never spoke of Him as from a distance . . . The attributes of God were drives, challenges, commandments, rather than timeless notions detached from His Being. They did not offer an exposition of the nature of God, but rather an exposition of God's insight into man and His concern for man.[26]

This means that the Hebrews

> experienced the word as a living manifestation of God, and events in the world as effects of His activity . . . Knowledge of God was fellowship with Him, not attained by syllogism, analysis or induction, but by living together.[27]

Heschel calls this understanding of history as being within the overwhelming presence of God the 'pathos of God'. Pathos, for Heschel, denotes

> not an idea of goodness, but a living care; not an immutable example, but an outgoing challenge, a dynamic relation between God and man; not mere feeling or passive affection, but an act or attitude composed of various spiritual elements; no mere contemplative survey of the world, but a passionate summons.[28]

God is not only to be understood as primal Creator of heaven and earth and the ordainer of history but as personally involved in and intimate with the world, such that at different times and in different situations different aspects of the divine personality are demonstrated. Heschel says,

> He does not simply command and expect obedience, he is also moved and affected by what happens in the world, and reacts accordingly. Events and human actions arouse in Him joy or sorrow, pleasure or wrath. He is not conceived as judging the world in detachment. He reacts in an intimate and subjective manner, and thus determines the value of events.[29]

Heschel's understanding parallels the process panentheistic understanding of God articulated earlier: a God who does not stand impassively outside the realm of creaturely suffering and sorrow, but who is both personally involved with creation and even genuinely affected by creaturely actions. The pathos of God, therefore, is what transcends the gulf between Creator and created; it is what relates God to humanity by being deliberately and actively involved in history. The distance between God and humanity is balanced by the reciprocity of relationship, consisting of God's engagement with human beings as well as of their commitment to God in the covenant. Here again pathos is the key:

> Pathos is the focal point for eternity and history, the epitome of all relationships between God and man. Just because it is not a final reality but a dynamic modality, does pathos make possible a living encounter between God and His people.[30]

The situation with which apocalyptic is most concerned is one characterized most fundamentally by alienation, imbalance, enmity; it is a situation in which the forces of evil hold sway, cutting human beings off from one another, the earth, and their Creator; it is a situation, too, in which God is most vulnerable because the all-embracing consequent aspect of the Godhead absorbs into itself the sinful activities and rebelliousness of humanity. Unable to be indifferent because God cares, God, like humanity, suffers in apocalyptic times; God, like humanity, is pained, and like the elect upon the earth seeks vengeance, retribution, a renewal of justice. Reacting to the growing evil God spills forth a holy wrath, a divine judgment.

When one considers the notion of the wrath of God, which the apocalyptists saw pouring out upon humanity, it should not be seen as an anthropomorphic transference of lower human emotions to God but as an aspect of the divine pathos itself. This means, says Heschel, that divine wrath

> is conditioned by God's will; it is aroused by man's sins. It is an instrument rather than a force, transitive rather than spontaneous. It is a secondary emotion, never the ruling passion, disclosing only a part of God's way with man.[31]

In discussing the same point, Moltmann asserts that God's wrath

> is injured love and therefore a mode of his reaction to men. Love is the source and the basis of the possibility of the wrath of God. The opposite of love is not wrath, but indifference. Indifference towards justice and injustice would be a retreat on the part of God from the covenant. But his wrath is an expression of his abiding interest in man.[32]

The wrath of God should not be seen as antithetical to the love of God but as part of it, as serving it. Wrath is integral to God's pathos; it is part of God's personal way of relating in a caring way with creation. This concept is central to understanding the antinomial character of God. Again, recalling the analogy of light refracted through a prism, we know that all colours are necessary to make up the totality of light. Thus the wrath of God, which spills unimaginable destruction upon the earth, must be understood as integral to the divine pleroma.

When, therefore, Deutero-Isaiah speaks of the Lord as creating evil as well as good, war as well as peace (Isa. 45.7), the emphasis should be not so much on the fact that the hand of God is in all these aspects of human reality, but on the fact that 'I the Lord do all these things'. Not only is there no element in the entire range of human emotion or actuality that is unworthy of God or beneath God's dignity to permeate and control, but there is no element in the range of emotions characteristic of personality or type of action possible for sentient creatures that God does not at certain times express for reasons known only to the divine will. All the possibilities of human emotion, action, and thought, therefore, are also possibilities for the Divine itself.

That God is in every sphere of life is an insight brought out starkly and forcefully by Elie Wiesel in his description of his experience in Auschwitz:

> The SS hanged two Jewish men and a youth in front of the whole

camp. The men died quickly, but the death throes of the youth
lasted for half an hour. 'Where is God? Where is he?' someone
asked behind me. As the youth still hung in torment in the noose
after a long time, I heard the man call again, 'Where is God now?'
And I heard a voice in myself answer 'Where is he? He is here. He
is hanging there on the gallows . . .'[33]

God suffered death at Auschwitz. God was pathetically present
in that suffering, able through divine pathos to become vulnerable
to even the magnitude of evil perpetrated by the Nazi Final Solution.
Wiesel's understanding was shared by the apocalyptists; they, too,
saw God as present, as still sovereign in the face of the Antichrist,
as still omniscient in the face of human refusal to obey the divine
will, and as still willing to react and relate in the face of revolt,
apostasy, overwhelming sin.

Apocalyptic evil, like the reality of Auschwitz, forced the visionaries to reflect whether there was a limit to the presence and suffering
of God; whether there were even realms of conduct and human
situational realities that God simply would not bear to behold. Their
answer, given at a time in which evil was triumphant over the good,
when apostasy had replaced devotion, and when the elect were
being hounded, persecuted, and killed, was that nothing was outside
God's awareness and participation. Indeed they, as well as other
Old Testament writers, went even further in their exploration of the
pathos of God, and demonstrated, according to Walther Eichrodt,
'*the forcefulness with which every single happening in the world is
attributed to God as its sole and ultimate cause*'.[34]

The apocalyptists realized that even within the outpouring of evil
the handiwork of God could be seen; indeed, interwoven with the
manifestation and outpouring of evil was to be seen the outpouring
and manifestation of divine wrath. What Satan and human beings
were capable of, God was not only capable of but able to manifest
in far more powerful ways. While human and satanic moral evil was
being done because of the infection of sin, however, the divine
destruction was stemming from a wrath which served divine love.
The wrath was not coming forth because God was rejecting history
or cutting Divinity off from humanity; rather, it was pouring forth
in these apocalyptic times, interwoven in more than equal measure
with the evil of humanity and of Satan, because God cared.

That God's wrath must be seen within the context of divine
pathos, divine caring, and divine love is important to bear in mind
because as I suggested earlier, it is always a very difficult and painful

task to distinguish the outpouring of satanic evil from the outpouring of divine wrath interwoven with that evil. Moreover, what is unfathomable about the wrath of God is that it is not commensurate with the evil done but generally runs far in excess of any seemingly just retribution. For a finger, it seems as if God seeks a hand, or even an arm.

What emerges as expressive of God's wrath are forces of darkness that far exceed and utterly vanquish anything contrived by Satan and his hosts. There are earthquakes (II Bar. 27.7; 70.8), famines (II Bar. 27.6; 70.8; II Esd. 6.22), destruction by fire (II Bar. 27.10; 70.8; II Esd. 5.8), the violent uprising of the natural order (II Esd. 6.22; I Enoch 80.2,3; Jub. 23.18; I Sib. Or. III. 539ff.), the appearance of fearful and mysterious portents on earth as well as in heaven (Rev. 6.12–13; 8.12; Matt. 24.19; Isa. 13.10; Ezek. 32.7; Joel 2.31; 3.15; Ass. Moses 10.5; II Esd. 6.21; I Enoch 80.4–5,6; Sib. Or. III. 801–803; II Esd. 5.4,5; II Macc. 5.2–3). The result of this outpouring of wrath is suffering, devastation, ecological disruption and death, all characteristics of the rule of Satan and his fallen angels; indeed, while perhaps different in terms of motivation, the manifestation of the wrath of God seems to be virtually the same as that of satanic or human moral evil. Any difference would lie in the quantity and magnitude of the wrath of God over against anything Satanic power can achieve, God demonstrating far more efficiency in the utilization of dark forces.

I wish to make three comments about this description of the wrath of God. The first is that in many cases it is bound together with deliberate action on God's part to blind the people involved in order that they do not repent; this allows God to give full vent to divine wrath in such a way that divine sovereignty is affirmed.

The classical paradigm of blinding people so that wrath can be poured out unimpeded upon them, and the sovereignty of God affirmed, can be found in the Exodus account of the ten plagues. Here Yahweh makes it clear to Moses that the divine intent is to demonstrate to Israel and to the Egyptians the glory and power of God. In order to do this, God is willing to harden Pharaoh's heart, because if left on his own Pharaoh would let the Israelites go (7.3). 'Then I will lay my hand upon Egypt and bring forth my hosts, my people the sons of Israel, out of the land of Egypt by great acts of judgment. And the Egyptians shall know that I am the Lord . . .' (7.4,5).

In demonstrating to Egypt and the Israelites the power of the Lord, Yahweh unleashed plagues such as had never been seen in

Egypt before: the rivers were turned to blood; swarms of frogs appeared; the dust turned to maggots; flies infested the land; the grazing herds of horses, cattle, donkeys and sheep were struck down with pestilence; boils infected every Egyptian, human and beast; a hailstorm descended; hordes of locusts invaded the land; and finally the first-born male child of each Egyptian household was struck down in the night. Throughout the plagues Yahweh reminds Moses: '. . . I have hardened his (Pharaoh's) heart and the heart of his servants, that I may show these signs of mine among them, and that you may tell in the hearing of your son and of your son's son how I made sport of the Egyptians and what signs I have done among them; that you may know that I am the Lord' (10.1,2).

In assessing this notion of God hardening the heart of Pharaoh to demonstrate divine power, Brevard Childs makes several points. First of all, he argues that the hardening is neither a psychological idiom used to describe an inner human resistance to divine will, nor is it concerned, as F. Hesse maintains, with 'the almighty power of Yahweh and the sinful action of man in an unrelievable tension'.[35] Rather, the formula 'that you may know that I am the Lord' is the central notion. The signs are given to reveal the knowledge of Yahweh to both Pharaoh and Israel alike. This is true both for the timing of the sending of the plagues and for their removal. In 5.2, Pharaoh asks: 'Who is the Lord that I should heed his voice and let Israel go?' The Lord answers with vengeance, making 'sport' of the Egyptians so that Israel in particular will witness the fact that Yahweh is Lord of Lords. The plagues, therefore, are not to be seen as the result of Pharaoh's hardening; rather, Pharaoh's hardening is required by Yahweh as part of the context for the plagues through which the divine glory will be revealed.

There are two strands of tradition in the narrative, J and P, Childs indicating that in J hardness prevents the signs from revealing the knowledge of God while in P the hardness results in the multiplication of the signs as judgment.[36] The profundity of the signs was missed by the Egyptians who had been hardened against them. This gave rise to a multiplication of the plagues with the prior divine intention to impress Israel with the power of their God. Both hardening of hearts and opening of eyes, then, are seen as aspects of divine glory, revealing the fact that the wrath of God, no matter how terrible, is always being carried out within a larger overall purpose that is ultimately salvific. This understanding is given more poetic clarification in Deuteronomy 32.39, where God challenges Israel to

See now that I, even I, am he,
and there is no god beside me;
I kill and I make alive;
I wound and I heal;
and there is none that can deliver out of my hand.

What emerges from this is that, contrary to the notion that it is always being experienced in terms of goodness, mercy, love, and compassion, God's glory is also experienced in displays of raw anger that destroy, that make sport of entire nations by slaughtering their livestock and killing their people, and that even go so far as to blind people deliberately so that this anger can not only be poured out but be multiplied. The vengeance of the Lord upon those who displease the Infinite is integral to understanding the wrath of God.

Yet the problem does not remain so clear cut. In the Exodus account of God hardening Pharaoh's heart, it is said that Pharaoh was ready to repent and let Israel go but that Yahweh deliberately further hardened him so that more signs could be shown for Israel's benefit. And yet the paradox of this action was that Yahweh was hardening even the people the plagues were intended to impress. Deuteronomy 29.2–4 makes this clear. It is part of the last address of Moses to the people of Israel after wandering in the desert for forty years. He tells them:

You have seen all that the Lord did before your eyes in the land of Egypt, to Pharaoh and to all his servants and to all his land, the great trials which your eyes saw, the signs and those great wonders, but to this day the Lord has not given you a mind to understand, or eyes to see, or ears to hear.

Vengeance and repentance alone do not suffice to explain the wrath of God. There is something deeper going on within the Godhead itself, something that defies conventional morality or even covenantal promises. It suggests a certain intention on the part of Yahweh to give vent to a dark side of the Divine even as Yahweh gives vent to a lighter side: both seem to be an integral part of divine glory and an indispensable part of the way in which God deals with humankind.

That this aspect of Divinity is far beyond the comprehension of human beings to fathom rationally can be seen in the narrative of David's sin in numbering the people of Israel. II Samuel 24.1 reads: 'Again the anger of the Lord was kindled against Israel, and he incited David against them, saying "Go, number Israel and Judah".'

Although nothing in the text indicates that David would have thought of numbering the people on his own, the Lord incites him to do so and then considers David's numbering a 'transgression'. It is interesting to note that I Chronicles 21.1 attributes the same incitement to Satan rather than to God. This indicates that there was ambivalence in the Hebrew mind as to who should bear responsibility for David's temptation.[37] In both cases, however, it is David who must repent and ask the Lord to 'take away the iniquity of thy servant' (II Sam. 24.10; I Chron. 21.8). The punishment for an action David did at the Lord's incitement: 70,000 men were struck down from Dan to Beersheba.

Caspari terms the incident the result of an 'anger for an unknown reason' because it is never clear why numbering the people was a sin in the first place nor why the Lord, either directly or through the instrumentality of Satan, would in anger provoke David to do something the Lord would then punish him for doing.[38] It gives an insight into an inexplicable dimension of divine wrath, however, and into the inscrutability of the divine will.

I Kings 22 and Isaiah 6 both testify further to the willingness of God to blind people's minds. The theme is fundamental to the gospel witness to the ministry of Jesus; indeed, Isaiah's prophecy is mentioned in all four gospels in interpreting the hardness of people's hearts. John 12.37–41 states:

> though he had done so many signs before them, yet they did not believe in him; it was that the word spoken by the prophet Isaiah might be fulfilled: 'Lord, who has believed our report, and to whom has the arm of the Lord been revealed?' Therefore they could not believe. For Isaiah again said, 'He has blinded their eyes and hardened their heart, lest they should see with their eyes and perceive with their heart, and turn for me to heal them.'

Mark 4.11 is quite explicit in saying that the reason people were hardened against Jesus was '. . . lest they turn again and be forgiven'. In Luke 24 it is specifically stated that even the disciples themselves were subject to the blinding will of God, 24.16 recording that the eyes of two of them while on their way to Emmaus after the crucifixion were 'seized', 'mastered', so as to prevent them from recognizing Jesus. It was only after Jesus had interpreted to them all the scriptural passages concerning himself and had also made himself 'known to them in the breaking of the bread' that their eyes were 'opened', and they recognized him as the risen Christ (24.31). Later,

Jesus opened the minds of all the disciples to understand the scriptures (24.45).

In I Corinthians 2.8, Paul points to the deliberate intention of God to keep the mystery of the divine purpose in Christ secret and hidden from the rulers, for 'if they had (understood), they would not have crucified the Lord of glory'. This implies that if the rulers did not know what they were doing, it was because God willed that they should not. This is clear, for as Paul insists in 2.10ff., only the Spirit can know and reveal the purposes of God. If God, therefore, in divine freedom deliberately chose not to give the rulers who crucified Jesus the Spirit to know the truth, then they could not possibly have recognized who Jesus really was.

Further, while I Corinthians 2.8 exemplifies the notion of God choosing not to reveal the divine purpose before the time appointed, particularly to the rulers who crucified Jesus, Romans 11.8 (a conflation of Isa. 29.10 and Deut. 29.4) states quite categorically that even when the *testimonium* of Christ *was* revealed, God deliberately chose to give certain people 'a spirit of stupor, eyes that should not see, and ears that should not hear, down to this very day'. Barth comments on this by saying that Paul is here representing a God 'who in revealing His mercy, so mercilessly utters His "No"; who in turning His face towards all, so sternly excludes all; who, in making Himself known, remains "hidden" and is first known as the Hidden God . . .'[39]

In considering the notion of blindness and hardening generally, three aspects need to be noted. First, there is the notion reflected in Deuteronomy 29 that God chose not to give to the Israelites eyes to see and ears to hear; secondly, there is the revelation of the implications of the mystery of election at the centre of God's salvific will, something reflected in Isaiah 6.9–10 and 29.10, that God deliberately hardens hearts and closes minds to the saving work of the Divine. In Romans 11.8, this aspect of Isaiah 29.10 governs the use of Deuteronomy 29.2–4. Thirdly, there is the notion reflected in I Corinthians 2.7–10, that God deliberately chooses not to reveal what has been foreordained and that those who have not received the revelation of truth play an integral role in the overall purposes of God.

What emerges from all three aspects of God's selective and deliberate blinding of people and/or keeping them blind is one central point: that God's wrath and God's use of hardening to allow for and receive that wrath is inextricably connected with the notion of God's *election*, of God's *purpose* for creation. The blinding and hardening of hearts is inseparably bound up with election, and can only be dealt with in that context.

In I Corinthians 2.8, for example, the ignorance of the rulers is central to the purposes of God. In Romans 11, Paul also makes this clear, that the interaction of God's blinding of Israel on the one hand, and Israel's sin and rebelliousness on the other – as well as the salvation of the Gentiles and eventually even of Israel herself – all need to be interpreted in the light of a revelation that God is weaving these strands of historical reality within the framework of divine purpose and election; i.e., all of history must be seen as 'in God', a point stressed in articulating the hermeneutic of engagement.

The issue of divine wrath, then, blinding people so that they cannot repent, pouring forth destruction far in excess of the deed done, trapping people such as David unawares and manipulating their reality, and hardening the hearts of people such as Pharaoh in order to make 'sport' of them, indicates that the wrath of God has as much to do with the internal dynamic of the Godhead itself as with a retributive response to human sinfulness. In other words, we have traditionally understood the wrath of God as arising in response to human beings breaking the covenant; it seems equally true that the wrath of God, like the love of God, simply emerges from the Godhead for reasons inscrutable to us and certainly independent of human stimulus. The wrath of God seems to be as much a part of the glory of God as is the mercy of God, both equally effective and both equally undeserved from the human vantage point, arising from reasons hidden in the Godhead. This is to say, in reference to apocalyptic, that the apocalyptic time of alienation and outpouring of darkness is as much an action and revelation of *God's* nature and purpose as it is the result of *human* actions. We are blinded by sin; we are at times blinded by God. We are in a sea of anomie; so, it appears, is God, for at times, seemingly without cause, divine wrath spills forth. And there are times when within us dark forces emerge, antithetical to the forces of light; so, too, with God, who forms the light and creates darkness; who makes peace and creates evil (Isa. 45.7).

What is important to realize, however, is that in the biblical tradition the wrath of God, activated to be sure for reasons hidden within the sovereign freedom of the Godhead, is set within the context of a divine sovereignty that spills forth this wrath for a specific purpose, a purpose foreordained 'since before the creation of the world', a purpose having ultimately to do with the election and nurturance of a Chosen People, a community of the faithful who will give confessional witness to the belief that God is above all gods and acts salvifically in their history, ultimately for all humanity.

The second comment arises directly from the first: that in speaking of the wrath of God, one must be aware above all that one is dealing with a dimension of Divinity beyond the rational and beyond the moral. Rudolf Otto stresses this point:

> . . . this 'Wrath' has no concern whatever with moral qualities. There is something very baffling in the way in which it 'is kindled' and manifested. It is, as has been well said, 'like a hidden force of nature', like stored-up electricity, discharging itself upon any one who comes too near. It is 'incalculable' and 'arbitrary'. Any one who is accustomed to think of deity only by its rational attributes must see in this 'Wrath' mere caprice and wilful passion.[40]

Thus the wrath of God is analogous to the religious idea in general of a mysterious *ira deorum*, and is an essential aspect of the *mysterium tremendum*. We can know this aspect of the Godhead because we experience it but we cannot rationally understand it. The wrath of God, therefore, constitutes a unique moment in the religious experience, a moment peculiarly daunting and awe-inspiring which directly challenges the notion of God as being merely love, goodness, gentleness and mercy. God is much deeper than any such monopolar prejudice allows, much more complex than the platitudes derived from discourse based on moral reasoning which describes Divinity as the sum total of human logic. Rather, as Otto observes, 'something supra-rational throbs and gleams, palpable and visible, in the "Wrath of God", prompting to a sense of "terror" that no "natural" anger can arouse.'[41]

Eichrodt points out in this regard that the inward fire of the wrath of God in the Old Testament is described by the Hebrew words meaning snorting, foaming, boiling, or breaking forth under pressure. All the depictions connote a non-rational, highly emotive element, Eichrodt adding that in times of unexpected and terrifying disasters a term is used, meaning a 'blow' from Yahweh as a sign of displeasure.[42]

The third comment arises, in turn, from the second. While Israel is aware of the unpredictability and non-rational nature of the wrath of the Lord, the Hebrews never fall victim to the despondency of the so-called 'Babylonian Job' who sees the contradictions of evil and goodness within the relationship of God to humanity to such a point that he is led to say:

What to man seems good, that to God is evil: and that which in his heart is iniquity, to his God is good. Who is able to know the will of the gods in heaven? The counsel of God, who can understand it?[43]

Israel never succumbs to explaining the wrath of God in terms of despotic caprice or demonic savagery, but rather gives testimony to the notion that *'supreme power which is sinister in its intentions (is) no truly integral element in the divine nature'.*[44] For this reason, the wrath of God, though ferocious and bloodthirsty, never becomes a stumbling block to faith, and the will of God, though opaque and at times contradictory to the covenant, never becomes a pretext for cynicism. While the wrath of God plays a fundamental role in the divine pleroma, God finally weaves the strands of divine action, of mercy and of wrath and of sinful human action into a creative integration which is ultimately salvific.

This can be seen in virtually all the accounts which bear witness to the wrath of God. In the case of David being incited to number the people, for example, perhaps the most puzzling of all the cases mentioned, the angel of the Lord, after smiting the 70,000 men, comes to rest by the threshing place of Araunah the Jebusite. The Lord then commands David to build an altar there. It is on this site that Solomon builds the Temple. The other examples mentioned turn out the same way. From out of the crucible of the plagues of Egypt, Israel is delivered to take possession of the Promised Land; out of the affliction of the Philistines over the ark of the covenant, Samuel is able to persuade the children of Israel to put away their Baalim and Ashtaroth and serve the Lord only; and from out of the intricacies of blinding and keeping blind various people to enact the crucifixion come the resurrection and glorification of Christ Jesus. The wrath of God is always to be interpreted in the context of the love of God.

The wrath of God impresses upon us, however, that we are contingent beings, that our personal destinies must be subordinated to the inscrutable will of God, whatever that will might be. As Eichrodt puts the matter: 'Yahweh's subjects enjoyed no privileged exemption from the enigmatic chances of human life and the natural course of things.'[45] Indeed, it can be said that the wrath of God, the blinding will of God, affirms that God's ways are full of power and glory, and yet are 'totally beyond man's understanding, calculation and measure of judgment, for they appear to him as an arbitrary and violent transgression of the order he has worked out for his life'.[46]

Again, this point challenges any rationalistic categorization of reward and punishment. God is not at our disposal: God does not have to fit into our definitions and estimations of the 'right' and the 'wrong'. God's overwhelming majesty is beyond the confines of even the Mosaic covenant; indeed, it is beyond the reach of any human apprehension at all. Barth is quite right, therefore, in saying that in the presence of God

> the valleys are exalted and the high hills made low. Ended is the conflict of good and evil, for men are ranged upon one line, and their secrets . . . are judged before God and before Him only.[47]

As such, then, God is

> precisely no 'thing-in-itself', no metaphysical substance in the midst of other substances . . . On the contrary, He is the eternal Origin of all things. As their non-existence, He is their true being.[48]

The wrath of God is part of a *mysterium*, therefore, that is of positive value solely in terms of itself; before it we can make no claims; we can only become conscious of it and appreciate it for what it is: 'a value inexpressible, positive and "fascinating" '.[49]

The apocalyptists, perhaps more than most, were conscious of this *mysterium*, for it was their only place of refuge. They awaited its action, knowing that when it came all of history would be wiped away. For them, a single stroke from eternity was of greater import than the sum total of the realm of finite things, for having seen the vision of the coming wrath and the inevitable judgment of God, they knew that all the falsehood and evil structurings of a human race gone astray in rebelliousness and pride were a mere speck compared with the sovereign power of a wrathful God. In the face of the Absolute the relativity of a corrupted world would not stand. And the Absolute was coming in judgment.

The totality of God's judgment is dealt with by Barth:

> The judgment of God is the end of history, not the beginning of a new, a second, epoch. By it, history is not prolonged, but done away with . . . God speaks: and He is recognized as the Judge. By His speech and by His judgment a transformation is effected so radical that time and eternity, here and there, the righteousness of men and the righteousness of God, are indissolubly linked together.[50]

In commenting on the wrath and judgment of God, however,

Barth observes a paradox to which we must now turn. On the one hand, 'the difference between that which lies beyond the judgment and that which lies on this side of it is not relative but absolute: the two are separated absolutely';[51] on the other hand, 'the new is also the goal; the Redeemer is also the Creator; He that judgeth is also He that restoreth all things.' What this means, says Barth, is that

> What is new is also the deepest truth of what was old. The most radical ending of history, the negation under which all flesh stands, the absolute judgment, which is the meaning of God for the world of men and time and things, is also the crimson thread which runs through the whole course of the world in its inevitability. Thus the final subjection to the wrath of God is faith in His righteousness: and then God is known as the Unknown God.[52]

From out of the darkness of evil, a new creation was to appear for the apocalyptists, a creation of purity, righteousness and light and in which the apocalyptists placed their final hope.

The wrath of God can be seen as deadly yet positive, inexplicable and arbitrary yet sovereign and ultimately creative, because it is always placed within the overall purpose of election of and salvation for God's chosen people. This is particularly true in apocalyptic: the dramatic conflict between *civitas dei* and *civitas diaboli*, the outpouring of divine anger upon a lawless and rebellious humanity, and the blinding and hardening of hearts and eyes and ears so that this rebellion intensifies and the resultant wrath continues, are all to be seen as coupled with an expression of hope in God's final triumph. The 'Day of Yahweh', in which God's will is vindicated and the elect are justified, is always seen as the culmination of whatever blindness or darkness or evil is present in the existing order. The New Age is only considered accessible through the pain of the Old. Indeed, the name given in later Jewish and Christian writings to the time of waiting just before the End – when the wrath of God and the evil intents of Satan and the Antichrist have reached their highest pitch – is 'travail pains of the Messiah'.[53]

All that fills the vision of the apocalyptists, therefore, from the evil forces impinging upon the world and the evil inclination of the human heart to the outpouring of the wrath of God, must be seen as fitting into a pattern of history, ordained by God, which leads inextricably to the creation of a new world order, sometimes established by God directly but more often brought to fruition through a Messianic figure who is to be seen as representational of God. The goodness, bliss and beauty of this New Age, however, is only brought forth from the womb of the evil times of the Old Age. There must be death before there can be a new life; there must be the wrath of God before God can manifest divine love; there must be a crucifixion before the resurrection. God is clearly Lord of both, creating the evil, making the light, bringing the war, ensuring the peace (Isa. 45.7). What is more, this dynamic of erasing the old to bring forth the new is not something that involves merely humanity or planet earth but the entire cosmos.[54]

Frost points out that for the apocalyptists the vision of the New Age invoked fear as well as excited anticipation. On the one hand, he says,

> we can understand the delight which the apocalyptist had in picturing that holocaust of a universe in ruins, for he found in it real solace for his soul, since only in an End on such a scale as that could he find any ground of hope whatsoever.[55]

On the other hand, however, the apocalyptists were aware that they had yet to go through the purifying wrath of God. There was not only delight, therefore, but fear and dread: 'he himself must pass through the flame, he himself endure the woes that should precede the End, he himself be present when the solid earth should melt away in fervent heat'. Only then would the New Age of beauty, bliss and harmony be born, when a new heaven and a new earth would be created, filled with the very presence of God and ruled by God's own representative, the Messiah, in a reign that would last for ever.

VI

The Synthesis of Hiroshima and Apocalyptic

A. INTRODUCTION

We are currently being confronted with 'the second great break in the history of humankind', i.e., with a great revelation of God amongst us. This event, symbolized by the dropping of the atomic bomb on Hiroshima, is dramatically radicalizing our ancient conceptualizations of apocalyptic. I pointed out in the last chapter that classical apocalyptic perceived the world as overflowing with evil and as corrupted to the point where its history would soon be terminated by the judgment of a wrathful God. It was a conception based on a strict determinism which saw all things as being done by the fiat of a Divine Controller. Hiroshima, however, has humanized the eschaton; it has given to human beings the power to enact what the apocalyptists believed only God could do: terminate human history and destroy the world. This means that the referent for the apocalypse must no longer be seen solely in terms of a wrathful God outside ourselves but also in terms of a wrathful humanity inside ourselves. The atomic age has catapulted human beings into an epoch where we can, with God, enact the apocalypse.

What is of equal importance to bear in mind is that Hiroshima says as much about God as it does about humanity. Indeed, what will emerge from the following discussion is that God and humanity are in fact co-creating the apocalypse together; i.e., while we are fashioning the instruments of our own self-destruction, we are doing so not only because of our own evil inclinations but because God is instilling within us the divine lure to enact the apocalypse. This is a hard statement, for it means that God and humanity must both be perceived as integral to the Hiroshima event. Nevertheless, given what we have just discussed concerning the shadow dimension of the wrath of God, it is clear that God can and does enter into every aspect of life, whether light or dark.

In this chapter I shall be exploring the synthesis of Hiroshima and apocalyptic within the context of humanity and Divinity co-creating the 'end of time'. It will be a difficult synthesis, for, above all, Hiroshima confronts us with the imperative to take the antinomial character of God seriously. It necessitates that we at long last give up our monopolar prejudice concerning God being merely the expression of the traditional notion of the *Summum Bonum* and recognize that God is the God of all possibilities; that God utilizes all the instruments of power – including blinding and keeping blind, including the deliberate committing of destructive acts, and including the ruthless disregard for covenantal morality. This is to say that even as Hiroshima confronts us with new dimensions of human depravity, it also confronts us with deeper dimensions of the shadow side of God.

Therefore the synthesis between Hiroshima and apocalyptic challenges us to explore the coming together of humanity and God in our new found powers of global destruction. It is important to stress the co-creative character of the apocalyptic possibilities in our day. Hiroshima humanizing the apocalypse means that if the wrath of God must come it is human hands which will push the button; and if the righteousness of God will replace the old order with a new age it is human work which will create it. In history, God never works alone, but always in conjunction with human beings. Therefore, it is imperative to find the locus of the Divine/human interface within the human realm.

Because Hiroshima has humanized the eschaton and for the first time placed the capability to destroy the world in human hands, it is important to discern that locus in which three things occur: first, in which the human realities of darkness and light are felt most strongly; second, in which these human feelings and drives engage with, and are affected by, God; and third, in which some type of synthesis can occur not only between the forces peculiarly human but also between the human and the Divine.

The locus in which all these three dynamics occur is the human psyche, for it is here that the active inner and spiritual life of human beings takes place; where religious experience takes place, meaning our inner encounters with God; and where we can synthesize the contradictions within us to achieve some type of reconciliation. As I said, Hiroshima has made imperative this journey inward; therefore, theology, if it is to internalize adequately the historical event

Hiroshima represents, must take seriously the psychic dimensions of human experience. Not only does our psyche influence what we perceive, receive, mediate and express in terms of our spiritual life, but it is only as we find reconciliation within the psyche that we can deal adequately with the polarities inherent in the external world. A *psycho-theology* has, since Hiroshima, become inescapable in understanding the dilemma we are confronted with. I made this point initially in the discussion of the *hibakusha* and our organic connection with what they experienced.[1] We all are survivors of Hiroshima and Nagasaki because we have all had 'engraved' in our psyches the death immersion the atomic bombing of Japan represents. As Lifton points out, this death immersion has caused a 'psychic mutation' in us all.

In exploring our psychic reality I have chosen to follow primarily the discoveries of C. G. Jung because I believe it can be shown that he, above all, appreciated the psyche as the locus in which the human and the divine meet, mutually affect one another, and cocreate.

I agree with Eleanor Bertine in her remark that

> All down the ages the existence of a supreme value has been attested by religious and mystical people, but Jung's great gift to his generation is the discovery that this value lies within the human psyche itself. Moreover, he has elaborated a method by which it can be sought there, without the necessity of any dogma or belief, and in addition can be formulated in terms consonant with the best of modern science.[2]

This is true for two reasons. First, I believe that it can be demonstrated that Jung's analytical psychology reveals most deeply the inner workings of psychic life, revealing the psyche to be not only as empirically real as our physical existence but also an autonomous force within us that shapes our conscious perceptions and theological statements. Jung offers an anthropology that can deal with our spiritual reality more adequately than any other at the present time.

This last remark raises the second important reason for using the work of Jung to explore the human psyche: namely, that in describing psychic reality, Jung, in contradistinction to most modern scientists, takes the religious dimension of human life seriously. If Hartshorne is the 'God-intoxicated philosopher', Jung must surely be the 'God-intoxicated psychologist'. Indeed, as Victor White observes, 'whereas for Freud religion is a symptom of psychological disease, for Jung the *absence* of religion is at the root of all adult psychological disease'.[3] Jung himself stated in 1932 that he had not had one patient

> whose problem in the last resort was not that of finding a religious outlook on life . . . every one of them fell ill because he had lost that which the living religions of every age have given their followers, and none of them has been really healed who did not regain this religious outlook.[4]

To utilize Jung's depth psychology does not imply that I follow him uncritically. Quite the contrary, as with my use of Whitehead and Hartshorne in delineating process panentheism, although I believe Jung's basic concepts are sound, I have critically modified and adapted his insights into my own schema.

I am mindful of James Heisig's comment, that

> Jung's writings drag the reader so hastily back and forth across the frontiers of philosophy, theology, psychology, mythology, philology and anthropology that, willy nilly, one tends either to stumble dizzily into a position of naive discipleship or else break free and stalk off in sceptical, defiant indifference.[5]

In order to avoid these extremes, Heisig rightly suggests that 'it is necessary to approach Jung slowly and patiently, cautious of generalizations and reconciled to the aim of making but a few humble steps'.

Heisig himself is highly critical of Jung's methodology, asserting that Jung's most serious fault lay in his failure to clarify properly the relationship between fact and theory.[6] It was Jung's opinion that he gathered his data objectively, free of prejudice, but Heisig, rightly in my opinion, points out that if Jung's position is to be consistent, that one can never know the *Ding an sich* but only as it is filtered through one's own psyche, then it must be acknowledged that all his data were filtered through his own intuitive insights.[7]

Moreover, Jung's literary style and method of argument do not lend themselves easily to dissection by rationalist analysis. Aldous Huxley, for example, although he much preferred Jung to Freud, accuses Jung of 'turgid copiousness'.[8]

An important point to bear in mind when approaching Jung from a rationalist perspective is that Jung can best be described as an 'introverted-thinking type' with intuition as the dominant auxiliary function in both his method and style.[9] His writings prefer imagery to concrete factuality, and in the place of rigorous and systemic argumentation there is a quasi-poetic flow of thoughts. This yields an almost prophetic quality in his work rather than a rationalistic detachment. In fact, Jung deliberately used equivocal language as he felt either rational reductionism or symbol alone was inadequate in describing psychic reality.

Jung's interpretative framework and hypotheses are clearly intuitive. His logic is always to be found at work in the context of the complex and paradoxical insights of his intuition. Moreover, being intuitive, Jung runs counter to the demythologizing approach of many current theologians and philosophers, for to Jung myth is the indispensable tool of the unconscious.

Being aware of both the criticisms and limitations of Jung, nevertheless find him helpful. Jung offers a practical and open model of the psyche which must be taken seriously. Most importantly, Jung grappled with profound clarity and perception in the area that concerns us – the reality of evil. It is in this dimension that rationalist logic is weakest, for what we shall be exploring are those areas precisely not amenable to the neat categorizations of sequential logic. The central question of this work is why it is that after several thousand million years of life on this planet our species, in our generation, has brought this life to the brink of extinction through thermonuclear war. We are dealing with the problem of evil, with the shadow aspect of reality, not only in ourselves but in God. The discussion is yielding an affirmation of the antinomial character of God, a reality in which a 'both . . . and . . .' complementarity of opposites is much more constructive than the 'either . . . or . . .' dichotomy of logical reasoning. In this realm, Jung's empirical data in the selection and interpretation of which his intuition plays a major role, will be helpful.

Like Hartshorne's neo-classical metaphysics, Jung understands reality to be much more of a 'both . . . and . . .' continuum rather than an 'either . . . or . . .' dichotomy. Like Hartshorne, too, Jung takes as fundamental the law of dipolarity, applying it to the psyche as Hartshorne does in articulating his dipolar theory of God. Jung sees polarity operative in different ways, however, and therefore offers insights which will have application to what we have been discussing thus far concerning the antinomial character of God, an area Hartshorne does not discuss.

In particular Jung is helpful in deepening our understanding of the hermeneutic of engagement I discussed earlier. I have asserted that in understanding scripture it is imperative to bear in mind that the biblical tradition interweaves the facts of history and the confessional witness into a single continuum which can be responded to authentically only by faith. The profane and the sacred, the historic and the mythic are both essential components of what actually occurred. Thus the historical fact of Jesus dying on the cross and the mythic formulations concerning Christ crucified for our redemption become a seamless robe that cannot be undone if Christians are truly to appreciate divine action in human history. Both poles are present in the divine event without contradiction. If we are to continue to bear witness to the Logos in the modern age, we must reflect this antinomial complementarity in the structure and character of our witness.

Jung gives us a clue as to how to engage with the mystery of the nature of scripture. This model of the psyche is based on the interaction of consciousness with unconsciousness and the interaction of the logic of time, space and causality with symbols and mythic images. Consciousness uses the categories of time, space and causality; the unconscious uses symbols and mythic images. The interrelationship between these two aspects of the psyche form a *complexio oppositorum*, a tension of opposites, which can be integrated only by the self – the unifying force in the psyche – if we are to reach the goal of wholeness. To reduce symbol to rational logic or mythic images to the literalism of the categories of time, space and causality on the one hand or to swallow up the reality of the world of time, space and causality into symbol and myth on the other, is to miss the real profundity and dynamic power of the psyche. The same holds true for scripture: on the one hand, to reduce divine action in history to either literalism or demythologized rationalism, or on the other hand, to deny the physical historical truth of Jesus of Nazareth by swallowing it up in symbol and myth, is to emasculate the mystery of the biblical witness. My hermeneutic of engagement holds both historical fact and confessional response in creative tension. Jung's model of the psyche does the same. Consciousness is in tension with the unconscious and the categories of time, space and causality are in tension with the expressions of symbol and myth. The resulting *complexio oppositorum*, while not amenable to rationalistic reduction, leads us closer to an appreciation of the mystery of scripture and the antinomial reality of God.

I shall endeavour to make clear two points within the theological/psychological interface Jung points toward: first, that it is within our psychic reality that we encounter God; and second, that the images of God we do encounter in our psychic depths are of an antinomial nature, i.e., composed of both light and dark dimensions. This will in turn allow for a deeper understanding of the synthesis of Hiroshima and apocalyptic in our day.

The remainder of this chapter, then, is divided into two parts first, there will be a discussion of Jung's depth psychology as i relates to the subject at hand; and second, there will be a re examination of the synthesis of Hiroshima and apocalyptic in the light of the insights we will have derived from Jung as well as the ontology of God set forth in Chapter III.

B. JUNG'S DESCRIPTION OF THE PSYCHE

1. *The psyche as objectively real*

Hans Schaer observes that

> the moment you start on Jung's psychology you have the feeling of entering into a spacious new world that contains wide tracts of unknown territory and many secrets, and that accordingly holds out all sorts of possibilities of discovery. This new world is the world of the soul or the psychic, these terms being understood in their broadest sense.[10]

Over the last several decades we have been shown through the research done in physics and astronomy that matter extends to the infinitely great and the infinitesimally small without our being able to discover limits at either end or even an overall hierarchical structure.[11] There appears to be no micro or macro limit to physical reality. Jung has demonstrated that the same assertions hold true for the human psyche, that it, too, is infinite in extension. Schaer calls this assertion one of 'almost Copernican proportions'[12] because the psychological and anthropological notions concerning the human psyche or soul before Jung were, by and large, like physics before Heisenberg and Einstein. The psyche, if it was posited at all was seen as a monad-like substance enclosed by, and limited to, the individual human being in which it dwelt.

For Jung, the psyche is as substantive a part of, and affective upon, reality as the physical aspects of the world. It is real because it can be empirically observed to *act*; moreover, Jung states categorically that 'the psyche has a peculiar nature which cannot be reduced to anything else'.[13] This is of fundamental importance to grasp, for there are those who still operate under the prejudice that the psyche is either a mere epiphenomenon of a bio-chemical process in the brain or that it is merely a personal matter constructed by individual subjectivity. These prejudices must be overcome, says

Jung, for like our physiology, the psyche is a relatively 'self-contained field of experience' to which we must attribute a quite special importance because it includes the phenomenon of *consciousness*. Counterbalancing our physical aspects, therefore, which are an indispensable condition of existence, are our psychic aspects which include our consciousness. Indeed, 'without consciousness there would, practically speaking, be no world, for the world exists for us only in so far as it is consciously reflected by the psyche. *Consciousness is a precondition of being*.'[14] Thus the psyche is endowed with the dignity of a 'cosmic principle' co-equal in importance with physical reality in understanding the human being.

The relationship between these two 'cosmic principles' Jung understands in much the same way that modern physics understands the relationship between the observer and the observed: namely, that what we know of the surrounding physical world we experience through our psyche. We have no immediate knowledge of physical reality at all, only replicas of it in the psyche. We never know the *Ding an sich*, only the *Ding an sich* as it is mediated by our consciousness.[15]

This debate between truth as objectivity or subjectivity is of course an old one, falling between those who, following Plato, support a realist point of view, that the universal concepts have existence in themselves; and the nominalists, who assert that the so-called universals are nothing but names. Jung was familiar with the philosophical arguments on both sides; he was also aware of the philosophical solution offered by Aristotle and Aquinas who supported the notion of *universale in re*, that the idea exists as the universal 'form' of the concrete object. Jung dismissed this position as 'primitive concretism'.[16] He appealed instead to Kant, focussing on the psychic image of the objective reality. He repeatedly quoted Kant's statement throughout his works that 'there can be no empirical knowledge that is not already caught and limited by the *a priori* structure of cognition'.[17]

As Jung understood it, 'to the extent that the world does not assume the form of a psychic image, it is virtually non-existent'.[18] He agreed with Heisenberg and the physicists in asserting that we never see the world as it is but only as it is mediated through our faculties of observation.[19]

The 'tragic thing' about this, says Jung, is that 'psychology has no self-consistent mathematics at its disposal, only a calculus of subjective prejudices'.[20] The result has been that '*the* category of existence, the indispensable *sine qua non* of all existence, namely the psyche, (is) treated as if it were only semi-existent'.[21] This state of affairs is due to the fact that while a science such as physics can observe the physical world from the viewpoint of the psyche, translating the physical into the psychical, the psyche can only observe itself from itself and can therefore only translate the psychic by the psychic. There is thus no medium for psychology to reflect itself through.

Nevertheless, Jung is insistent in bringing out the fact that while

> physics . . . is in a position to detonate mathematical formulae . . . and kill seventy-eight thousand persons at one blow . . . we can, in all modesty, point out that mathematical thinking is a psychic function, thanks to which matter can be organized in such a way as to burst asunder the mighty forces that bind the atoms together – which it would never occur to them to do in the natural course of things, at least not upon this earth.[22]

While 'only a calculus of subjective prejudices', therefore, 'the psyche is a disturber of the natural laws of the cosmos, and should we ever succeed in doing something to Mars with the aid of atomic fission, this too will have been brought to pass by the psyche'.

This means not only that all knowledge of the world is mediated by the psyche but also that the psyche is fully capable of intervention in the existing natural order. 'The psyche,' says Jung, 'is the world's pivot.'[23] How true this is, that the psyche not only mediates reality but can dramatically disturb it, will emerge as our discussion proceeds.

In order to understand better what Jung means by 'psyche' it is necessary to delineate briefly some of the categories and terms he uses to describe it. I shall contextualize the discussion as much as possible within the religious dimension, although I will offer examples from physics to help clarify certain points. In speaking of the psyche the use of spatial language is necessary; however, it is important to bear in mind that such language is to be taken metaphorically, not literally. The psyche is not a container in which psychic experiences happen any more than God is a secondary being 'up there' whom we can point to. Nevertheless, spatial images remain essential in discussing both these phenomena.

2. The unconscious

Fundamental to Jung's concept of the psyche is the concept of the unconscious, a term first used by C. G. Carus in the nineteenth century to describe that part of our psychic reality which is real yet invisible to our ego-consciousness.[24] His ideas were not readily taken up by psychology, as they were based more on intuitive insight than empirical data, although Edward von Hartmann worked with them philosophically. It was not until Freud that the notion gained widespread acceptance that there is a major portion of our psyche that is hidden from us. As Freud presented it, the unconscious is where human beings deposit all the psychic contents of their lives which for one reason or another they cannot or do not want to keep in consciousness. Experiences which are too painful to dwell upon, such as childhood traumas, are repressed and forgotten, at least by consciousness. But they do not thereby disappear; rather, they become part of an unconscious reservoir of impulses, drives, memories etc. that make themselves felt in consciousness again through dreams, fantasies, 'Freudian slips', symptoms, and complexes of all kinds. Many of these repressed psychic elements can lead to neuroses and can only be cured if they are made conscious again and dealt with.

Although Jung agreed with the Freudian assertion that the unconscious contained repressed material, he felt compelled to go beyond it. As with Carus, he discerned that the unconscious is an autonomous reality in our psyche upon which both consciousness and the ego float. By *ego* Jung means the 'complex of representations which constitutes the centre of my field of consciousness and appears to possess a very high degree of continuity and identity'.[25] Elsewhere, he terms the ego 'the subject of consciousness'.[26] He defines consciousness as 'the function or activity which maintains the relation of psychic contents with the ego'.[27]

The level of the unconscious containing those aspects of an individual's life that are either forgotten, repressed or subliminally perceived Jung terms the *personal unconscious*.[28] Beyond this lies the *collective unconscious* which does not include acquisitions particular to individual egos. Whereas the personal unconscious is *post*-birth, therefore, the collective unconscious is *pre*-birth, being composed of contents resulting from the inherited possibility of psychical functioning in general. The collective unconscious is an inheritance as it were which is common to all human beings; it therefore constitutes the basis of every individual psyche.[29]

The collective unconscious is thus the 'primal datum' out of which all other aspects of our psyches emerge: the personal unconscious, consciousness and ego.

The central energy, which Jung termed *libido* and referred to as the 'unfathomable ground', permeates all sectors of psychic life, remaining essentially unchanged, whatever stratum it energizes. As defined by Jacobi, this central energy is 'the total force which pulses through all the forms and activities of the psychic system and establishes a communication between them'.[30] Above this 'unfathomable ground' lies the deposit of our animal ancestors and human ancestors. Each segment represents a further differentiation of the collective psyche until after animal and human ancestry emerge ethnic group, nation, tribe, family and finally, individual. Being the last and highest segment, each individual carries in his or her psyche the collective memory of all that has gone on before. This can be understood perhaps more clearly by recalling that in physical terms, each baby in the womb undergoes a development which takes it through all the stages of evolution; only during the last stages of the embryonic journey is its development explicitly human. The same is true in terms of our psyche, says Jung: 'The collective unconscious contains the whole spiritual heritage of mankind's evolution born anew in the brain structure of every individual.'[31] He explains it another way as well by saying that

> Just as our bodies still retain vestiges of obscure functions in many of our organs, so our minds, which have apparently outgrown these archaic impulses, still bear the mark of the evolutionary stage we have traversed, and re-echo the dim bygone in dreams and fantasies.[32]

Despite the vitality of the collective and personal unconscious, neither one can be directly observed; they can only be known through their effects upon our consciousness. Freud observed the personal unconscious through the symptoms of hysteria, dreams, jokes, paraplexes, etc. He thereby penetrated into what he termed the 'concealment of the actual' (*Verborgenheit des Eigentlichen*). Jung puts the existence of the unconscious this way:

> The existence of an unconscious psyche is as likely . . . as the existence of an as yet undiscovered planet, whose presence is inferred from the deviations of some unknown planetary orbit. Unfortunately we lack the aid of a telescope that would make certain of its existence.[33]

This forced Jung to say that although actual, the processes of the unconscious must be called 'hypothetical'.[34]

What this means, says Goldbrunner, is that 'experience is the sole basis of our claim to speak . . . of the collective unconscious'.[35] These experiences he divides into four categories: the hallucinations and behaviour of mental patients; dreams, visions and fantasies; the wisdom of Oriental mysticism; and the analysis of the background of the psyche.[36] While agreeing with this categorization, Schaer, Jacobi and others, following Freud, call dreams the 'royal road' to the unconscious.[37] Dreams serve to illustrate the point. We do not acutally perceive the unconscious processes in the dreams, only their reflections; but since dreams are spontaneous expressions of psychic activity beyond the control of conscious volition, they express the actual state of our unconscious in symbolic form, the language of the unconscious, particularly the collective unconscious. Dreams, therefore, arise through unconscious activity; yet while dissociated from our egos and consciousness they are nevertheless observable by consciousness and the ego. Through proper dream interpretation, therefore, we can discern unconscious processes. Dream interpretation is not a straightforward process, however, for while the language of dreams is symbolic, the language of the ego and consciousness is in terms of time, space and causality. The ego and consciousness must speak rationally of the symbols of the unconscious; therefore, what is passed down from generation to generation is our rational description of symbol, not the reality itself to which the symbol points.

What Jung observed beyond this is that analogous images and motifs occur not only in dreams and fantasies and the other areas mentioned by Goldbrunner, but in art, mythology and comparative religion. He discovered that wherever human beings have lived and given symbolic account of their inner reflections of God and the world there have been basic patterns, symbols and motifs that have been shared as they expressed themselves in their art, mythology and religion. This similarity occurs regardless of cultural, geographic, racial, economic, linguistic or religious differences. Jung termed this similarity a 'universal parallelism'[38] and inferred from this that there are in the human make-up typical unconscious 'dispositions' which arrange the contents of consciousness in accordance with certain structural forms. Jung termed these inner dispositions *archetypes* and characterized the conscious contents and motifs ordered by them as *archetypal images*.

3. The archetypes

The concept of the archetypes in the human psyche is considered by many to be Jung's greatest single achievement. L. Stein writes: 'The more I have studied Jung's works, the more I have come to see that the essence of his greatness lies in this concept of archetypes with their contrasting and complementary meaning.'[39]

Jung took the term 'archetype' from the Greek term meaning 'prime imprinter', specifically from the *Corpus Hermeticum*[40] and from the *De Divinis Nominibus* of Dionysius the pseudo-Areopagite.[41]

Above all, Jung was drawn to Augustine's notion of the *ideae principales*, the Latin equivalent to the Greek term. Augustine writes:

> For the principal ideas are certain forms, or stable and unchange-able reasons of things, themselves not formed, and so continuing eternal and always after the same manner which are contained in the divine understanding. And though they themselves do not perish, yet after their pattern everything is said to be formed that is able to come into being and to perish, and everything that does come into being and perish. But it is affirmed that the soul is not able to behold them, save it be the rational soul.[42]

Taken psychologically, archetypes generally refer to the patterns of human life which shape the life of the psyche and therefore influence the direction and character of conscious conduct. Although they are continually alive because they work in the realm of the collective unconscious, the archetypes remain hidden and are only discernible as they impinge upon consciousness through the medium of dreams and images.[43] Archetypal motifs, therefore, like birth, death, love, motherhood, God, the hero and the wise old man are knowable but the archetypes themselves, which stand behind the archetypal motifs, producing them, remain unknown. What this means, says Jung, is that

> An archetypal content expresses itself first and foremost in metaphors. If (it) should speak of the sun and identify with it the lion, the king, the hoard of gold guarded by the dragon, or the power that makes for the life and health of man, it is neither the one thing nor the other but the unknown third thing that finds more or less adequate expression in all these similies, yet – to the perpetual vexation of the intellect – remains unknown, and not to be fitted into a formula . . . Even the best atttempts at explanation are only more or less successful transformations into another metaphorical language.[44]

I might point out that this method of constructing scientific models is not unusual. The atom, for instance, is an entity that cannot be represented as it is but physicists have been able to construct accurate models of it from its observable effects.[45]

As with the unconscious, however, Jung was hesitant to state the metaphysical existence of archetypes, particularly prior to existence: 'Whether this psychic structure and its elements, the archetypes, ever "originated" at all is a metaphysical question and therefore unanswerable.'[46] 'The only thing that can be said with certainty,' writes Aniela Jaffé,

> is that they are inherited as irrepresentable dispositions in the unconscious, the timeless constants of human nature. On the other hand, the arrangements they produce are formed anew in each individual life as time-conditioned variants of the timeless motif.[47]

Jung understood archetypes to be of a dual nature. On the one hand, he drew a comparison between archetypes and biological instincts, stating that 'to the extent that the archetypes intervene in the shaping of conscious contents by regulating, modifying, and motivating them, they act like instincts'.[48] Jacobi calls the archetypes 'self-portraits of the instincts'.[49] In this sense archetypes act similarly to the instinctual star grid Portmann observed in the blackcap[50] and can be characterized as 'inherited, instinctive impulses and forms that can be observed in all living creatures.'[51] Taken as instincts, says Wolfgang Hochheimer, archetypes represent a special psychological instance of the biological 'pattern of behaviour'.[52]

This is not to say that archetypes are instincts; on the contrary, while instincts are modes of existence, archetypes are modes of apprehension; and while instincts are natural impulses expressed as regular and typical modes of action/reaction, archetypes are dominants which emerge into consciousness from unconsciousness as ideas and images that can be shaped and changed.[53]

On the other hand, Jung discerned that the archetype was an 'authentic element of spirit',[54] and as such serves as a kind of unconscious 'knowledge' which represents a 'spiritual model' in the Platonic sense. This spiritual dimension is most apparent when the archetype is *experienced*, for when experienced, the archetype engenders 'an experience of fundamental importance'.[55] As we shall see in later discussion, this 'experience of fundamental importance' has all the qualities attributed to the numinous by Rudolf Otto. Because of this, Jung states that the archetype 'deserves the epithet "spiritual" above all else'.[56]

Jung describes the simultaneous instinctual and spiritual character of the archetype thus:

This term is not meant to denote an inherited idea but rather an inherited mode of psychic functioning, corresponding to that inborn *way* according to which the chick emerges from the egg; the bird builds its nest; a certain kind of wasp stings the motor ganglion of the caterpillar; and eels find their way to the Bermudas. In other words, it is a 'pattern of behaviour'. This aspect of the archetype is the biological one – it is the concern of scientific psychology. But the picture changes at once when looked at from the inside, that is, from within the realm of the subjective psyche. Here the archetype presents itself as numinous, that is, it appears as an experience of fundamental importance. Whenever it clothes itself with adequate symbols, which is not always the case, it takes hold of the individual in a startling way, creating a condition of 'being deeply moved', the consequences of which may be immeasurable.[57]

This duality, says Jung, is an instance of the 'problem of the opposites that is profoundly characteristic of the psyche'.[58] Jaffé points out in this regard, however, that 'fundamentally, it is less a question of opposites than of antinomies, of self-complementary models of manifestation'.[59]

It was because of this complementary nature of the archetypes that Jung asserted in 1946 that 'archetypes . . . have a nature that cannot with certainty be designated as psychic.'[60] From then on, therefore, he described the archetypes as *'psychoid',* meaning that they were as much non-psychic as psychic.

This concept opened up entirely new vistas, for being psychoid, the archetype could indeed be a possible 'bridge to matter in general',[61] abolishing any rigid distinction between the psychic and physical aspects of the human totality. In 1951, Jung put the matter thus:

> The deeper 'layers' of the psyche lose their individual uniqueness as they retreat farther and farther into darkness. 'Lower down', that is to say as they approach the autonomous functional systems, they become increasingly collective until they are universalized and extinguished in the body's materiality, i.e., in chemical substances. The body's carbon is simply carbon. Hence 'at bottom' the psyche is simply 'world'.[62]

What I noted earlier about the fundamental reality of the psyche along with the reality of our physical characteristics to explain human life and behaviour must now be restated. The psyche and

ody are not only equally real as 'cosmic principles' but they are
separably inter-connected. Archetypes are present in the highest
aches of spirit and the lowest reaches of matter, uniting the world
d spirit into one singularity. Because of this, Jacobi defines the
chetypes as our 'gestalt' in the broadest sense.[63]

I have taken the time to go into the psychoid character of the
chetypes because I believe that in many ways, at least as far as we
e concerned here, it is the most important aspect of the archetypes.
ay this because if I am to demonstrate that the psyche is the realm
which God and humanity meet, then I have to discern that point
here they conjoin and co-create together. What we are ultimately
scussing here is the nexus where incarnation begins to make sense
something scientifically possible; i.e., that place within us that is
pable of being wholly divine and wholly human simultaneously.
as not this the ultimate mystery and profundity of Christ, that he
as 'very God yet very Man', all within the one singularity of Jesus
Nazareth? I am not making a statement here about Christ,
though I think the concept I am proposing opens up fruitful
scussion; rather, what I am saying is that the archetype, being
sychoid, offers us the nexus point where the 'divine lure' of God
nnects with our materiality and gives direct impetus to our
ncretization of the 'lure'.

This being the case, it is important that we be clear about what
ccurs when the archetype arises from our unconscious and begins
have an impact upon our consciousness. In the first place, it would
ppear that an archetype never arises from the unconscious unless
is seeking to be actualized; i.e., an archetype does not arise
ccidentally' or simply because of capricious psychic pressures
hich would push its image into consciousness and then withdraw it
ain. In coming to consciousness, an archetype is seeking to take
n corporeal form, i.e., it wants to give shape to human conduct and
ought: to become human, as it were. Put theologically, the
rchetype, as the 'divine lure', only begins to have an impact upon
s when it desires to transform us in some way. This raises the
uestion of will within the psyche. It is clear that our conscious ego
as will but so, too, it would appear, does the unconscious, which
ems to work through the archetypes in an intentional way. Within
e psyche, therefore, there seems to be two wills, that of the ego
nd that of the archetype. This inevitably leads to dialectical tension,
equently to conflict.

This is an important consideration, for the most important arche-
ype is that of the Self, that deepest and most comprehensive symbol

of totality that shapes and gives direction to each individual life. T
archetype of the Self contains within itself all the polarities of psych
life and is, as will be discussed shortly, empirically synonymous wi
God.

The second characteristic which is important to understand
relation to an arising archetype is that archetypes are bi-polar, the
are composed of a pair of opposites. While still unconscious th
oppositional character cannot be easily discerned; if the archety
emerges into consciousness, however, its inherent polarity can t
clearly seen.

The polarity I am ascribing to the archetypes is not peculiar on
to them; all of psychic life is governed by a necessary opposition.
For Jung, there is no balance or system of self-regulation in th
psyche without opposition. In making this assertion, he clear
acknowledges his debt to Heraclitus, who first recognized th
regulative function of opposites. He called this interplay *enantio*
romia, meaning, according to Jung, 'a running contrariwise, t
which he meant that sooner or later everything runs into its oppo
ite'.[65] Oppositional tension is fundamental and constitutes th
quintessence of life. This is so because it is the tension between tw
opposites which is the source of psychic energy; the greater th
tension, the greater the energy.[66] Opposites are therefore the key i
understanding the dynamics of the human personality; indeed,
another writer, Ralph Waldo Emerson, suggests, opposites are th
key to life itself:

> Life itself . . . as well as the proverbs of all nations, give point t
> the same thing. All things are double, one against the othe
> dualism bisects nature so that each thing is a half, and sugges
> another to make it whole.[67]

Put psychologically, as Jung would, this means that 'every psychc
logical extreme secretly contains its own opposite or stands in som
sort of intimate and essential relation to it.'[68] And again: 'Everythin
human is relative because everything rests on an inner polarity.'[69]

Because consciousness and the ego cannot see into the uncor
scious, it is invariably the case that consciousness will at first embrac
only one half of the archetype, making its presence felt as if it wer
the whole truth. Consciousness and the ego will 'cling to the one an
reject the other' as it were, thus setting in motion a monopola
prejudice that takes no account of the archetype's other half. Thi
other half is projected and perceived as external, almost always a
an enemy. It remains nevertheless in active dialectical tension wit

conscious half. This gives the unconscious a compensatory
~~r~~ationship to consciousness, for the opposites in psychic life are
~~ne~~ither antithetical nor contradictory; they are related and mutually
~~de~~pendent.[70] Being thus, they balance and temper one another,
~~en~~deavouring to complement one another so that psychic wholeness
~~ca~~n be achieved. What this means in concrete terms is that when
~~co~~nsciousness is too one-sided, the projected side of the archetype
~~ha~~s the ability spontaneously and autonomously to force the ego to
~~tak~~e it into account and grapple with it. Schaer explains:

When the conscious mind favours and fosters an attitude in a
one-sided manner that fails to satisfy the needs of the total
personality, an untenable psychic situation is gradually brought
about. If the conscious mind is unable to correct its onesidedness,
the compensatory activity of the unconscious sets about preparing
a new attitude which is then released at a certain moment and
transforms consciousness.[71]

~~Th~~e law of compensation is a corollary to the law of *enantiodromia*.
What is important to take note of concerning the compensatory
~~po~~wer of the unconscious is that it does not occur at the command
~~of~~ the ego or of consciousness. In the West, our one-sided, almost
~~alw~~ays rationalistically constructed consciousness, is blind to itself,
~~sen~~sing the unease of its imbalance but, because it is unable to see
~~the~~ unconscious or the archetypes, is unaware that it has neglected
~~the~~m and has not integrated this projected shadow side. Antonio
~~Mo~~reno brings out this point quite clearly:

Dangers and sufferings . . . are never solved exclusively by what
the rational man thinks of himself; only the suprahuman revealed
truths of the irrational archetypes intervene automatically, and
their coming into action is represented in the fantasy by helpful
images which are imprinted on the human psyche.[72]

It is only through the emergence of the archetype from the ~~un~~conscious – complexes completely independent of our ego per~~so~~nality – that the compensatory power of the unconscious can take ~~eff~~ect in order to move towards the integration of the total person. ~~Th~~e unconscious, therefore, that 'ultimate, undiversified and eternal ~~gr~~ound' of our being, directly influences our conscious life through ~~th~~e presence of archetypal motifs which arise from its depth and ~~be~~come formative and ordering factors in our conscious behaviour. ~~As~~ Moreno says, the archetypes come as 'revealed truth' by way of ~~dr~~eams, active imaginations, visions and fantasies – all the media by

which the archetypal motifs impinge upon our consciousness. Wh
they come, they come efficaciously, involving the total person. Sa
Jung: 'Archetypes were, and still are, living psychic forces th
demand to be taken seriously, and they have a strange way of maki
sure of their effect.'[73] They are as effective as they are in transformi
consciousness, asserts Jacobi, because they

> represent the sum of the latent potentialities of the human psyc
> – a vast store of ancestral knowledge about the profound relatio
> between God, man, and cosmos. To open up this store in on
> own psyche, to awaken it to new life and integrate it w
> consciousness, means nothing less than to save the individu
> from his isolation and gather him into the eternal cosmic process

The 'eternal cosmic process' in which we are enveloped, More
reminds us, is deep and immense:

> The archetypes are not obscure corners of the mind, but t
> mighty deposit of ancestral experiences accumulated over millio
> of years. They are the echo of prehistoric happenings to whi
> each century adds our infinitesimal amount of variation a
> differentiation. The archetypes bring to contemporary man t
> mind of our ancestors, their mode of thinking, feeling a
> experiencing life. They are the unwritten history of mankind fro
> time unrecorded, making the past to be present.[75]

While we rationalistically attempt to construct 'contemporary' re
ity and religion, therefore, the archetypes, as they emerge from t
unconscious, re-connect us with our roots, with the whole of wh
we are. While we may think in terms of years, maybe decades, t
unconscious thinks and lives in terms of millennia.[76]

Archetypes, therefore, bring us into an interface between t
ancient past and the contemporary present; they raise to o
conscious awareness the patterns our forebears used in dealing wi
similar situations. This perspective parallels the hermeneutic
engagement offered in Chapter III, section F, that the 'mighty ac
of God' can be structurally understood as the synthesis of t
historical event – the present reality in which the numinosity of Go
is interacting with us – and the confessional witness – the typolo
within our confessional heritage that is most appropriate to t
present situation and through which we can understand the hand
God in the situation. The numinosity of Hiroshima is only proper
fathomed within the context of the ancient category of apocalypti
The archetypes allow this interface. Through them, we are led ba

to paths trodden by our forebears since time immemorial, the milestones of which, Jung insists, are religious.

4. God and the unconscious

The hypothesis that the unconscious is the medium through which a hidden transcendental spiritual order affects human life brings psychology into the realm of religion. As the unconscious and the archetypes are autonomous, we cannot control them; rather, they impinge upon us from the 'beyond' as it were, overpowering our consciousness with their irresistible force. It is this overpowering-ness, this irresistibility, that gives the unconscious and the archetypes their numinosity, compelling us to describe the experience of their presence as divine. As Jung puts it:

> Recognizing that they do not spring from his conscious personal-ity, he calls these powers mana, daemon, or God. Science employs the term 'the unconscious', thus admitting that it knows nothing about it, for it can know nothing about the substance of the psyche when the sole means of knowing anything is the psyche. Therefore the validity of such terms as man, daemon or God can be neither disproved nor affirmed. We can, however, establish that the sense of strangeness connected with the experience of something appar-ently objective, outside the psyche, is authentic . . . Hence I prefer the term 'the unconscious', knowing that I might equally well speak of 'God' or 'daemon' if I wished to express myself in mythic language. When I do use such mythic language, I am aware that 'mana', 'daemon' and 'God' are synonymous for the uncon-scious – that is to say, we know just as much or little about them as about the latter. People only believe they know much more about them . . .[77]

The above passage comes from Jung's memoirs and serves to recapitulate what he said in numerous other writings over several decades. The primary point I wish to draw from it is the empirical synonymity between God and the unconscious. 'It is only through the psyche that we can establish that God acts upon us', says Jung,

> but we are unable to distinguish whether these actions emanate from God or from the unconscious. We cannot tell whether God and the unconscious are two different entities. Both are borderline concepts for transcendental contents.[78]

Both God and the unconscious, therefore, because they are both unknowable in and of themselves and because they both impinge upon our consciousness as though from the 'beyond' and with such an overwhelming power that we describe them as numinous, are empirically synonymous in so far as the psyche is concerned.

To assume the *synonymity* of God and the unconscious, however, is not to assume their *identity*. On the contrary, Jung is clear that to speak of the unconscious and God being empirically synonymous

> is certainly not to say that what we call the unconscious is identical with God or is set up in his place. It is simply the medium from which religious experience seems to flow. As to what the further cause of such experience may be, the answer lies beyond the range of human knowledge. Knowledge of God is a transcendental problem.[79]

What Jung is seeking to make clear is that there is a difference between what is subjectively experienced and that which exists in itself. The former is knowable through the means of psychology; the latter is a 'transcendental problem' upon which people may speculate metaphysically or otherwise but which cannot ultimately be known. I made this point earlier in discussing Jung's understanding of the psyche, that his epistemology is essentially Kantian: we cannot observe nature, the unconscious or God as they are in and of themselves; we can only have immediate knowledge of the psychic image in our consciousness. While Jung was certainly aware that 'the world inside and outside ourselves . . . is as certain as our own existence',[80] he nevertheless realized that the 'transcendental reality' beyond what we could subjectively experience remains for ever an unfathomable mystery. To speak of the synonymity of God and the unconscious, therefore, is to address the fact that as they are *experienced* they are indistinguishable.

5. God and the Self

The relation of the psyche to religious reality has led us to acknowledge the empirical synonymity of God and the unconscious as they are subjectively experienced, in particular through the symbols of the Self. These symbols represent for the psyche the essence of psychic wholeness and as such are empirically synonymous with God as well. As Jung puts it:

> Strictly speaking, the God-image does not coincide with the unconscious as such, but with a special content of it, namely the Self. It is this archetype from which we can no longer distinguish the God-image empirically.[81]

There are innumerable symbols of totality: anthropos, creator, a circle, a square, trinity. Many of them in fact have been used since ancient times to symbolize God. The archetype of the Self is experienced in the psyche as the *imago dei*.

As with God and the unconscious, to assert the empirical synonymity between God and the Self in terms of their representation to the individual of psychic wholeness is not to assert an identity between God and the Self. Jung is clear on this: 'When I say as a psychologist that God is an archetype, I mean by that the "type" in the psyche. The word "type" is, as we know, derived from *typos*, "blow" or "imprint"; thus an archetype presupposes an imprinter.'[82]

As already stressed, the 'imprinter' cannot be known in and of itself but only as it makes itself felt upon our psychic awareness: 'We simply do not know the ultimate derivation of the archetype any more than we know the origin of the psyche.'[83] Therefore Jung speaks of the Self in the following way:

> I may define the 'self' as the totality of the conscious and unconscious psyche, but this totality transcends our vision . . . In so far as the unconscious exists it is not definable; its existence is a mere postulate and nothing whatever can be predicted as to its possible contents. The totality can only be experienced in its parts and then only in so far as these are contents of consciousness; but *qua* totality it necessarily transcends consciousness. Consequently the 'self' is a pure borderline concept similar to Kant's *Ding an sich*. True, it is a concept that grows steadily clearer with experience – as our dreams show – without, however, losing anything of its transcendence. Since we cannot possibly know the boundaries of something unknown to us, it follows that we are not in a position to set any bounds to the self.[84]

The unconscious is synonymous with God and the symbols of the Self with God-images; in the first case this represents something completely unknowable and numinous; in the second, something which while unknowable in its totality can be known in part, even if as though 'through a glass darkly'.

This double aspect of Divinity, something infinite and beyond understanding and yet simultaneously finite in its historical manifestation, is structurally similar to the dual transcendence notion of God offered in my discussion of process panentheism. It is also an emphasis that finds striking parallels in the theology of Tillich, who, while referring to God as the 'ground of being', distinguished between the 'infinite source of all holiness' and a 'finite holiness',[85] the infinite source of all holiness being that which is unconditioned, inexpressible, transcendent; the finite holiness being that which is knowable, conditioned by history, experienceable by individuals.

What I would like to stress in relation to Jung is that in speaking about this dual aspect of God psychologically he is not thereby reducing God to a psychologism. In making this distinction between an unknowable aspect of God and a historical God-image, Jung was well aware that 'I am moving in a world of images and that none of my reflections touches the essence of the Unknowable.'[86] In fact, Jung was strongly critical of the way in which

Every theologian speaks simply of 'God' (and) intends it to be understood that his 'god' is *the* God. But one speaks of the paradoxical God of the Old Testament, another of the incarnate God of Love, a third of the God who has a heavenly bride, and so on, and each criticizes the other but never himself.[87]

In making this distinction, Jung was attempting to make clear that whatever God is in and of the Divine Self, God is also a concretely real phenomenon *inside* the psyche. Goldbrunner makes this point in a most interesting way. He points out that

If God had *not* been encountered in (the psyche) as a spiritual fact which can be experienced directly, He would never have been referred to at all since . . . natural science has not discovered a God anywhere and epistemology proves the impossibility of knowing God, but the soul comes forward with the assertion that it has had a direct experience of God. This inner experience is 'valid in itself'.[88]

6. Life in God: The process of individuation

For Jung, the meaning of life is seen in terms of the realization of the Self, that is to say, God. The ultimate meaning in life is therefore understood as the realization of the 'divine' within us. The process through which this realization occurs, Jung terms *individuation*. In his introduction to H. L. Philp's *Jung and the Problem of Evil*, Jung defines individuation as 'the life in God'.[89]

What individuation means psychologically is

becoming a single homogeneous being, and in so far as 'individuality' embraces our innermost, last, and incomparable uniqueness, it also implies becoming one's own self. We could, therefore, translate individuation as 'coming to selfhood' or 'self-realization'.[90]

Jane Singer describes individuation as 'the cosmic realization and integration of all the possibilities immanent in the individual'.[91] Put negatively, as Raymond Hostie does, individuation can be summed up in the saying that 'If a man wants to be happy he cannot live at odds with himself.'[92]

Paradoxically, it is when individuation is put negatively that individuation begins, for it involves the realization of the polarities within us, which, when they are unsynthesized, put us at odds with ourselves, such that 'the things I would do I do not, and the things I would not do I do'. Individuation is the uniting of forces normally at odds, a point emphasized by Moreno: 'In individuation, conscious and unconscious factors have equal rights. Therefore open conflict and collaboration are essential requisites of human growth.'[93]

The process of individuation invariably begins when we become aware of our shadow, that 'other side' of our personality that negatively mirrors our *persona*.[94] Our *persona* is the image of ourselves we present to the world; the shadow is the inferior personality as it were and is made up of everything that will not fit in with the laws and regulations of conscious life nor with the *persona* we project to others. It is difficult to discern not only because we focus our consciousness on what it is that we do want to present of ourselves but because, as the inverted opposite of *persona*, the shadow remains hidden in the unconscious, retaining our repressions, our guilt-ridden personality – all those aspects of our personality that we cannot or will not consciously deal with. The shadow is also composed of the latent half of the archetypes which have emerged into consciousness. The shadow is not to be seen as something necessarily or intrinsically evil, therefore, but rather as the aspect of all those things that our consciousness will not allow to surface; it can include a number of good qualities such as normal instincts and reactions, perceptive insights and creative impulses.[95]

Although the shadow represents primarily the contents of the personal unconscious, there is also an archetypal dimension of the shadow which, when it appears, according to Jung, offers a rare and shattering experience of the face of absolute evil. Often the contents of the personal shadow merge with the archetype of the shadow. When this occurs and when the shadow then emerges into consciousness, even the most rational and 'good' *persona* is overwhelmed.[96]

Like all psychic factors, the shadow has the character of personality and appears in consciousness either as a projection upon a suitable external object or as personified in some mythic way. In this personification is represented everything the individual and/or the society refuses consciously to acknowledge. The shadow is personified in dream symbolism often as a black snake, although when the contents of the personal shadow merge with the archetype of the shadow the personification can assume grotesque and horrible forms. The psychological elucidation of these images will lead us into the depths of religious phenomenology, for as Jung asserts and I shall argue, the grotesque images in the Revelation of St John are shadow contents of the Christ symbol; i.e., the figure of the Antichrist is none other than the shadow side of Christ.

I raise the concept of shadow now to help explain individuation, however, and to make the point that the unconscious compels consciousness to face the shadow when consciousness has become too one-sided. Unconscious projection of the shadow has the effect of changing the world into a replica of one's 'unknown face', a phenomenom which initially isolates and alienates the subject from the environment. Paradoxically, however, this is necessary if individuation is to occur, for the shadow forces consciousness in time to grapple with its own unknown face.

An important characteristic of the shadow is that while it possesses an emotional nature, it is not capable of conventional moral judgment; it only compensates consciousness. The surfacing of the shadow, therefore, poses a moral problem that challenges the entire ego-personality, for it is real and must be dealt with, but often – precisely because it is the shadow – it contradicts our moral norms.

The problem is complicated because we are in a culture that has taught us to seek good and reject evil, resulting in represssion of the shadow and a systemic refusal even to give evil substantive reality, much less parity with the good. But the more the shadow is repressed, the darker it becomes, until finally, despite the efforts of the consciousness to marginalize it, the unconscious begins the inexorable process of compensation.[97]

The only way to deal with the shadow is through the path of self-knowledge.[98] This is not an easy process, for as Aquinas observed centuries ago, we do not face self-scrutiny without resistance and much painstaking work.[99] If not scrutinized, however, the shadow will possess our minds. 'Consequently,' says Moreno,

> it is imperative to discover our shadow, because insofar as it is conscious there is always a possibility of correction; if repressed, there is no possibility at all, and, on the contrary, it is liable to burst forth suddenly in a moment of unawareness, upsetting the ego and breeding neurosis.[100]

When the shadow emerges in the collective consciousness of entire societies and cultures, the result can be catastrophic.[101] This is a point I shall explore in the section on Wotan.

Jung asserts that the neurosis that is brought on when the shadow overturns consciousness without being properly assimilated is always a substitute for 'legitimate suffering'[102] and only serves to intensify the evil of the shadow until such time as it can destroy the person and/or the society. In dealing with the shadow, therefore, what one has to do, says Jung, is

> to expose oneself to the animal impulses of the unconscious, without identifying oneself with them and without running away. Identification would mean that one lives out his bestial impulses without restraint; running away, that one represses them.[103]

The middle way between these two is

> to make them conscious and to recognize their reality, whereupon they automatically lose their dangerousness . . . One must stay with the unconscious, and the process which began by self-observation must be lived through in all its developments and joined on to consciousness with as much understanding as possible.[104]

The question therefore becomes not how to get rid of the shadow, for to try to repress or ignore it only serves to strengthen and darken it, but how to assess its real strength, its character, and how to assimilate it without ourselves becoming dark. Writes Moreno: 'Shadow and consciousness have to live together, even in an admittedly precarious unity, for opposition and polarity are sources of psychic energy.'[105] Jung is more emphatic, stating simply that evil cannot be overcome; it works in the psyche to complement the good and should be understood to be as positive a factor as good.[106]

The shadow can be as positive as the good because it has no moral content in and of itself. In addition to evil it can also contain the hidden side of whatever is being emphasized in consciousness and emerges from unconsciousness only to compensate for conscious one-sidedness; therefore, it performs a fundamental role in the process of individuation by making the individual aware that he or she is not complete but that the polarities of the psyche have to be assimilated before wholeness can be achieved. The shadow is often labelled 'bad' because it does not conform to the particular sense of morality embraced by the collective authority which shapes our consciousness and our *persona*; but when many of its contents have emerged into consciousness and have been embraced by the ego they can, in their time, be transformed into the 'good', until such time as they, too, need to be compensated for by their shadow. Above all, the shadow is a *complexio oppositorum* of good and evil dimensions.

As can be seen from the above, the unfolding of the numinous archetype of the shadow in the initial stages of individuation is a dynamic of grave consequence because it is so deeply transformative. Moreno stresses this point, saying that

> When we are dealing with the unconscious we have to be cautious, for consciousness is like a fertile field exposed to a raging torrent by the bursting of a dam. If the consciousness of man is weak, the unconscious swallows the ego and a pathological inflation may ensue, which is dangerous because it presupposes the identification of consciousness with the collective contents of the unconscious.[107]

As we shall see in the section on Wotan, one of the greatest dangers to the psyche that is possible when the shadow begins to compensate for too one-sided a consciousness, is that of confusing individuation with becoming a demi-god; i.e., the ego, completely unaware that it is being engulfed in the torrent from the bursting dam, actually thinks it is in control and able to control the sudden burst of energy and power it feels. This danger can only be avoided if the ego-personality can come to terms with the shadow as well as the Self without losing sight of the reality of human limitation and finiteness. Inflation results when the ego identifies with the archetypal image instead of engaging with it dialectically.

The process set in motion with individuation, therefore, is a powerful one, one that can easily destroy the personality but which can also lead to wholeness; indeed, although the unconscious and its shadow contents are dangerous and forceful, the necessity for the unconscious to compensate for the one-sidedness of consciousness transcends the dangers involved.[108] The larger issue, consequently, is not the shadow but the Self and the path of individuation towards wholeness of which dealing with the shadow is but the first stage. The Self transcends the shadow because as the ultimate *complexio oppositorum* it contains both the shadow and the conscious contents the shadow is compensating for. It is a unity that does not negate any component of the psyche but as the symbol of totality seeks to synthesize the polarities of conscious/unconscious, anima/animus, flesh/spirit, shadow/*persona* and many others into a complementary whole. Indeed, this is why the God-image is empirically indistinguishable from the archetype of the Self – precisely because it performs this function, called by Jung a *coniunctio oppositorum*, and in this sense also serves the highest function of religious symbolism.[109]

What this means, according to Ira Progoff, is that

> The ego remains the centre of consciousness but the Self emerges as the centre of the psyche as a whole. It is a process that takes place within the individual, but its essential meaning is that it gives personality a larger aspect, opening beyond the particularities of the individual.[110]

Put theologically, as Bertine does, this means that

> God becomes the focal point in one's universe. Psychologically expressed . . . God may be defined as that which is the centre and ordering-point of one's life . . . the unconditioned value, the consideration which, if it conflicts with any other, whatsoever it be, will be given precedence.[111]

Jung speaks of the 'passion of the ego'.[112] For in the process of individuation it is the fate of the ego to be confronted by the greater existence of the Self and robbed of its illusion that *it* is the centre of the psyche. The ego 'suffers, so to speak', says Jung, 'from the violence done to him by the Self',[113] meaning that individuation from the ego's point of view is 'as much of a fatality as a fulfilment'.[114]

Through this dialectical relationship with the Self the ego gains an inalienable sense of freedom which is not only the prerequisite of human dignity but of human moral responsibility. Through its virtual total dependence upon the Self, therefore, the ego lives out its role as the centre and pivot of consciousness in an increasingly effective way. Above all, the ego is the essential ingredient for all experience and without it there could be no individuation. 'In this sense,' comments Jaffé,

> the Self is in a position of relative dependence on the ego: the ego creates it, as it were, by the conscious realization and actualization of unconscious contents. It discerns the images of the Self in dreams and its patternings in life, and, through this observation and acceptance of the observed, it lifts the Self out of the darkness of the unconscious into the light of consciousness.[115]

While the Self completely surrounds, sustains and gives life to the ego, therefore, the ego it is that brings the Self out of the darkness of the unconscious 'depth' of being into the light of consciousness. God and the Self are dependent upon us for their historical actualization. Again, Jung's psychological description parallels the theological description of process panentheism.

What emerges is that the process of consciousness involves a paradox. For individuation to be real the individual must give up claims to his or her ego-personality being the centre in favour of the Self as the supraordinate presence: the ego must die so that the Self can live, thus necessitating the 'passion of the ego'. However, it is also true that the Self is dependent upon the ego due to the fact that unless the ego submits to the Self and thereby raises the Self from the unconscious to the conscious there is no way for the Self to be actualized in the individual human being.

It is also within the context of the 'passion of the ego' that human freedom should be seen. Like the apocalyptists, Jung asserts that we are virtually completely determined by the Self (God) and yet are nevertheless free agents:

> Psychology must reckon with the fact that . . . man does enjoy a feeling of freedom, which is identical with autonomy of consciousness. However much the ego can be proved to be dependent and preconditioned (by the self), it cannot be convinced that it has no freedom. An absolutely preformed consciousness and a totally dependent ego would be a pointless farce . . . The existence of ego consciousness has meaning only if it is free and autonomous.[116]

Jung acknowledges that in saying that the ego stands to the Self as the moved to the mover while at the same time maintaining that the existence of ego consciousness has meaning only if it is free and autonomous, he has set up an antinomy. 'In reality,' he says, 'both are always present: the supremacy of the Self and the hubris of consciousness.'[117]

We are not free to decide what our destiny will be; that the Self lays out for us. But our consciousness is free to accept or reject this destiny as a task laid out for it. Jung puts it thus:

> So far as I can see, no relevant objection could be raised from the Christian point of view against anyone accepting the task of individuation imposed on us by nature, and the recognition of our wholeness or completeness, as a binding personal commitment. If he does this consciously and intentionally, he avoids all the unhappy consequences of repressed individuation. In other words, if he voluntarily takes the burden of completeness on

himself, he need not find it 'happening' to him against his will in a negative form. This is as much as to say that anyone who is destined to descend into a deep pit had better set about it with all the necessary precautions rather than risk falling into the hole backwards.[118]

In the same section Jung puts the question of freedom more starkly:

The psychological rule says that when an inner situation is not made conscious, it happens outside, as fate. That is to say, when the individual remains undivided and does not become conscious of his inner opposite, the world must perforce act out the conflict and be torn into opposing halves.[119]

If we accept the challenge of individuation actively rather than passively, voluntarily submitting to the Self (God), our freedom is not lost with the sacrifice. Rather, only in ego-sacrifice is our freedom discovered. Only in death with Christ can we be born anew in Christ, now creatures liberated in the spirit rather than bound to the lusts of the flesh. With Paul we can say 'I have been crucified with Christ; it is no longer I who live, but Christ who lives in me' (Gal. 2.20) In Christ crucified we have the deepest and most complex symbol of the relationship between the ego and the Self. Ego-sacrifice becomes an affirmation of the destiny set before the ego by the Self; it carries us beyond the 'natural man' to the 'spiritual man', thus enabling us to live on the plane of authentic existence. Put concisely: the Self condemns the ego to undergo the passion of surrender in order to destine it to freedom.[120]

C. JUNG AND PROCESS PANENTHEISM

Any reading of Jung leaves little doubt that for him religion and the processes of the psyche are inseparably bound together. Whatever else it may be, religion is an empirically psychic occurrence for Jung and therefore is accessible to psychology. Of primary importance in this regard is the significance Jung attaches to the role of the unconscious; indeed, Jung's final statement on the matter would be that the unconscious is the seat of the religious function.[121] It is from the depths of the unconscious that the 'inner voice' of revelation comes that is so important in religious life. Revelation Jung defines as 'an opening of the depths of the human soul, a "laying bare", a psychological mode pure and simple,'[122] although he hastens to add, as he always does, that this statement 'says nothing about what *else* it could be. That lies outside the bounds of science.' Whatever the ultimate source of revelation, then, what we experience comes to us as from the unconscious. Coming from the unconscious, the religious factor 'is a dynamic agency or effect, not caused by an arbitrary act of will . . . it seizes and controls the human subject who is rather its victim than its creator'.[123]

In understanding religion as an overwhelming and transformative experience, not as either belief in approved dogma or membership in some ecclesiastical congregation, Jung clearly stands in the definition of religion offered by Otto, that it is a *numinosum*: 'Its nature is such that it grips or stirs the human mind with this and that determinate affective state.'[124] In and of itself, however, it is 'perfectly *sui generis* and irreducible to any other; and therefore, like every absolute primary and elementary datum, while it admits of being discussed, it cannot be strictly defined.'[125] Indeed, Otto asserts there is only one appropriate expression for the religious *numinosum*: *mysterium tremendum*.

> . . . the feeling of it may at times come sweeping like a gentle tide, pervading the mind with a tranquil mood of deepest worship. It may pass over into a more set and lasting attitude of the soul, continuing, as it were, thrillingly vibrant and resonant, until at last it dies away and the soul resumes its 'profane', non-religious mood of everyday experience. It may burst in sudden eruption up from the depths of the soul, with spasms and convulsions, or lead to the strongest excitements, to intoxicated frenzy, to transport, and to ecstasy. It has its wild and demonic forms and can sink to an almost grisly horror and shuddering. It has its crude, barbaric, antecedents and early manifestations, and again it may be developed into something beautiful and pure and glorious. It may become the hushed, trembling, and speechless humility of the creature in the presence of – whom or what? In the presence of that which is a mystery inexpressible and above all creatures.[126]

In the face of this all-determining *tremendum*, our only choice is whether to submit actively or passively. To submit actively allows us to help shape the impact of this symbol or archetypal image on us and so to give it meaning for us; to submit passively is to be dominated, possibly victimized by it. This understanding by Jung of the presence of God within us as something irresistible and overpowering is similar to what I was expressing in my critique of Whitehead's and Hartshorne's notion of divine lure. I concur with Jung also in his equally strong insistence that despite the overwhelmingness of God, we still have the freedom to co-create with the archetypal image emerging from our psychic depths. Thus our self-determining freedom is a reality within the context of an infinitely powerful and free God.

To submit actively to the divine presence within us and therefore give the psychic process direction and meaning is where Schaer asserts 'religion comes in, for in the last analysis religion consists not in merely experiencing the suprapersonal forces of the soul as such, but in adopting – psychically – an active attitude'.[127] This active participation in the unifying symbol emerging from the unconscious to compensate for our conscious one-sidedness is the essential meaning of individuation, for it brings together our consciousness and ego-personality with the contents of the unconscious in an intimate union of complementarity. It is a dynamic in which the unconscious begins to thrust upon our consciousness an archetypal image; by our active participation in the ensuing transformation of the psyche that results from unconscious compensation of consciousness, we help shape the archetypal image, give it direction, and discern its meaning.

This is an important concept in the light of the discussion in Chapter III concerning process panentheism. In that discussion I attempted to make three basic points: first, that God is not completely impassible and distinct from the world but is integrally connected with it, the world being in God, though not identical with God; secondly, that God is relative as well as absolute Being, co-creating with humanity each creative advance on our planet, thus necessitating an I-Thou relational encounter as the fundamental operative dynamic between Creator and created; thirdly, that God is affected by what occurs in creation, that while there is indeed an absolute dimension of the Divine whence the realm of possibilities emerge (the archetypes if you will, that provide the 'divine lure' to the creatures), there is also a consequent aspect which is contingent, vulnerable and malleable and which responds to and cares about all our actions, whether they be good or bad.

The individuation process is in effect a co-creation of consciousness with unconscious. In asserting God to be an autonomous complex and a symbol whose affects are psychologically measurable, God is bound to become relative, for if God is placed in an intimate relation to the soul, God in effect becomes dependent on the soul. In so far as God is to have any communication with us and be psychologically effective, God must be mediated through an image within the psyche; i.e., through a symbol.

Symbols, however, arise in the human psyche, evolve to a certain point where their content becomes explicable in some other way, and then they die. Such is the case with the recent demise of the God-image presented by theism – it is an image whose time is past; therefore, 'God is dead' says the theologians. However, a new image is in the process of arising. Note that I am not saying arising through our actions, but taking shape of its own accord. I stress the overwhelming role of God in any symbol formation. We can only actively participate in what is already occurring at its own initiative. This evolving of God-images, while certainly not affecting the absolute dimension of God, certainly establishes that there is a consequent aspect very much subject to human participation. Within the context of process panentheism, Jung is quite right in asserting that

> 'Absolute' means 'detached', to regard God as absolute is tantamount to placing him outside all human relationships. In that state man cannot influence God, nor God man. A God of this sort would be of no consequence at all. We can in fairness only speak of a God who is relative to man, as man is to God. The Christian idea of God as a 'Father in heaven' puts this relativity in an exquisite way.[128]

Jung posits that the classical urge to regard God as absolute derives solely from the fear that in being made relative, God would become 'psychological', too much dependent upon human 'subjectivity'. As I have attempted to show, however, it is only once God becomes psychological that God becomes truly real. We cannot relate to an absolute God, totally other.

Jung is therefore in consonance with process panentheism when he insists upon the relativity of God to denote

> a point of view that does not conceive God as 'absolute'; i.e., wholly 'cut off' from man and existing outside and beyond all human conditions, but as in a certain sense dependent on him; it also implies a reciprocal and essential relation between man and God, whereby man can be understood as a function of God and God as a psychological function of man.[129]

This is to say that our God-image is a symbolic expression of a certain psychic state, thereby making God dependent upon us; but the entire impetus comes from God, thereby making us dependent upon God for the unifying symbol that will give us an experience of wholeness. Jung puts it this way:

> From the metaphysical point of view God is, of course, absolute,

existing in himself. This implies his complete detachment from the unconscious, which means, psychologically, a complete un-awareness of the fact that God's action springs from one's own inner being. The relativity of God, on the other hand, means that a not inconsiderable portion of the unconscious process is registered, at least indirectly, as a psychological content.[130]

This insight can only come about, however, when the psyche is taken for what it is: a fundamentally real component of human individual and collective reality that is fully capable of acting upon us from a basis beyond our conscious ego. The consequence of this is that the contents of the unconscious are withdrawn from being projected on to objects and become endowed with a conscious quality that makes them appear as integral to the subject.

Traditional theology, of course, is inclined to regard revelation as unique and finished, particularly certain Protestant groups who assert Jesus Christ to be God's ultimate revelation and the sixty-six books of the Bible to be the only source of revelation about the Divine. In theory, Catholicism recognizes continued revelation, but in practice recognizes as revelation only what concurs with earlier revelations receiving ecclesiastical approbation, thus forcing 'revelation' to affirm the tradition rather than transform it.

I have utilized the hermeneutic of engagement to suggest that in attempting to assess any given event, we must utilize certain typological categories from our confessional heritage that are appropriate, but we must reckon on the fact that any new movement of God in our midst will fill our old skins with new wine, bursting them asunder. I have attempted to bring this out, first, in the discussion of Deutero-Isaiah and now, in the discussion of Jung: that God lives within our souls, the psyche, as a continually creative power.

God cannot any longer be seen as a being who revealed the Divine Self 'once and for all' several thousand years ago. Rather, God is continually moving within us, emerging from the unconscious with an overwhelming and numinous power that appears as fate. This 'fate', however, is malleable and can be moulded into an image appropriate to us, if we actively participate in the individuation process into which the unifying symbol from the unconscious seeks to draw us.

In conclusion, I should like to stress that to engage with Jungian depth psychology in order to appreciate the psychic reality facing us since Hiroshima is not a capricious decision on my part. Rather, it is the logical conclusion of, first, beginning from a metaphysical discussion of process thought and panentheism which sought to make these same points through the matrix of philosophical theology; secondly, proceeding to the hermeneutic of engagement which brings the historical and confessional axes together to discern the actual presence of God at work in our history; thirdly, turning from the abstract model of this hermeneutic based on the prototype of Deutero-Isaiah to examine the confessional axis of apocalyptic and its radicalization by the Hiroshima event, the assertion being that Hiroshima has humanized the eschaton, challenging us to go within our psyches to discern the wrath and mercy we formerly attributed to a God outside ourselves; and finally, seeking to delve into the psyche itself, but only doing so in a way consonant with the previous discussion. Jung meets these criteria in a way which explains the inner psychic dynamic of what I have tried to describe metaphysically and structurally under the terms process panentheism and the hermeneutic of engagement. This is to say that while process panentheism asserts *that* God is absolute yet relative; *that* God co creates with the creatures; *that* God moves us through a 'divine lure' and yet is still vulnerable to our actions as a result of our interface with this lure, Jung complements this by offering a credible empirically based explanation of *how* God is actually relative to us; *how* God is dependent upon us and affected by our actions. It is as though Jung provides a description of the *inner* experience of which process panentheism describes the *outer* reality.

The parallelism is obviously not perfect but it does demonstrate the internal relatedness of Jung's depth psychology to the process panentheistic ontology of God I am proposing.

D. WOTAN

When a new symbol is brought into the history of a people, it may be adopted owing to the exigencies of the moment and for seemingly short-term parochial reasons, but it has in fact arisen after much preparation in the depths of the collective unconscious of that people. What counts is the demise of the previous unifying symbol and the psychic readiness of the society for a new one.

In attempting to make clear the hermeneutic of engagement, I offered as a prototype the prophecies of Deutero-Isaiah. Once the model was clear structurally, it was easier to proceed with the contemporary components of the model. Here again I feel it necessary to make clear in a structural way what happens when an archetype arises in history to 'possess' a people.

I wish to explicate this point by examining the experience of Germany under the Nazis. I do so not only because the Nazi situation offers perhaps the classic case of archetypal 'possession' but because the archetypal experience in question was one consisting almost in its entirety of its shadow aspect. This is the element of the archetype we are ultimately concerned with: namely, the Antichrist.

In a lecture delivered in Cologne and Essen in February, 1933, Jung stated that 'just as for the individual a time of dissociation is a time for sickness, so it is in the life of nations. We can hardly deny that ours is a time of dissociation and sickness.'[131] He then went on to term this sickness a 'crisis', meaning the time when 'the sickness has reached a dangerous climax'.

The sickness Jung saw was a general one infecting Europe: a 'state of degradation' resulting from

> the accumulation of urban, industrialized masses – of people torn
> from the soil, engaged in one-sided employment, and lacking
> every healthy instinct, even that of self-preservation.[132]

This degradation Jung measured in many ways, particularly by the growing dependence he saw of individuals upon the state:

> Dependence on the state means that everybody relies on everyone
> else (=state) instead of on himself. Every man hangs on to the
> next and enjoys a false feeling of security, for one is still hanging
> in the air even when hanging in the company of ten thousand other
> people. The only difference is that one is no longer aware of one's
> insecurity . . . it means that the whole nation is in a fair way to
> becoming a herd of sheep, constantly relying on a shepherd to
> drive them into good pastures.[133]

The problem, Jung points out, is that 'the shepherd's staff soon becomes a rod of iron, and the shepherds turn into wolves'.[134] What a tragedy it was, therefore, to see 'the whole of Germany heave a sigh of relief when a megalomaniac psychopath proclaimed, "I take over responsibility" '![135]

As time went on, Jung became increasingly disturbed by the state of affairs in Germany. He saw the Nazi phenomenon as a 'possession', one that clearly indicated to him as a psychologist that Germany was being possessed by archetypal forces from its collective unconscious. In March 1936, he published an article entitled 'Wotan' in which he stated that a 'curious' phenomenon was occurring; namely, that an ancient god of storm and frenzy, the long quiescent Wotan, should awake, like an extinct volcano, to new activity, in a civilized country that had long been supposed to have outgrown the Middle Ages.[136]

According to E. Tonnelat, writing in the *New Larousse Encyclopedia of Mythology*, the origin of Wotan can be found in the widespread belief throughout Germanic lands that on certain particularly stormy nights the tumultuous gallop of mysterious horsemen could be heard in the sky.[137] Believed to be the phantoms of dead warriors, they were called in the legends the 'furious army' and the 'savage hunt'. Leading this army was a god whose name was derived from the very word the Germans use to express frenzy and fury: *wuten*, meaning to rage.

Jung observed Wotan's characteristics in Nazism in general but particularly in the German Youth Movement. It was, he said, a movement of passion that was literally bringing Germany to its feet and producing a spectacle of unashamed racism, militarism and xenophobia.

While certainly mindful that as modern thinking people 'we are always convinced that the modern world is a reasonable world, basing our opinions on economic, political, and psychological factors',[138] Jung ventured the 'heretical suggestion' that the 'unfathomable depths of Wotan's character explain more of National Socialism than all three reasonable factors put together'.

Jung summed up the Wotan phenomenon under the term *Ergriffenheit*, meaning a state of being seized or possessed, a term postulating not only an *Ergriffener* – one who is being seized, but an *Ergreifer* – one who seizes: 'Wotan is an *Ergreifer* of men', said Jung, 'and, unless one wishes to deify Hitler – which has indeed actually happened – he is really the only explanation.'[139]

According to Jung, 'Wotan is a Germanic datum of the first importance, the truest expression and unsurpassed personification of a fundamental quality that is particularly characteristic of Germans.'[140] As an autonomous psychic factor, Wotan produced effects on the collective life of Germany, revealing both Germany's inner nature and his own. Because of this enormous impact upon the German psyche, we can speak of Wotan as an archetypal image, for Wotan has a peculiar biology of his own, quite apart from the nature of human beings. Moreover, it is only from time to time that Wotan surfaces to overpower individuals and societies with his irresistible influence. Germany under National Socialism was one such time.

Jung points out that with the 'conversion' of the teutonic tribes to Christianity, Wotan was changed into a devil, and forced to live on only in fading local traditions as a ghostly hunter wandering through the sky on stormy nights. Wotan the god did not die, however, Jung argues, but was only repressed back into the teutonic collective unconscious:

> He simply disappeared when the times turned against him, and remained invisible for more than a thousand years, working anonymously and indirectly. Archetypes are like riverbeds which dry up when the water deserts them, but which it can find at any time. An archetype is like an old watercourse along which the water of life has flowed for centuries, digging a deep channel for itself. The longer it has flowed in this channel the more likely it is that sooner or later the water will return to its old bed.[141]

Since Wotan was the principal god of the pre-Christian Teutons with a cult prevailing over all others, his power was firmly entrenched and not to be wiped away.

As a psychic force, therefore, Wotan remained alive even if latent. Remaining subterranean, he formed the shadow of the superficial layer of Christianity the German consciousness embraced, biding his time until Germany had become so 'civilized' that it lost all contact with its roots. Then, as the laws of compensation and *enantiodromia* came into effect, Wotan surfaced as Wotan *redivivus* with the fantasies of Nietzsche, becoming historicized in the person of Hitler. Says Jung:

> Apparently he really was only asleep in the Kylfhäuser mountains until the ravens called him and announced the break of day. He is a fundamental attribute of the German psyche, an irrational psychic factor which acts on the high pressure of civilization like a cyclone and blows it away.[142]

Jung added at the time, however, that 'a hurricane has broken loose in Germany while we still believe it is fine weather'.

Jung acknowledges that it might be more palatable to speak of the Nazi phenomenon as a *furor teutonicus*. However,

> we should only be saying the same thing and not as well, for the *furor* in this case is a mere psychologizing of Wotan and tells us no more than that the Germans are in a state of 'fury'.[143]

But more than a 'fury' is happening, Jung maintains; what we must reckon with is the fact that 'a god has taken possession of the

Germans and their house is filled with a "mighty rushing wind" '.
This can be seen because of the phenomenon of the *Ergreifer* and
the *Ergriffener*: 'one man, who is obviously "possessed", has
infected a whole nation to such an extent that everything is set in
motion and has started rolling on its course towards perdition.'[144]

The horrors of the 'perdition' into which the Nazis led the world
have been adequately described elsewhere. What struck Jung *after*
the war was over, however, was how such a depraved man as Hitler
and such utterly barbaric policies as the Final Solution could be
accepted by an entire nation almost without reaction. In an article
entitled 'After the Catastrophe', written in 1945, Jung stated that he
could only explain this virtual total possession of the Germans by
the Wotan archetype as the result of a 'hysterical disposition' in
which the opposites inherent in every psyche, especially those
affecting character, are further apart than in normal people.[145]

All these hysterical ingredients can be found in Goethe's Faust,
Jung suggests, in whom we see the same 'hungering for the infinite'
born of inner contradiction and disharmony; the same eschatological
expectation of the Great Fulfilment.[146] In Faust, too, we experience
the loftiest flights of mind and the greatest descents into the depths
of guilt and darkness, descents so low that Faust is reduced to a
wholesale murderer as a result of his pact with the devil. Moreover,
Faust is dichotomized within himself, setting up evil as an external
object and alibi personified as Mephistopheles. There is never the
impression that Faust has genuine insight into his depravity or
suffers remorse, choosing rather to worship success to such a degree
that the ethical conflict is obscured, and Faust's moral character is
clouded.

What is important to grasp, Jung reminds us, is that what happened
to Faust can happen to entire nations:

> The phenomenon we have witnessed in Germany was nothing less
> than the first outbreak of epidemic insanity, an irruption of the
> unconscious into what seemed to be a tolerably well-ordered
> world. A whole nation, as well as countless millions belonging to
> other nations, were swept into the blood-drenched madness of a
> war of extermination. No one knew what was happening to them,
> least of all the Germans, who allowed themselves to be driven to
> the slaughterhouse by their leading psychopaths like hypnotized
> sheep . . .[147]

And thus it happened that the Germans allowed themselves to be
deluded like Faust by 'the age-old temptations of Satan, instead of

turning to their abundant spiritual potentialities, which, because of the greater tension between the inner opposites, would have stood them in good stead'.[148] Forgetting their Christianity, 'they sold their souls to technology, exchanged morality for cynicism, and dedicated their highest aspirations to the forces of destruction'.

What is fundamental to understand in this, Jung argues, is that this hysteria is not limited to Germany. While Wotan is certainly the dominant archetype in the German psyche, it lurks throughout Europe. We must realize, therefore, that 'the German catastrophe was only one crisis in the general European sickness',[149] and that the breakup of traditional values, the decline and decay of the orthodox God-image and the resulting anomie is something that has infected us all. 'Did not Nietzsche announce that God was dead and that his heir was the Superman, that doomed ropedancer and fool?'[150]

With the orthodox Christian God dying, the numinosity and power previously seen in God become absorbed into the human being, inflating that human to 'god-like' proportions. But ' "God-almightiness" does not make man divine', says Jung,

it merely fills him with arrogance and arouses everything evil in him. It produces a diabolical caricature of man, and this inhuman mask is so unendurable, such a torture to wear, that he tortures others. He is split in himself, a prey to inexplicable contradictions.[151]

What occurred in Germany was that 'fate' confronted the Germans with their own 'God-almightiness'; Faust was put face to face with Mephistopheles and could no longer say: 'So that was the essence of the demonic.' Rather Faust must confess instead, 'Mephistopheles is my other side, my alter ego, my own inner shadow, which, because I did not see it, has possessed me.'[152] But what fate brought upon the Germans is in store for all those nations for whom 'God is dead', for the same psychological laws apply. The loss of our God-image, the loss of the centrality of Christianity in our lives, is an event whose awesome consequences are still to come:

Christianity was accepted as a means to escape from the brutality and unconsciousness of the ancient world. As soon as we discard it, the old brutality returns in force, as has been made overwhelmingly clear by contemporary events. This is not a step forwards but a long step backwards into the past . . . Who throws Christianity overboard and with it the whole basis of morality, is bound to be confronted with the age-old problem of brutality. We have had bitter experience of what happens when a whole nation finds the moral mask too stupid to keep up. The beast breaks loose, and a frenzy of demoralization sweeps over the civilized world.[153]

The paradox within this 'frenzy of demoralization' is that the society can appear to be in many ways 'perfectly normal' – so normal that the frenzy seems almost absent, gnawing at the conscience of certain individuals perhaps but not enough to arouse them from their stupor. Even the craziest person is not completely crazy, a point even truer of hysteria where nothing appears to be really wrong beyond a few 'excesses' here and there, coupled with the paralysis of normal functions to mitigate these excesses. In mass movements, therefore, we can expect many parts of the psychic body politic to appear entirely normal even while the overall analysis can only be that the collective is in the grip of hysteria.

This is an important point to internalize because it means that in cases of possession, when entire nations are transformed from civilized human beings to barbaric murderers as Germany was, many individuals caught up in this maelstrom are not individually transformed; rather, most continue living quite normal lives and if challenged about being part of a 'hysterical mob' would probably deny it, certainly denying their participation in it.

In his Terry Lectures at Yale in 1937, Jung commented on this phenomenon of individual normalcy within the grip of collective hysteria:

Look at all the incredible savagery going on in our so-called civilized world: it all comes from human beings and their mental condition! Look at the devilish engines of destruction! They are invented by completely innocuous gentlemen, reasonable, respectable citizens who are everything we could wish. And when the whole thing blows up and an indescribable hell of devastation is let loose, nobody seems to be responsible. It simply happens, and yet it is all man-made. But since everyone is blindly convinced that he is nothing more than his own extremely unassuming and insignificant conscious self, which performs its duties decently and earns a moderate living, nobody is aware that this whole rationalistically organized conglomeration we call a state or a nation is driven on by a seemingly impersonal but terrifying power which nobody and nothing can check.[154]

What happens is that, like Faust, each of us, because we do not acknowledge the existence of the unconscious, nor how much it controls us, projects its contents, including the shadow, upon our neighbouring countries, races, religions. Once this projection is complete, and both sides are doing it, it then becomes the sacred duty of both to have the biggest guns and the most destructive weapon systems in order to defend themselves against the evil they see on the other side. While in the grip of the problem, therefore, each group, by projecting its shadow upon the enemy, psychologically absolves itself of any guilt and can continue to build up destructive weapons systems under the illusion that it is in fact the solution. And therefore German companies could calmly discuss improved models of gas chambers within the meetings of their boards of directors, even competing amongst themselves for the government contracts to build them; and German soap companies could go so far as to argue for more Jewish children to be gassed because they had discovered that making soap from the bodies of young Jews was cheaper than making it by normal means.

The great tragedy of post-war Europe is that the willingness to own up to one's own guilt and recognize the inner existence of the shadow has not happened. We are for ever forgetting this truth, says Jung,

> because our eyes are fascinated by the conditions around us and riveted on them instead of examining our own heart and conscience. Every demagogue exploits this human weakness when he points with the greatest possible outcry to all the things that are wrong in the outside world. But the principal and indeed the only thing that is wrong with the world is man.[155]

The fanaticism of the Germans against the Jews has been replaced by the anti-communism of the West in general, the Americans in particular, only now the weapons are not gas chambers but nuclear weapons and the other side is not meekly going to the slaughter but is equally armed and dangerous, caught up in its anti-capitalism. The conflagration that broke out in Germany was the outcome of psychic conditions that are universal, only while the Germans threatened a single people with genocide, the nuclear arms race threatens the entire human race with extinction. The situation is about the same, says Jung, 'as if a small boy of six had been given a bag of dynamite for a birthday present. We are not one hundred per cent convinced by his assurances that no calamity will happen.'[156]

He then asks:

How can we save the child from the dynamite which no one can take away from him? The good spirit of humanity is challenged as never before. The facts can no longer be hushed up or painted in rosy colours. Will this knowledge inspire us to a greater inner transformation of mind, to a higher, maturer consciousness and sense of responsibility?[157]

Although hopeful in one sense that collective individuation could take place, Jung was somewhat pessimistic, particularly since he saw about him the death of the Christian religion and symbols:

> If metaphysical ideas no longer have a fascination effect as before, this is not due to any lack of primitivity in the European psyche, but simply to the fact that erstwhile symbols no longer express what is now welling up from the unconscious as the end result of the development of Christian consciousness through the centuries. This end-result is a true *antinimon pneuma*, a false spirit of arrogance, hysteria, woolly-mindedness, criminal amorality, and doctrinaire fanaticism, a purveyor of shoddy spiritual goods, spurious art, philosophical stutterings, and utopian humbug, fit only to be fed wholesale to the mass man of today. That is what the post-Christian spirit looks like.[158]

Jung saw more deeply than any that 'God is dead'; but he also saw what others did not see, that given the inexorable law of *enantidromia*, Christ's spirit was being replaced by that of the Antichrist, symbolized by the atomic bomb.

In the face of this, in the face of nuclear annihilation, the time has come to turn our minds to fundamental things and stop projecting our shadow selves on to others. And yet, because we are refusing to come to grips with our collective guilt, because we are refusing to acknowledge the power of the unconscious over us, we have produced a world in which the question has at last become one of existence or non-existence – for all of us. It is an issue that demands to be addressed, for as Jung points out, 'the danger that threatens us now is of such dimensions as to make this last European catastrophe seem like a curtain-raiser'.[159]

E. AN ANSWER TO JOB

To understand the phenomenon of nuclear weapons and the Age of Overkill for which the atrocities of World War II were only a 'curtain-raiser', it is necessary to go back deeply into the roots of Western culture, even as in understanding the Nazi phenomenon it was necessary to go back more than 1,500 years to when Wotan ruled the teutonic pantheon. Only by going back to the beginnings will we be able to understand the archetypes that are only now making themselves felt upon us.

Jung feels it essential to begin by re-examining the paradigm of Job. In Job one finds all the ingredients of anomie that we are today facing: violence pouring forth at an unparalleled level; the inability of the existing religious orthodoxy to explain and cope with this evil; and the painful realization that what is being experienced is coming from the hand of God.

Job is fundamental in understanding our present predicament, says Jung, because its portrayal of violence is such that

> the violence is meant to penetrate man's vitals, and he succumbs to its action. He must be affected by it, otherwise its full effect will not reach him. But he should know, or learn to know, what has affected him, because in this way he transforms the blindness of the violence on the one hand and of the effect on the other into knowledge.[160]

1. The context

In my discussion concerning the wrath of God, I attempted to lay the scriptural foundations for a perception of God which sees both the light and the darkness as integral to the divine pleroma. I would like to focus the question by returning to the story told by Elie Wiesel about watching the young Jewish boy hanging on the gallows at Auschwitz. He realized that yes, God was there, God was hanging on the gallows – God was sharing in their suffering. I would now like to pose another question: *Can we also see God in the SS who hung the boy; and in the boy, one of the Chosen People, a symbol of Christ crucified*?

This is a hard question, for we can readily enough acknowledge God's *allowing* evil, God's *utilization* of evil, even God's *suffering* from evil; but are we willing to accept that God *brings about* what we experience to be intrinsic evil, that from out of the divine pleroma darkness as well as light issues forth, both equally real, both having equal impact upon human reality? Are we able to understand the words of Isaiah 45.7, that 'I form the light and create darkness: I make peace, and create evil: I the Lord do all these things?'[161]

There are two things that are important to note about this verse. The first is that the verb *bārā'*, 'to create', is the same as that used to describe the divine action in Genesis 1.1. I pointed out in previous discussion that this verb is used exclusively for divine creativity.[162] The second note of importance is that what God is understood to be creating in Isaiah 45.7 is *ra'*, 'evil'. The Brown, Driver, Briggs *Hebrew and English Lexicon of the Old Testament* defines *ra'* as moral wickedness, connoting bad, evil, malignant, worse than bad, distress, misery, injury, calamity, etc.[163] This same word is used in Genesis 2.9, 17; 3.5, etc. in referring to the tree of the knowledge of good and 'evil'; in Genesis 6.5 and 8.21 it is used to refer to the 'wickedness' of man; and in Genesis 13.13 *ra'* refers to the 'wickedness' of Sodom.

In his commentary on the verse, Claus Westermann wonders why this startling assertion does not bother biblical commentators more than it seems to, for in contradistinction to the usual claim that darkness and evil come from a source outside God, Deutero-Isaiah is clearly stating that 'each and every thing created, each and every event that happens, light and darkness, weal and woe, are attributable to him (God), and to him alone'.[164]

Unless we can come to grips with these words I do not believe we shall be able to appreciate the full profundity of the fact that God has appeared to us for a second great time in human history as Emmanuel, only this time God comes not as a suffering servant to lay down his life as a ransom for many but as the force which was integral in unleashing the atomic bomb and who now seeks to destroy the world even as Jesus sought to save it.

The God we worship is a terrible God, full of power and might, and as fully capable of manifesting light and darkness as we, God's creatures, are. Indeed, if we, the creation of God, made in the divine image, are composed of light and darkness and capable of deeds of great mercy as well as acts of horrible cruelty, why are we so slow in 'allowing' for God the same capabilities we ourselves possess, particularly when throughout our scriptures we are clearly told that it is a fearful thing to fall into the hands of a living God; that ours is a jealous God, a wrathful God – even as ours is a God whose goodness is as perennial as the grass and whose truth endureth to all generations?

This is not to say that as we do, so God does, for only humans sin; i.e., the evil perpetrated by human intention is invariably for short term gain at the expense of others and hence for the purpose of ego gratification. Evil used by the ego is ultimately destructive and therefore sinful. However, evil used by the Self, by God, is invariably ultimately creative. Evil used by God is always done so within the context of God's holiness. This is an important reminder because it is not always easy in particular situations to know God's ultimately creative intention.

An example of what I mean can be seen in God's attempt to kill Moses.[165] It can also be seen in Exodus 19 when the Lord first appeared to the Israelites at Mount Sinai. The text states that 'Mount Sinai was wrapped in smoke, because the Lord descended upon it in fire; and the smoke of it went up like the smoke of a kiln, and the whole mountain quaked greatly' (19.18). God called Moses from the smoke, telling him that none of the people or the priests should touch the mountain 'to come up to the Lord, lest he break out against them' (19.24). The presence of the Lord is here described as a fiery furnace, striking death to any who would even touch the mountain. Before this, the people trembled, knowing their God to be a Holy God, a *mysterium tremendum* of fearful power and might. The Lord had just completely devastated the Egyptians, destroying their land and killing their animals and firstborn sons. Now Yahweh comes to teach them through the fire, the smoke and the shaking of the sacred mountain that the fear of the Lord was an integral part of the worship of the Lord.

In time God leads these people into the 'promised land' flowing with milk and honey. What is often overlooked, however, is that this land, while promised to the Israelites, was already peopled by the Hittites, the Amorites, the Canaanites, the Perizzites, the Hivites and the Jebusites (Josh. 12.8). Yahweh shows neither mercy nor compunction in ordering the wholesale slaughter of these indigenous peoples – every man, woman and child and all their flocks. There is no talk of loving them, converting them, dwelling in peaceful co-existence with them; rather, God ordered the Israelites to do to the people in their 'promised land' what Hitler was in time to attempt against them: commit genocide.

This implacable fury of God is not isolated to the taking of the promised land. II Kings 1, for instance, tells how King Ahaziah was told by Elijah he would die because he had inquired of Baalzebub, the god of Ekron. The king sent fifty of his men to bring Elijah to him. He did not order them to kill Elijah. They found the prophet sitting on the top of a hill, and their captain ordered Elijah to go with them to the king. Refusing, Elijah answered: 'If I am a man of God, let fire come down from heaven and consume you and your fifty' (1.10). Fire immediately descended and consumed the men alive. Twice this happened. Only with the third group did Elijah agree to come down and meet with the king. The story is important because it illustrates the point being made concerning the darkness of God's might. A man of God, because he is a man of God, orders down fire to destroy over a hundred soldiers only following orders to bring him to the king, something he eventually agrees to do. If he could bring down fire he could have escaped just as easily, or struck them blind, or even caused them to laugh themselves off their horses. But he did not, he killed them all – with God's obvious blessing – to demonstrate that he did in fact speak for the Almighty.

Paradoxically, this same Elijah was commanded prior to this event to 'Go forth, and stand upon the mount before the Lord' (I Kings 19.11). This involved a forty day fast for Elijah, at the end of which

> the Lord passed by, and a great and strong wind rent the mountains, and broke in pieces the rocks before the Lord; but the Lord was not in the wind: and after the wind an earthquake; but the Lord was not in the earthquake: and after the earthquake a fire; but the Lord was not in the fire; and after the fire a still small voice (19.11,12).

It was in the 'still small voice' that the Lord God came to the prophet.

God can appear anywhere; God can do anything; God can work in whatever God desires to work in: a consuming fire, a devastating earthquake, a 'still small voice'. We cannot delimit the Infinite, for the Infinite can be just as easily hanging on the gallows as doing the hanging – not only in different times and places and for different reasons, but simultaneously. Perhaps nowhere is this made clearer than in the life and death of Christ: God preaching the goodness of God, healing the sick, forgiving the sinners; God pleading with God to 'remove this cup from me: yet not what I will, but what thou wilt' (Mark 14.36); God crucifying God; God resurrecting God. Evil in the hands of God creatively activated the redemption of Christ. In the final analysis it was 'Abba' God who made the implacable demand that the sins of humanity be expiated with the blood sacrifice of the 'only begotten of God'. It was an implacability, as I have already pointed out, which deafened the people listening to Jesus so they could not understand even his parables; which kept the rulers in their darkness, for 'had they known they would not have crucified the Lord of glory' (I Cor. 2.8); and which, even after the resurrection, blinded the Jews so that the message could be taken to the Gentiles.[166] This theme of the crucified God as the ultimate statement of the light and darkness inherent in the Godhead is a theme to which I shall return. I raise it now to suggest that the creativity of God in terms of light and darkness is not merely an Old Testament phenomenon which can, as Marcion argued, be dispensed with by asserting that the New Testament portrays a different God, one much more enlightened and loving. On the contrary, the life of Christ epitomizes the contradictions and tensions within the Godhead that appear throughout the law and the prophets. In Jesus all the strands came together, and in one complex event the wrath of God and the love of God intermingled and cosmic sacrifice became cosmic redemption. Without the one the other could not have happened.

What one discerns from the above is that even in the darkest events, Israel perceived the handiwork of God. Walther Eichrodt is clear on this point:

> As in the revelation of the covenant he (God) shows himself to be the limitless Giver, so on the other hand he shows himself as the One who incomprehensibly deprives and rejects . . . In Israel the responsibility of the contradiction between blessing and threat to life falls upon the God who has called man to serve him and jealously watches that no other power is allowed to influence the life of his community. That is why something of the uncanny and the demonic enters into the portrayal of his power.[167]

Eichrodt makes two comments on this:[168] first, that this view stemmed from the early strong effort to see beyond a purely negative perception of evil, as to what ought not to be, to a recognition that evil also played a positive role in the total view of human destiny; and second, that Israel's inflexible concern with truth, which did not allow it superficially to harmonize incompatibles, compelled it to pause in awe before the inexplicable fact of suffering.

Basic to the struggle with the reality of evil was Israel's conviction that the origin of suffering had to do with the displeasure and wrath of God and that this divine wrath was due to the sins of humanity. God's wrath was expressed primarily as righteous retribution for the violation of well-known laws. Indeed, particularly in the prophetic tradition, it is possible to discern in the sending of divine evil God's saving will, warning the guilty to repent while there was still time. Within this context, suffering is seen to be a purifying experience. The story of Joseph exemplifies this educative value of punishment.

If this were the only cause for evil and suffering in the world, the contradiction between suffering and the divine goal for human life could be smoothed away. But what of the suffering of the innocent? How was the suffering of those who clearly had not violated the covenant to be explained? This was the question asked by Job.

2. *The question of Job*

Although some writers argue to the contrary, Hartshorne in particular,[169] the majority of commentators concur with von Rad's point that both Job and his friends are equally convinced that the suffering inflicted upon Job comes from God.[170] It is on the basis of this agreement that their dialogues are held.

The basis of the argument of Job's friends is that no one is pure before God, not even the angels. Whatever Job is suffering, therefore, is due to God's judgment for Job's sin. Their exhortation to Job is for him to 'submit to this divine correction and admit that God is just'.[171]

Von Rad points out that the exhortation of Job's friends follows the 'judgment doxology'[172] of the day, whereby an individual or community afflicted by a misfortune acknowledged their suffering as a beneficial and judicious act by God. By doing this, the supplicant hoped to bring to a halt God's judgment and receive the beginning of God's blessing.

Job is equally convinced that his suffering is from God; indeed, E. Dhorme observes that Job's disease, consisting of foul ulcers, was considered one of the divine scourges.[173] However, Job refuses to admit he is in the wrong and proclaims his righteousness before God: 'I was at ease when he shattered me',[174] he insists, and demands that his case be dealt with directly by God. 'But I wish to speak with the Almighty, and I desire to argue my case with God' (13.3ff.; cf.23.3–5). If only God would let him speak to the divine pleroma itself, Job argues, then he would ask without fear: 'Let me know why you contend against me' (10.2; cf. 13.24). After all, was not God his creator (10.3, 8–11,18) and the helper of all who suffer? (13.16).

The novelty of this demand by Job is in the fact that he appeals to God against God. While on the one hand recognizing God's injustice to him, he also is certain that it is from God that he will receive justice. 'Even now, behold, my witness is in heaven, and he that vouches for me is on high' (16.19).

Despite this hope, the more consistent theme in Job's discourses is the lament that it is hopeless and impossible to expect only justice. God is clearly free of human morality; God establishes justice by different criteria: 'It is all one; therefore I say, he destroys both the blameless and the wicked. When disaster brings sudden death, he mocks at the calamity of the innocent' (19.22,23). Buber points out here that Job believed, with Deutero-Isaiah, in a 'God that hides

Himself'.[175] 'This hiding, the eclipse of the divine light', remarks Buber, 'is the source of his abysmal despair.'

What is galling for Job is that there is not an arbitrator other than God before whom he can take his case. God is the only arbitrator, and yet God is free and arbitrary: 'Lo, he passes by me, and I see him not; he moves on, but I do not perceive him. Behold, he snatches away; who can hinder him? Who can say to him "What doest thou?"' (9.11ff., 32–35).

God finally accepts Job's challenge to answer him and appears to Job in the same manner as when Job's children had been killed: in the whirlwind.

In the tempest of divine almightiness, Yahweh demands to know 'Who is this that darkens counsel by words without knowledge?' (38.2). In view of what has been happening, however, it is perhaps appropriate to ask who is darkening what counsel. It is clear that Job is not darkening anything, least of all a counsel; rather, it is Yahweh that has been darkening the very covenant made with Israel. Moreover, from the whirlwind there comes no enlightenment. Yahweh appears content to flaunt his divine power before Job: 'Where were you when I laid the foundation of the earth? . . . have you commanded the morning since your days began, and caused the dawn to know its place . . . Declare, if you know all this' (38.4,12,18, etc.).

This appearance of Yahweh must surely have confused Job, for he was never in doubt concerning God's might; rather, he had believed that God's might was always an instrument of God's right. But God in the whirlwind breaks out of this narrow human conception. God has set the mornings; God has laid the foundations of the ocean; God has created the beauty of the ostrich and the valiance of the horse; God has fashioned the power of Behemoth and the fierceness of Leviathan; God brings life to whom God wills; God brings misfortune to whom God wills; God controls all, the actions of the Divine are boundless. As Leonard Regaz puts it: 'What is God's answer? It is powerful, at once crushing and uplifting, and, as far as it goes, of eternal validity: it is God Himself.'[176]

Sitting in ashes, scraping his boils with potsherds, Job answers the Lord: 'I know that thou canst do all things, and that no purpose of thine can be thwarted . . . I had heard of thee by the hearing of the ear, but now my eye sees thee; therefore I despise myself, and repent in dust and ashes' (42.2,5,6).

Job had heard with his ears the traditions of the Lord being good and perfect beyond the understanding of human beings; he had heard that it was the sin of people that brought down the wrath of God. What Job saw with his eye, however, was the numinosity of the Divine itself: a numinosity from which both the evil befalling him and his redemption issued forth – a single antinomial totality as capable of committing evil as of sustaining the good. Seeing this, experiencing this, Job fell to his knees in worship for the first time. He 'despised' himself, for he realized that while he had been demanding that God be called into account because God had violated his sense of morality, he had in fact been an individual human focus for the intense conflicts and tensions that characterize the process of antimony at the heart of humanity's full experience of the Godhead. Completely marginalized and dwarfed, Job could do nothing else than repent in dust and ashes.

In this experience, Job sees that the *mysterium tremendum* is not a phenomenon subject to human morality but a phenomenon that is unbounded. God is as God is, at one moment behaving irrationally in a cataclysm; at another demanding love, loyalty, worship; at another coming in the whirlwind; and at another whispering in a still small voice. In the face of this we can make no demands, we can only keep our integrity and bend the knee. As Dhorme points out, 'Man cannot know the nature of this God, for it exceeds all dimensions . . . God does whatever He wills.'[177] What this means in the case of Job is that 'If Job is struck by God, it is then solely because God has willed to treat thus one whom He has called His servant.'[178] As the apocalyptists rightly pointed out, all is under the control of God except for that one dimension of human experience wherein free will exists: the moral choice of whether actively or passively to submit to the will of God and to see within the apocalypse the handiwork and salvation of God.

3. Comment

Several points emerge from the experience of Job that are pertinent to our over-all discussion of evil and the workings of God in human history. The first is that in reading Job one cannot but affirm that he stands face to face with a new experience of God. As Job himself put it in 16.12–17:

> I was at ease, and he broke me asunder;
> he seized me by the neck and dashed me to pieces;
> he set me up as his target, his archers surround me.
> He slashes open my kidneys, and does not spare;
> he pours out my gall on the ground.

> He breaks me with breach upon breach;
> he runs upon me like a warrior.
> I have sewed sackcloth upon my skin,
> and have laid my strength in the dust.
> My face is red with weeping, and on my eyelids is deep
> darkness; although there is no violence in my hands, and my
> prayer is pure.

Job's experience, says von Rad, depicts God

> as the direct enemy of men, delighting in torturing them, hovering
> over them like what we might call the caricature of a devil,
> gnashing his teeth, 'sharpening' his eyes (the Greek translation
> mentions 'daggers of the eyes') and splitting open Job's
> intestines.[179]

As Paul Weiss puts the matter: 'What shocks us and should shock us
is not Job's blasphemies, but God's.'[180] This was a new revelation of
God which was as incalculable as it was fearful, and against which
Job's friends and their judgment doxology were helpless. Moreover,
as Dhorme points out,

> The trial of Job began when God permitted it, and ends when
> God so determines. It was not the consequence of sin and it is not
> conversion which causes it to cease. God alone knows the motives
> of His own decrees.[181]

Secondly, although realizing that it is from the hand of God that
the evil has come upon him, Job nevertheless continues to appeal to
God for vindication and redemption. Herein is the greatness of Job,
that faced with a manifestation of God seemingly in complete
contradiction with the description of God handed down to him by
his tradition, Job does not doubt the unity of God. He clearly
experiences God as in an internal conflict, so much so that Job feels
free to call upon God for an advocate against God. This is not
dualism. It is rather the perception on the part of Job that God can
only be experienced as an antinomy, a totality of opposites which in
their dialectical tension produce Yahweh's tremendous dynamism
and unpredictability.

Thirdly, the over-all impact of this experience upon Job is to make
him aware that if it is God who gives and who takes away, the
believer is irresistibly pushed again and again towards God. What
Job does, therefore, is to place the question of suffering within the
context of the question of God. This does not remove or resolve the

contradictions involved in evil and in the suffering of the innocent, for they will always remain the great 'nevertheless . . .' But the experience undergone by Job does challenge us to recognize the proper context for addressing these contradictions. The problem of evil and suffering in the world is not in the final analysis a problem derived from either human free will or the temptation of demonic forces alone; it is only properly addressed within the reality of God. What this attitude indicates, according to Eichrodt, is

> the awakening of a wholly new readiness to take the authoritative presence of God seriously – a presence to whose hidden depths suffering also belongs – and to renounce every theory which does not come within reach of the divine richness. Here one can certainly no longer be self-assured in the possession and disposal of one's life; but one must simply stand and wait, in the human existence which one knows to be provisional, surrounded and upheld by the eternity of God.[182]

Fourthly, it is in speaking about 'the eternity of God' that I wish to make a point about God's omnipotence. It may seem that in using such language I am attributing to God *de facto* omnipotence. This is not the case. Von Rad points out that at the end of God's discourse to Job, God clearly wants Job's acknowledgment. God has clearly turned to Job and Job immediately understands that he has been confronted by the Holy. God had bet on Job and had won. Had Job closed his mind, God would have been the loser.[183]

The fifth point is that to recognize God as the context in which evil and suffering are to be addressed, is not to be resigned either to the sceptical despair of the 'Babylonian Job' or to the notion that God is amoral.[184] Even in the presence of the inexplicable tribulations of life, there was in Israel the ever-present awareness that the fundamental will of God was beneficent. Thus after Job had been tested, he was redeemed and restored to glories far beyond what he initially had. In the discussion of the wrath of God I termed this dynamic the 'creative integration' of God and argued that it is the proper context within which to understand the notion of God as the *Summum Bonum*. Though clearly the prime cause of what humans experience as intrinsic evil and intrinsic good, God invariably uses intrinsic evil instrumentally for a higher purpose. The antinomy of God must therefore be seen as complementary aspects within the over-arching beneficence of the will of God.

Receiving evil at the hand of God thus makes suffering something to be reckoned with in the context of eschatological fulfilment.

Indeed, suffering within an eschatological context offers God the most effective way of establishing Lordship over history, for only God can take all the evil, of both divine and human origin, and weave all the strands together. As Eichrodt puts it:

> It is in suffering that the afflicted man is nearest to God, and that the painful calculation of the scheme of retribution is brought *ad absurdum*. The way of the cross becomes the true straight way to glory, the way by which honour remains with God alone.[185]

What this means, according to Rowley, is that 'It is the essence of its message that Job found God *in* his suffering, and so found relief not *from* his misfortunes, but *in* them.'[186]

Finally, a word about Job in Christian theology. The 'patience of Job' has always had a place in Christian preaching, but what of the awareness of evil contained in the poetic dialogues? Its impact has been slight, according to Francis Anderson, in part because 'Job does not resort to a line of thought that has been paramount in Western Christianity since the triumph of Augustine over Pelagius.'[187] Apart from a few isolated cases, Luther's 1524 Preface,[188] for example, one is faced with the fact that neither the theology of Job nor his penetrating questions have been given the serious consideration they deserve. Recognizing this, von Rad asked

> whether the church, if it had also remained open over the centuries to the theological perspectives of the book of Job, might not have been able to confront the fierce attacks of modern man more effectively and more calmly.[189]

F. *THEOLOGIA CRUCIS*

This recognition of a God beyond the God of the Mosaic covenant who is of both light and dark dimensions resulted in an unprecedented transposition of values between God and humanity that shook the very foundations of the Old Testament. Paul Ricoeur asserts that Job 'shattered' the Mosaic concept of blessing for good, condemnation for evil.[190] Frank Cross argues that in many ways Job brought the Mosaic covenant to an end by challenging its undergirding assumption of the justice of God.[191]

With the passing of one God-image, movement began in the minds and hearts of the Jewish seers to articulate a new vision, one that would establish a new union between created and Creator, a new testament. This finally occurs in the incarnation of God in Jesus

Christ. The paradox of the new testament, however, is that when Christ hung in agony upon the cross, ridiculed by humanity and forsaken by God, then it was that Divinity itself chose to drink of the same cup Job had been forced to drink. Like Job, Jesus experienced the anomie of being made 'to be sin who knew no sin' (II Cor. 5.21; Job 1.1). 'Abba' God did to Jesus of Nazareth what Yahweh did to Job: both were abandoned; both were God-forsaken. Job was stripped of family and possessions, wealth, friends, health – until he lay in ashes scraping his boils with potsherds; Jesus in Gethsemane was 'greatly distressed and troubled' (Mark 14.33), and on Golgotha died with 'loud cries and tears' (Heb. 5.7). His last words, according to Matthew and Mark, were 'My God, my God, why hast thou forsaken me?' (Matt. 27.45; Mark 15.34).

These words interpret most profoundly the antinomial reality of being made to be sin who knew no sin. At this point, totally immersed in the sin of the world and therefore totally separated from God, the mission of Jesus and therefore of Divinity itself was completed. Sin had been conquered from within.

The key difference between the experience of Job and that of Jesus is that while in Job God 'crucifies' a human being, in Jesus God crucifies God. As Moltmann points out, the last cry of Jesus means 'not only "My God, why hast thou forsaken me?" but at the same time, "My God, why hast thou forsaken *thyself*?" '[192] In Job the left hand of God meets the right hand of a human being; in Jesus the left hand of God meets the right hand of God, and the torment of his torments is his awareness that he is being abandoned by what he most ultimately is. What Job can only *see*, therefore, is gruesomely *experienced* by Jesus for all the world to behold: that God is in a perpetual antinomial tension of opposites, even as God is One.

Because he completely experienced this antinomy, Jesus also completely experienced the resolution of the antinomy in the resurrection. Resurrection is the seal that in the depths of antinomy the *Summum Bonum* is at work, creatively using the good and evil present in the antinomy for a higher salvific purpose. We can experience this if we, like Jesus, grapple as fully as we are able with the antinomial reality of God. As Paul himself says 'It is the Spirit himself bearing witness with our spirit that we are the children of God, and if children, then heirs, heirs of God and fellow heirs with Christ, provided we suffer with him in order that we may also be glorified with him' (Rom. 8.16,17).

What can be discerned from this is that a living faith is an experience *with* Christ, not a belief *about* Christ. It is the willingness to become immersed totally in the antinomial reality of God, in the darkness as well as the light, in the trust that whatever we experience at the hands of God, there will we find our Redeemer also. This is difficult because it is impossible to experience God as *Summum Bonum* before experiencing God as antinomy.[193] The crucifixion of Jesus had to be totally complete, Jesus completely dead, before the miraculous power of the resurrection could shine forth. Therefore with the author of Hebrews we say that our faith is the substance of things hoped for, the evidence of things not seen. But just as surely as the dawn follows the night so we will experience God as *Summum Bonum* after we experience God as antinomy if our faith is lived in our complete experience of God.

It is within the context of God crucifying God that the purpose of the incarnation and crucifixion of Christ must be re-examined. Christian orthodoxy, in part because it has been so indelibly stamped by the doctrines of the *Summum Bonum* and the *privatio boni*, has long asserted that the incarnation and death of Christ were necessary to deliver humankind from sin, for which it was largely, if not wholly, responsible. Since 'all have sinned and fall short of the glory of God' (Rom. 3.23), and since the wages of sin are death, all of humanity stands condemned. But God is also seen as a God of love; indeed, 'God so loved the world that he gave his only son that whoever believes in him should not perish but have eternal life' (John 3.16). The incarnation and death of Christ have always been seen in terms of human salvation.

It is not my intention to negate this orthodox view. However, when one considers that sin was originally activated in the scheme of things by Satan,[194] who sat on the divine council, and one considers further that the Divine itself dispenses what we experience as intrinsic evil,[195] there must be something deeper going on in the incarnation and atonement of Christ than redemption from sin. Often the traditional understanding of Christ's coming and death implies that God was forced to take unexpected rescue action after the Fall and that the atonement was God's answer following on human sin. This implies that sin had no part in the original divine plan, and that the atonement was to make things as they were in the beginning, perfect and without blemish. Certainly Christ died to save us from our sins. But was it not also the purpose of the atonement to engage humanity in the antinomial tension at the heart of divine activity, so that believers reflect this creatively in the way they participate in human activity?

The scriptures affirm that in the beginning God created the

heavens and the earth. But the scriptures also affirm that redemption is always the context for *interpreting* creation. Whether Jew or Christian, we can only truly approach creation from the perspective of grace, of election sealed in redemption and participation in a covenantal relationship with God. That is why Genesis is the first book of Moses, to whom the Divine revealed itself in the first instance as redeemer and Saviour (Ex. 3). Only from the vantage point of a chosen, redeemed and covenanted people was insight given to Israel into the true nature of creation and fall in the purpose of God. As the apocalyptists so poignantly said, all of creation, both in its evil and in its weal, was ordained before the foundation of the world to serve the purposes of God.[196] Rev. 13.8 speaks of 'the Lamb slain before the foundation of the world'.[197] The cross is inherent in God's purpose for creation from the beginning. It also gives the ultimate clue to the mystery of life's meaning.

The mystery of sin and evil, of the blindness and disobedience of Israel and the sufferings of Job, are not to be seen as antithetical to the will of God but integral to its antinomial character. They are not to be interpreted as playing no part in the divine intention and reality; on the contrary, to those whose eyes are opened to see, they are revealed as central to God's purpose and plan from the beginning. The crucifixion of Christ compels us to see these, the weal and the woe, in the light of the antinomial character of God's actions. Indeed, if Christ crucified is the central fact of human existence, then the whole of reality needs to be seen and interpreted through this prism alone. This is what compelled Paul to say: 'I decided to know nothing among you except Jesus Christ and him crucified' (I Cor. 2.2); and John to say of the Word which became flesh, and whose glory is revealed on the cross: 'all things were made through him, and without him was not anything made that was made' (John 1.3).

In the light of Hiroshima, we became aware that the deeper purpose of the incarnation and the atonement is to provide the essential basis for the integration into individual lives and into history as a whole of the antinomial character and action of God as experienced in the human psyche. All opposites are of God: light and dark, good and evil, crucifixion and resurrection. The incarnation signalled that humanity must now bend to this burden. To be 'in Christ' means to be open to possession by the 'oppositeness' of God.[198] Even as Jesus was led to endure the polarity of the divine will that he who is the resurrection and the life must suffer crucifixion, so must we be ready to become vessels filled with divine tension. It is the tension of the opposites in God that produces the suffering of Christ, and although we hesitate to describe such a painful experience as the means of our redemption, it has nevertheless been the cross, upon which hangs the suffering yet glorified figure of the Christ, that has been the central symbol of the Christian faith. The principle of polarity must be the cornerstone of any theology of the cross.

How this tension of opposites is redemptive is obviously paradoxical.[199] Redemption will always remain a mystery, a merciful bestowal on the part of a loving God. However, viewing it merely as salvation from hell in no way does justice to the mystery. Redemption thus perceived amounts to little more than fire insurance. Understanding redemption as bringing within human experience the antinomial nature of God is a far more profound appreciation of the Christ event. It also reveals the nature of the life that we are called to live in response to the redemption that is given through Christ crucified. Redemption 'in Christ' offers us the awareness of God's antinomial character in which we are called to participate if we are willing to be wounded and crucified with Christ on the poles of the opposites. Only in the grip of the cruciform nature of reality, revealed so profoundly by the cross, does the Christian experience deliverance into Divinity. As St Paul puts it: 'You have died, and your life is hid with Christ in God' (Col. 3.3). To offer oneself up to be ravished and glorified as the antinomial nature of God works its will within and through us, is to accept the burden of being marked out as a 'Christian'. In this way alone is the *imago Dei* manifested in us and God's purpose to become fully human in sinful humanity is advanced.

This understanding of the incarnation and redemption allows us to bring fresh insight into the sixth and seventh petitions of the Lord's Prayer: 'Lead us not into temptation but deliver us from evil'. Many commentators argue that God does not actually tempt us, although God may permit us to be tempted.[200] I would argue that Jesus is here demonstrating an awareness that it is from the hand of God that temptation arises and evil comes.[201] In this connection it is worth remembering St Matthew's witness that 'Jesus was led up by the Spirit into the wilderness to be tempted by the devil' (4.1).

In the Lord's Prayer, Jesus does not ask his 'heavenly father' to keep Satan from tempting us; rather it is God who is asked to deliver us from evil; and it is God who is asked not to entice us into committing evil. Jesus feels the need to remind 'Abba' in prayer of his destructive inclinations towards humankind and to beg him to desist from them.

The incongruity of this with the traditional notions of God being the *Summum Bonum* is so colossal that were this petition not part of the Lord's Prayer one would call it blasphemous. Nevertheless, it is there in all the ancient traditions.[202] By teaching his disciples this prayer, it is clear that Jesus was trying to bring to our attention that while we receive our daily bread from God, so, too, might God lead us into temptation.

This awareness of evil coming from the Godhead is given its most painful expression in Gethsemane when Jesus realizes that the crucifixion he is about to undergo comes not only from the Pharisees and Sadducees but also from his 'Abba' in heaven. He even makes the point to his disciples on the way to Gethsemane, that he was going up to be crucified by God; 'for it is written, "I will strike the shepherd, and the sheep will be scattered" ' (Mark 14.27).[203] Jesus therefore makes the plea, 'Abba, all things are possible to thee; remove this cup from me; yet not what I will, but what thou wilt' (Mark 14.36; cf. Matt. 26.39; Luke 22.42). That 'Abba' does strike the shepherd and scatter the sheep; that 'Abba' does crucify his only begotten indicates that it does not seem to be in the divine purpose to exempt us from conflict or from the direct attack of evil. Far from it. It would seem to be the divine will to drive us into situations of conflict filled with temptation and evil as the central way of working out the divine purpose of redemption. Jesus himself is clearly calling us to walk in this way when he says 'If any man would come after me, let him deny himself and take up his cross daily and follow me' (Luke 9.23).

'Abba' God ultimately demands that Jesus offer himself up to be crucified. 'For this purpose I have come to this hour' (John 12.27). We know of this tendency of God from Gen. 22 where, to test his faith, Abraham is commanded to kill his own son.[204] Like Job, Abraham is not spared the savage gauntlet thrown down by God but is tested to the ultimate point when his knife is raised above Isaac's body. With Christ there is no ram caught in the thicket; his life is not spared by the loving 'Abba' by whom he has made the lame to walk and the blind to see. He who manifests the ultimate in the love of God is offered as willing victim to the ultimate in the wrath of God in a blood sacrifice for the redemption of the world. He who is sinless freely enters into the deepest recesses of sin to the very root and suffers in his being the full judgment of God upon sin, unto death, that humanity might live by grace ever more fully in God (II Cor. 5.21).

In articulating any theology of the cross we must keep before us the fact that God, in love, suffers unto death under the judgment of God on sin, perhaps in profound recognition of ultimate divine responsibility and purpose behind the presence and power of sin in creation. In Christ, Divinity, wrestling with its own dark side, seeks to experience and at the same time to transcend, the full antinomial tension of opposites in a fully human life.

When Jesus promised to send the Paraclete to guide the community of believers after he was gone, he clearly realized that the battle with darkness would continue after his self-sacrifice. Indeed, to send the Paraclete is in a paradoxical way to continue the same antinomial tension of opposites on the poles of which Christ was crucified.[205] In dwelling within the hearts of the believing community, the Holy Spirit makes Christ crucified and risen a present reality. The Holy Spirit confronts us implicitly and inescapably in the depths of our being with the antinomial character of God. With Christ, God clearly wants to be begotten in creaturely humanity in a continuing way. The indwelling of the Holy Spirit in humanity signifies the continuing presence of God in humanity. On the one hand, this represents a tremendous shift in the status of human beings, for in Christ we are raised by grace to the position of children of God and joint heirs with Christ of God's glory. On the other hand, in Christ, we are put in the position of mediators, called to live out the tension as fully and as creatively as possible of God's antinomial purpose and will as experienced in the depths of human life.

As mediators of the antinomial character of God's purpose and will revealed on the cross, we are inevitably involved in evil. Evil is the inescapable shadow side of freedom, whether human or divine.[206] The freedom given in Christ crucified does not lead us away from evil but empowers us, even commands us, to engage with evil and transcend it. We are called to go to the limit of the freedom rooted in and given by Christ crucified. We are called to do so by participating in the sin and evil of the world, that we may be channels of the divine grace which is seeking to redeem, from within, any situation infected with evil and sin through the misuse of freedom.

Further, it was the Holy Spirit who after the Christ-event awakened the early Christians to the fact that not only was evil still unfettered but there was still to come 'in the last days' another great outpouring from God, an outpouring which was to bring about the final consummation of history and the apocalyptic end of the world. It was the Holy Spirit who not only kept the words of Christ in the remembrance of the believing community but who created a disturbance deep in their hearts to bring to their attention that Christ was in time to be balanced by Antichrist.[207] This disturbance gave rise and shape to the Apocalypse of John and the prophetic foresight that the antinomial character of the will of God would again be fully and explicitly manifested in human history.

The Apocalypse of John seems strangely paradoxical in the light of the orthodox notion that Christ's death overcame evil once and for all. It also seems odd that after the miracle of the incarnation and the redemption of humanity through the death of Jesus, God would unleash evil once again upon the human race. One is compelled to ask why this forbearance toward Satan? Why this continual unleashing of evil upon the world? Why not pull evil up by its roots?

The reason is that evil is not something outside the purpose of God. God cannot pull up evil by the roots because the roots are within the very purpose and will of God as experienced by humanity. Thus at the end of the Bible it is revealed that the dark aspect of the Divine is to spill upon humanity, obliterating the world, even as it works its will in Christ on the cross. If Divinity, through the continuing indwelling of the Holy Spirit, is to incarnate fully its antinomial nature, then the dark as well as the light will always have to be made manifest.

G. THE REVELATION OF JOHN

The portents of things to come begin in Revelation 5 when the seer sees 'a Lamb standing, as though it had been slain'. (5.6). This is an obvious reference to Christ, but what the Lamb of God proceeds to do is the complete opposite of what one would have expected from him during his earthly ministry. Now he comes, not as a forgiving and merciful healer preaching the goodness of God's love, but as the opener of seven seals from which are set loose the four devastating horsemen upon the earth: the first to conquer; the second to take peace from the world; the third to upset the balances of human trade and commerce; and the fourth, whose name was Death and Hades, to kill with sword, famine, pestilence and by wild beasts a full quarter of all those living on earth. Christ came originally to bring down the kingdom of heaven; he now unleashes the kingdom of hell.

Then the Lamb opens the fifth seal, and the 'souls of those who had been slain for the word of God and for the witness they had borne' cry out, not for forgiveness or mercy for those who have wronged them, but to demand of God: 'O Sovereign Lord, holy and true, how long before thou wilt judge and avenge our blood on those who dwell upon the earth?' (6.9,10).

When the Lamb of God opens the sixth seal the vengeance comes:

> And behold, there was a great earthquake; and the sun became black as sackcloth, the full moon became like blood, and the stars of the sky fell to the earth as the fig tree sheds its winter fruit when shaken by a gale; the sky vanished like a scroll that is rolled up, and every mountain and island was removed from its place (6.12–14).

Before this onslaught, all the peoples of the earth hide under rocks and in caves, calling upon the mountains: 'fall on us and hide us from the face of him who is seated on the throne, and from the wrath of the Lamb; for the great day of their wrath has come, and who can stand before it?' (6.16,17).

When the Lamb of God opens the seventh seal, the wrath of God is multiplied sevenfold. Seven angels come forward with trumpets. The first angel blows his trumpet, 'and there followed hail and fire, mixed with blood . . . and a third of the earth was burnt up . . .' (8.7). With the second trumpet blast,

> something like a great mountain, burning with fire, was thrown into the sea; and a third of the sea became blood, a third of the living creatures in the sea died, and a third of the ships were destroyed (8.8,9).

The third trumpet sends the star Wormwood hurtling to the earth, polluting the waters and indiscriminately killing human beings. The fourth trumpet strikes the sun and the moon, so that a third of their light is darkened.

At this point, the seer stops the account and says:

> Then I looked, and I heard an eagle crying with a loud voice, as it flew in midheaven, 'Woe, woe, woe to those who dwell on the earth, at the blasts of the other trumpets which the three angels are about to blow!' (8.13).

The fifth angel then steps forward before the Lamb of God and blows his trumpet. A 'shaft of the bottomless pit' is opened, out of which 'rose smoke like the smoke of a great furnace, and the sun and the air were darkened . . . then from the smoke came locusts' which were given orders to harm 'those of mankind who have not the seal of God upon their foreheads' (9.1–4). In describing these locusts, the text states that 'they have as king over them the angel of the bottomless pit; his name in Hebrew is Abaddon, and in Greek he is called Apollyon (or Destroyer)'.

With the sixth angel the announcement is made: 'Release the four angels who are bound at the great river Euphrates,' angels 'who had been held ready for the hour, the day, the month, and the year, to kill a third of mankind' (9.14,15).

With the slaughter of a third of the human race complete, the seer sees a

> mighty angel coming down from heaven, wrapped in a cloud, with a rainbow over his head, and his face was like the sun and his legs like pillars of fire . . . And he set his right foot on the sea, and his left foot on the land.

Instead of blowing the seventh trumpet, however, this angel 'called out with a loud voice, like a lion roaring; when he called out, the seven thunders sounded' (10.3). The devastation this unleashes upon the earth is never described. The seer is forbidden to write about this final manifestation of the 'mystery of God' (10.7).

All this horror comes from the Lamb of God. In Jesus the Lamb was slain for many; as described by John, however, the Lamb is the slayer of many, controlling Death, Hades and the king of the 'bottomless pit'. Such a description, asserts Jung,

> contradicts all ideas of Christian humility, tolerance, and love of your neighbour and your enemies, and makes nonsense of a loving father in heaven and rescuer of mankind. A veritable orgy of hatred, wrath, vindictiveness, and blind destructive fury that revels in fantastic images of terror breaks out and with blood and fire overwhelms a world which Christ had just endeavoured to restore to the original state of innocence and loving community with God.[208]

What is interesting to note is that the outpouring of wrath by the Lamb of God is quickly followed by an equally vicious outpouring by the Divine itself. An angel is sent forth from the throne of the Almighty with a sharp sickle and commanded:

> 'Put in your sickle, and gather the clusters of the vine of the earth, for its grapes are ripe.' So the angel swung his sickle on the earth and gathered the vintage of the earth, and threw it unto the great

wine press of the wrath of God; and the wine press was trodden outside the city, and blood flowed from the wine press, as high as a horse's bridle for one thousand six hundred stadia (14.17–20).

This 'harvest' does not placate the Almighty, for seven more angels appear with orders: 'Go and pour out on the earth the seven bowls of the wrath of God' (16.1). Devastation follows devastation as the bowls are emptied in a manner reminiscent of the plagues Yahweh sent upon the Egyptians: foul and evil sores inflict the people; the oceans and rivers are turned to blood; the sun scorches people with fire; the earth is plunged into darkness; frogs are unleashed; earthquakes rend the earth; and hailstones rain down.

In the end, as the final battle of the ages commences, the Lamb of God reappears. He rides forth upon a white horse and is called

> Faithful and True, and in righteousness he judges and makes war . . . His eyes are like a flame of fire . . . He is clad in a robe dipped in blood . . . From his mouth issues a sharp sword with which to smite the nations, and he will rule them with a rod of iron; he will tread the wine press of the fury of the wrath of God the Almighty (19.11–16).

Christ and his army defeat the beast and the 'evil' kings of the earth, and the birds that fly in mid-heaven are called to

> gather for the great supper of God, to eat the flesh of kings, the flesh of captains, the flesh of mighty men, the flesh of all men, both free and slave, both small and great (19.17,18).

Welcome to the 'great supper of God'!

After this feasting on the flesh of the vanquished, another angel appears, 'holding in his hand the key to the bottomless pit and a great chain' (20.1). He seizes 'the dragon, that ancient serpent, who is the Devil and Satan' and binds him in the pit – but only for a thousand years, during which time Christ reigns supreme upon the earth. After this reign, Satan 'must be loosed for a little while' and the entire sequence of violence, pillage, wrath and the outpouring of evil occurs yet again: the forces of Gog and Magog attack the heavenly armies and are consumed by fire sent down by God. The Devil is again thrown into perdition, only this time it is into 'the lake of fire and brimstone' and not merely for a thousand years but 'day and night for ever and ever' (20.10).

The purpose of these apocalyptic visions, says Jung,

> is not to tell John, as an ordinary human being, how much shadow

he hides beneath his luminous nature, but to open the seer's eye to the immensity of God, for he who loves God will know God . . . Like Job, he saw the fierce and terrible side of Yahweh . . . *God can be loved but must be feared*.[209]

What John sees is that the reign of Christ is to be followed by the reign of Antichrist. Given these depictions by John of the wrath of the Lamb of God, the wrath of the Divine itself and the fact that the reign of Christ would be followed by a resurgence of the Antichrist,

> could anyone in his right senses deny that John correctly forsaw at least some of the possible dangers which threaten our world in the final phase of the Christian aeon? He also knew that the fire in which the devil is tormented burns in the divine pleroma for ever. God has a terrible double aspect: a sea of grace is met by a seething lake of fire, and the light of love glows with a fierce dark heat of which it is said '*ardet non lucet*' – it burns but it gives no light.[210]

What emerges from the Revelation of John is that there is an overwhelming polarity between the love of God and the wrath of God. Jung calls this 'the eternal, as distinct from the temporal, gospel: *one can love God but must fear him*'.[211] This necessitates a fundamental re-orientation in the notion of apocalyptic presented in the previous chapter, for Antichrist can no longer be seen only as a personage (either historical or cosmic) who is completely separate from and antithetical to the forces of light represented by a messiah figure (either historical or cosmic). To speak of Antichrist certainly includes this notion, particularly when applied to such figures as Antiochus Epiphanes, but the sense that I am giving it here signifies that it must also be seen as an aspect of Divinity itself. There is a darkness in God which complements the lightness of God. God is therefore experienced most deeply as an antinomy in whom the Christ and Antichrist are seen to be 'sons'.

I realize that in raising Antichrist to a level comparable with Christ I am posing a serious challenge to those who consider the person of Christ the central revelation of God. As I have already pointed out, however, it is not Christ who is the central symbol of Christianity but *Christ crucified*: the cross is the Christian symbol, held up to the world, the stumbling block to the Jews, the laughing stock of the Gentiles. The cross is the context for the Incarnation. Christ was born to die.

The church, however, has often tended to concentrate upon the person of Christ rather than upon the action of God in the crucifixion and resurrection of Christ; therefore, it has read back into God its understanding of Christ (*Summum Bonum*), rather than seeing in Christ crucified the antinomial character of God.

What Hick terms the 'majority report' of the church tradition had focussed too much on Christ without the cross. Not seriously grappling with the antinomial nature of God in Christ crucified, it has produced an intolerable dualism which has severed darkness from the light, evil from the good, and relegated the former to the nether land of metaphysical non-substantiality – thus creating the need for a theodicy involving the doctrines of the *Summum Bonum* and *privatio boni*.

The cross is the ultimate issue we have to deal with. When one focusses on the person of Christ alone the traditional doctrines emerge; but when the focus is on Christ crucified, antinomy emerges. This is a critically important point in my overall argument, for what I shall be asserting in the following sections is that Hiroshima is the revelatory event in our day which is forcing us to confront as never before the antinomial character of the cross and of the actions of God in human history.

H. MODERN THOUGHT ON THE ANTINOMY OF GOD[212]

1. Theological comment

This notion of both evil and good as integral to God has been given clear expression in contemporary times. Of particular note has been Petru Dimitriu in his book *Incognito*, in which he details the Job-like trials of a party official who falls from grace and is subjected to imprisonment and torture. It was during the agony of pain and mental anguish while being tortured that he realized that God was the totality of what was happening to him. Learning he could say 'Thou' to his torturers, Dimitriu realized that he was attributing evil to God. Seeing God in everything, including his torturers, did not lead him to despair, however. Rather, he states,

. . .He is also composed of volcanoes, cancerous growths and tapeworms. But if you think that justifies you in jumping into the crater of an active volcano, or wallowing in despair and crime and death, or inoculating yourself with a virus – well, go ahead. You're like a fish that asks, 'Do you mean to say God isn't only water, He's dry land as well?' To which the answer is 'Yes, my dear fish,

He's dry land as well, but if you go climbing on to dry land you'll be sorry.'[213]

Here Dimitriu is stressing that in the Spirit we can be bold enough to perceive God's antinomial character at work. Indeed, if Jung is right, the Holy Spirit's purpose is to bring the reality of Christ crucified and the antinomy of God to life within the believing individual and community. In the Spirit, therefore, God's antinomial character can be seen bringing about intrinsic evil – which must always be judged evil in the Spirit. The fact that God is seen at work in any given situation does not make it 'good', therefore, even though in faith one believes God will somehow use the evil instrumentally to bring about a more creative movement in human life than had the evil never been committed.

For Dimitriu God 'is perfect, but He is also terrible and evil. He is both perfect and imperfect. He is all things, and He confines himself to none.'[214] Our response to both the 'perfection' and 'imperfection' of God, to both the right hand and the left hand of the Divine, must be that of acceptance. It must be an active acceptance, however, in which we 'vanquish lethargy' and manifest love. This is not an easy task:

> What is difficult is to love the world as it is now, while it is doing what it is doing to me, and causing those nearest to me to suffer, and so many others. What is difficult is to bless the material world which contains the Central Committee and the *Securisti*; to love and pardon them. Even to bless them, for they are one of the faces of God, terrifying and sad.[215]

John A. T. Robinson has been greatly influenced by *Incognito*, describing it as 'one of the most remarkable novels of our time'.[216] He is aware that Dimitriu's panentheism is 'doubtless heretical' according to the norms of orthodox Christian theology, but 'one is inclined to reply,' says Robinson, 'so much the worse for orthodox Christian theology'.

In his book, *Truth is Two-eyed*, Robinson stresses the point that Dimitriu's portrayal of God is fundamental in understanding panentheism. Only by recognizing that 'God is in everything and everything is in God' in a 'co-inherence between God and the universe which overcomes duality without denying diversity',[217] does God truly become the 'Thou' of our life with whom we can have the relational encounter which Robinson considers the cornerstone of the panentheistic concept. What this means in terms of evil, he writes, is that we must see that 'God is *in* the cancer as he is in the sunset, and is to be met and responded to in each. Both are among the faces of God, the one terrible, the other beautiful.'[218]

Because of this panentheistic perspective, Robinson is strongly critical of the notions of the *Summum Bonum* and the *privatio boni*. By detaching evil from the image of God or Christ and projecting it on to a Devil or Antichrist as the embodiment of evil *per se,*

. the Devil came to occupy a uniquely powerful, even obsessive, position. The absolutizing of evil in a totally malignant Being has been the dark side of the absolutizing of the good in ethical monotheism. Evil is utterly banished and excluded from God.[219]

Another theologian, Charles Davis, emphasizes the same point, stating that the ethical monotheism of the *Summum Bonum* is really a form of dualism:

In Christianity the dualism implicit in ethical monotheism came out into the open in its depiction of the Devil and its stress upon sin and hell. Because the Christian God refuses his shadow side and identifies himself with unalloyed goodness, the Devil emerges as God's unconsciously produced shadow. When Christians absolutize moral goodness, they are led to attribute ultimate seriousness to sin and evil. Hell becomes the counterpart of Heaven, the everlasting bliss of the just has its correlation in the everlasting torments of the wicked. The mystery of inquity is placed alongside the mystery of goodness.[220]

The result of this thinking, says Robinson, is that

The demons are silenced and cast out, as the scapegoat is driven off into the wilderness to bear away the sins of the people. Satan is hurled from heaven, trampled under foot, locked in the abyss, thrown into the lake of fire.[221]

This attempt to sever permanently good from evil has produced 'polarization and antagonism' theologically and disintegration and destruction psychologically. Unable to integrate evil into any single totality, we have had either to repress it or project it on to others. As I observed in the discussion of the Nazi phenomenon, this has had terrible consequences. Robinson concurs:

When evil is disowned it becomes monstrous and sadistic . . . Unacknowledged it becomes terrifyingly inhuman. And by this polarization not only does the Devil become remote and alienated

– 'out there' or 'down there' – but God himself, 'formed in the image of a self-righteous monarch, cut off from all the pain and suffering, the frailty and sin of this world, personified moral goodness made absolute,' becomes a very devil, Blake's Nobodaddy, rather than the God and Father of our Lord Jesus Christ.[222]

By splitting the Christ-image, by negating the shadow and relegating darkness and evil to outside the divine pleroma, the doctrines of the *Summum Bonum* and the *privatio boni* have weakened rather than strengthened the Christ-image:

> the effect is to make the Christ unreal as a man. He becomes an immaculate paragon, unsullied by any contact with evil, rather than a genuine man of flesh and blood who is 'made perfect', as the Author to the Hebrews boldly puts it, who achieves integration in the only way men can grow, by acceptance and incorporation of the whole self rather than by rejection or repression of a part.[223]

Davis amplifies this point by demonstrating out that not only do the doctrines of the *Summum Bonum* and the *privatio boni* deprive God and Christ of their totality but they have also made it difficult for Christians to accept themselves totally:

> If we take the polarity of good and evil as we find them in human existence and then identify God the Absolute with a goodness excluding evil, we make it impossible for us to accept ourselves radically. Instead of the radical self-acceptance required for a fully human life, the groundwork of our lives, of our thought and action, becomes anxiety; that is, the sense and terror of being ultimately wrong, the feeling that we are basically corrupt.[224]

When seen from this traditional perspective, says Davis, 'Satan is in effect human evil projected externally and refused integration. The Devil represents all that we will not acknowledge in ourselves.'[225]

In this connection I agree with Paul Ricoeur's suggestion that

> this reduction of the serpent to a part of ourselves does not, perhaps, exhaust the symbol of the serpent. The serpent is not only the projection of man's seduction of himself, not only our animal nature goaded by interdictions, maddened by the vertigo of infinity, corrupted by the preference each man gives to himself and to that in which he differs from others, and beguiling his properly human nature. The serpent is also 'outside' in a more radical fashion and in various ways.[226]

What 'outside' means for Ricoeur is that 'in the historical experience of man, every individual finds evil *already there*; nobody begins it absolutely.'[227] Even in the Garden of Eden, therefore, 'the serpent is already there; he is the other side of that which begins.'

Ricoeur calls the Satanic dimension of existence 'the pole of counter-participation'.[228] Ultimately there is nothing one can say about this pole, he says, 'except that the evil act, in positing itself, lets itself be seduced by the counterpositing of a source of iniquity represented by the Evil One, the Diabolical'.

Despite the mystery of evil, Ricoeur is definite in arguing for the objective reality of evil. Because of this he faults the Adamic myth for implying 'a prophetic accusation directed against man; the same theology that makes God innocent accuses man.'[229] He points out, however, that, while positing evil in human beings and in the serpent, the Jews must have been at least subliminally aware that their analysis was incomplete, because in time the Adamic myth was shattered by the experiences of Job. The Adamic myth and the Mosaic covenant yielded the 'ethical sense' in which God's holiness was judged innocent and God's covenant with Israel patterned on the *quid pro quo* of blessings for good, condemnation for evil:

> This ethical sense, which makes the Law the bond between man and God, reacts upon the conception of God himself; God is an ethical God. This 'ethicization' of man and God tends toward a moral vision of the world, according to which History is a tribunal, pleasures and pains are retribution, God himself is a judge. At the same time, the whole of human experience assumes a penal character. Now, this moral vision of the world was wrecked by Jewish thought itself, when it meditated on the suffering of the innocent. The book of Job is the upsetting document that records this shattering of the moral vision of the world. The figure of Job bears witness to the irreducibility of the evil of scandal to the evil of fault, at least on the scale of human experiences.[230]

With Job, therefore, 'suffering emerges as an enigma when the demands of justice can no longer explain it' and 'it becomes possible to turn the accusation back against God, against the ethical God of the accusation'. Put another way, as Frederick Sontag does in *The God of Evil*,

> *the flaws which lead to man's downfall must find their source in God's nature or else go unexplained.* The same tendencies in man, those in which non-being both reveals and threatens his existence, must be present at the root of the divine nature.[231]

It is at this point, observes Ricoeur, when we are unable to grasp that within the Godhead are the shadows of turning, 'there begins the foolish business of trying to justify God: theodicy is born.'[232]

The major attempts by Christian orthodoxy to construct a viable theodicy have involved the doctrines of the *Summum Bonum* and the *privatio boni*. The essential point of this section is that such a theodicy is not necessary; indeed, it deprives us of our full humanity and God of complete divinity.

Without such a theodicy, says Robinson, there emerges an understanding which

> makes God the personal, yes, the loving ground of *all* being, of the impersonal and evil as well as of the moral, of volcanoes and tape-worms and cancer as much as of everything else. This is *not* to say that God is morally evil but that his is the ultimate responsibility, through all the random movements of chance and necessity, for everything that happens.[233]

The 'ultimate responsibility' of God for evil means that while being the ground of all things, God is not their ground neutrally, but as love – 'a love which all along is taking up, changing, Christifying everything'. The evil that flows from God therefore has a creative purpose that only participation in the crucified Christ can reveal to us.

2. The contribution of Jung

It should be pointed out that Jung's insistence on the reality of evil is based on his empirical observations as a psychologist;[234] it is not based on the theological reflections offered in the last section. Therefore, in *Aion*, where he has a lengthy critique of the notions of the *Summum Bonum* and the *privatio boni*, he asserts that they are empirically false, even though from a certain metaphysical position they may be tenable. It is empirically true, argues Jung, that good and evil 'are a logically equivalent pair of opposites and, as such, the *sine qua non* of all acts of cognition'.[235] This is all that can be said, he maintains, that being co-existent halves of a moral judgment, good and evil do not derive from one another but are always present in any given situation. This means that if, as Basil reasoned, human beings are the originators of evil, we must also be the authors of good, although Jung stresses that it is more accurate to say that we are foremost the authors not of good and evil but of moral judgments.[236]

Jung is categorical in stating that on an empirical basis, evil has as objective a reality as good. He demonstrates this by examining Basil's assertion that evil has no substance of its own but rises from a 'mutilation of the soul'.[237] If the soul was originally created good, says Jung, then it must have been corrupted by something equally real or else there would have been no fall. Furthermore, if something is traced back to a psychic 'mutation', it is most definitely not reduced to nothing and thereby deprived of substance; rather, the mutilation has shifted to the plane of psychic reality, which, as already discussed, is as objectively real and important as our physical reality. For Basil to speak of evil as 'mutilation of the soul', therefore, is, for Jung, to speak not of nothing but above all of something.

It was clear to Jung after the Hitler phenomenon and the advent of the atomic age that this 'something' was not only real but a serious threat to all human life:

> There are things which from a certain point of view are extremely evil, that is to say dangerous. There are also things in human nature which are very dangerous and which therefore seem proportionately evil to anyone standing in their line of fire. It is pointless to gloss over these evil things, because that only lulls one into a sense of false security. Human nature is capable of an infinite amount of evil, and the evil deeds are as real as the good ones so far as human experience goes and so far as the psyche judges and differentiates them . . . Today as never before it is important that human beings should not overlook the danger of evil lurking within them.[238]

The net result of 2000 years of teaching the *Summum Bonum* and the *privatio boni* has been 'a too optimistic conception of the evil in human nature and a too pessimistic view of the human soul'.[239] Indeed, Jung argues that it has been the steadfast refusal to acknowledge the reality of evil that has blinded the Christian religion and paralysed it in a day when the reality of evil has become so great that the light of Christ has all but been snuffed out. In commenting on this, Bertine makes the point quite clearly:

> Of the great religions, Christianity has gone farthest in splitting the original unity of good and evil and cleaving exclusively to the good. This extreme emphasis on spirit as over against instinct was probably necessary to compensate the previous one-sided bondage to physical nature, which dominated paganism; but certainly it has in its turn constituted an act of violence against the psyche's

shadow side, and the price has been nothing less than the possibility of wholeness. This imbalance has led to a sense of incompleteness and guilt and, finally, to an inevitable swing of the pendulum to the opposite extreme. Thus we are now experiencing, in the wake of Christian civilization, a mass evil, perhaps greater than ever known before.[240]

Bertine's point is helpful in providing a proper context within which the doctrines of the *Summum Bonum* and *privatio boni* should be understood. They served a purpose in helping the church to focus on the light side of God in Christ. However, now, like theism, these doctrines must be transcended and balanced, for their continued presence has become negative rather than positive.

According to Jung, 'If we see the traditional figure of Christ as a parallel to the psychic manifestation of the Self, then the Antichrist would correspond to the shadow of the Self, namely the dark half of the human totality . . .'[241] The archetype of the Self must include both dimensions and 'cannot omit the shadow that belongs to the light figure, for without it this figure lacks body and humanity'.

It is interesting to note here that the ancient Gnostics taught that Christ 'cast-off his shadow from himself'.[242] It was precisely this cut-off counterpart, says Jung, that the Christian writers, specifically John the Divine, recognized as the Antichrist who would appear at the 'end of time'. He would be the true 'imitating spirit of evil', says Jung, 'who inversely parallels Christ's presence like a shadow following a body'.[243]

Fully to appreciate the presence of the Antichrist in the New Testament writings, as well as the ruthlessness of the Lamb of God and the wrath of God in the Revelation of John, it is necessary to realize that

It is nothing less than the counterstroke of the devil, provoked by God's Incarnation; for the devil attains his true stature as the adversary of Christ, and hence of God, only after the rise of Christianity, while as late as the Book of Job he was still one of God's sons and on familiar terms with Yahweh.[244]

Put psychologically: 'The dogmatic figure of Christ is so sublime and spotless that everything else turns dark beside it. It is, in fact, so one-sidedly perfect that it demands a psychic complement to restore the balance.'[245]

With the coming of Christ, therefore, the archetype of Antichrist is activated. Christ is without blemish; but right at the beginning of his career he encounters Satan – the adversary who represents the counterpart of that tremendous tension in the human psyche which the Christ event signified. We thus hear of the millennial reign of Christ and of the coming of the Antichrist, almost as if there were an arbitrary division of the world between two royal brothers.

Indeed, this polarity led very early to the doctrine of the two sons of God, the elder of whom was called Satanael.[246] In the hermeneutic writings of the Church Fathers, Christ has a number of symbols and allegories in common with Satan: the lion, snake, bird, raven, eagle, and fish.[247] It is also worth mentioning that Lucifer, Morning Star, means Christ as well as Satan.[248]

What emerges from an examination of these symbols is that Christ corresponds to only one half of the archetype of the Self. The Antichrist or Satan symbolizes the other half. 'Both are Christian symbols,' says Jung,

> and they have the same meaning as the image of the Saviour crucified between two thieves. This great symbol tells us that the progressive development and differentiation of consciousness leads to an ever more menacing awareness of the conflict and involves nothing less than a crucifixion of the ego, its agonizing suspension between irreconcilable opposites.[249]

Jung cites Origen on this point, who despite his advocacy of the *Summum Bonum*, wrote in his refutation of Celsus that 'it is fitting that one of these two extremes, and that the best, should be called the Son of God because of his excellence, and the others, diametrically opposed to him, the son of the evil demon, of Satan and the devil'.[250] Origen goes on to state that

> where there is evil . . . there must needs be good contrary to the evil . . . the one follows from the other; hence we must either do away with both, and deny that good and evil exist, or if we admit the one, and particularly evil, we must also admit the good.[251]

When John spoke in the Book of Revelation about a final outpouring of the vials of the wrath of God and the coming of the Antichrist, therefore, he was not just articulating a prophetic prediction of the future; he was also living out an inexorable psychological law. The incarnation of the light side of God in Christ gave rise in his mind to the archetypal *image* of the Antichrist, an archetypal image he foresaw would one day be historicized with an intensity equal to the incarnation of Christ. He thus outlined the programme for the whole of the Christian age, says Jung, 'with its dramatic enantiodromia, and its dark end which we have still to experience, and before whose – without exaggeration – truly apocalyptic possibilities mankind shudders'.[252]

Although Jung argues that what the appearance of the atomic bomb implies is a veritable incarnation of God's shadow side, even as Christ is an incarnation of God's light side, I do not agree. Rather, I will use the term 'revelation' to describe the present outpouring of divine wrath. There are two reasons for my disagreement with Jung on this point. First, nuclear weapons are objects while Christ is a person. Incarnation has no meaning in terms of non-moral agents. Much more to the point is that there is a prevailing spirit of evil which indicates the presence of the collective archetype of Antichrist similar to the archetype of Wotan which possessed the Nazis. Yet while Wotan became personified by Hitler, no such parallel phenomenon has occurred with the archetype of the Antichrist; rather, it has remained diffuse, permeating the decisions and activities of many nations, not just one.

Secondly, I believe that the primary focus of Hiroshima is not on itself as an incarnation would suggest. Rather, the focus of Hiroshima seems to be to direct Christian attention back to the Christ event, only this time not upon the person of Christ so much as upon the act of God in Christ crucified. We are being given in our day the experience of the wrath and the evil of God, co-mingling to be sure with our own depravity and sinfulness.

I have argued thus far that while the light side of God was incarnated in Christ, God's antinomial character was made manifest in the crucifixion of Christ. Through Hiroshima, God is calling us again to witness the antinomial character of the Divine and to assimilate Antichrist into the power of Christ. Only a solid basis in the light (God's incarnation in Christ) is sufficient to integrate God's antimony. Hiroshima therefore points back to Christ crucified in order to inform our present challenge more deeply.

The last 2000 years have been an indispensable preparation for this hour. The moral impact of salvation through Christ is the indispensable element needed to enable humanity to begin to grapple with the darkness of God in Hiroshima, a darkness to which the antinomial character of the cross bears silent and terrible witness and in which Christians discern in fear and trembling the nature of the vocation to which we are now called.

I. APOCALYPSE NOW

It is my conviction that the 'dramatic enantiodromia' to which the visions of John point is upon us. I have already traced the radical secularization of the Western world after the Enlightenment, pointing out that the concept of God, because it had been elevated to the highest point by the mediaevalists, fell the furthest, culminating in our day with the 'death of God' theology and the necessity of articulating an alternative God-image.[253]

For Jung, the ramifications of the Englightenment have produced a world-wide situation which can only be termed 'anti-Christian' in a sense that confirms the early Christian anticipation of the 'end of time':

> the dechristianization of our world, the Luciferian development of science and technology, and the frightful material and moral destruction left behind by the second World War have been compared more than once with the eschatological events foretold in the New Testament. These, as we know, are concerned with the coming of the Antichrist.[254]

It is germane here to recall the passages in I John 2.22 and 4.3: 'This is the antichrist, he who denies the Father and the son,' and 'every spirit which does not confess Jesus . . . is the spirit of antichrist . . .' I have argued previously that as the God-image is the highest value and supreme dominant in the psychic hierarchy, anything that happens to it affects the entire psyche.[255] Any uncertainty about or diminution of the God-image causes profound anxiety, although this anxiety is generally ignored because of its painfulness. What occurred with the fall of God after the Renaissance and the Enlightenment is that the West made a Faustian pact with the Devil, and the psychic need for an image of wholeness sought answer in scientific materialism, atheism, and other substitutes. These 'spread like epidemics', says Jung,

> They crop up wherever and whenever one waits in vain for the legitimate answer. The *ersatz* product represses the real question into the unconscious and destroys the continuity of historical tradition which is the hallmark of civilization. The result is bewilderment and confusion.[256]

Whenever an adequate God-image is deprived of its place as the dominant factor in the psyche, and the spirit of God is excluded from human consideration, an inadequate unconscious substitute takes its place that is debilitating to the human personality.

In commenting on this, White observes that

> being deprived of divine beings, we shall find that, willy-nilly, we are in practice attributing omnipotence to a State, a Leader, a Party, a relation, a neighbour, or that we ourselves are behaving as if we were God-almighty . . .[257]

These substitutes cannot and will not suffice for our psychic need for wholeness, however. The example of Nazi Germany more than proves the point. Indeed, what actually occurs, says Jung, is that 'the destruction of the God-image is followed by the annulment of the human personality'.[258] This is so because 'When God is not recognized, selfish desires develop, and out of this selfishness comes illness.'[259]

This is a realm of Antichrist: the negation of the God-image, the perversion of the human personality. The paradox in this, however, is that in negating God we discover God: one God-image replaces another. To quote White:

> The gods are dead indeed – at least to the consciousness of masses of Western men and women . . . But although they are dead, they will not lie down. And it is depth psychology itself which is exposing them again in all their potency – indeed in all their naked primitiveness and explosiveness as inescapable factors in the fashioning of human health and happiness, misery and destiny.[260]

Thus in Christ humanity discovered God. Now in our day with the revelation of Antichrist humanity is discovering God anew in the inexhaustible depth of our being from which emerge all the archetypal images which govern our conscious lives: images of the light, images of the dark.

As pointed out in the discussion of the wrath of God, the closer one comes to God, the greater the danger of being scorched by the divine flame and burned away. The Christ event dramatically changed history; the Hiroshima event is doing the same. One cannot be touched by the numinous without being transformed. In Christ it is our salvation that is at stake; in Hiroshima it is our very existence on earth. The one is invisible to all but those with the eyes of faith and so humanity can and does pass it by; with the latter the threat is visibly upon us all. We know the darkness of the Nazi Final Solution, but, as Jung points out, 'the danger that threatens us now is of such dimensions as to make this last European catastrophe seem like a curtain-raiser'.[261] Hitler was essentially a prophetic phenomenon: his damage was cruel but local; Hiroshima is essentially an apocalyptic phenomenon, for the damage possible is now global: all live under the threat of a radioactive Final Solution. As Jung puts it: 'The four sinister horsemen, the threatening tumult of trumpets, and the brimming vials of wrath are . . . waiting . . . the atom bomb hangs over us like the sword of Damocles . . .'[262]

Hiroshima and Christ form a neat oppositional parallelism. Christ is the symbol of the salvation of the world; Hiroshima symbolizes the destruction of the world. Hiroshima is the negation of Christ and is therefore to be understood as Antichrist, for it potentially marks the final death-knell of human history.

The Christian era began with what I have already described as the equation of the perfection of the person of Christ with the wholeness of the God-image, an assertion that was given philosophical justification with the doctrines of the *Summum Bonum* and the *privatio boni*. The power of the church, of Christ on earth, reached its highest point in the Middle Ages when Catholic dogma was undisputed and the pope, the vicar of Christ, claimed supremacy in both heavenly matters and earthly power. The architecture of this period with its Gothic spires lifting upwards to the sky represents the heights to which Christ as the symbol of God had climbed. With the Renaissance, however, the vertical orientation of human consciousness began to become increasingly horizontal.[263] The planet, humanity, the past were re-discovered, and voyages of discovery, experiments in natural science and the secular power of the state began to replace the church, Christ and God as the focus of human attention. Anthropocentricity replaced theocentricity. The Enlightenment took this re-orientation one step further by replacing objective 'revealed truth' as given by the Bible and the church with the subjectivity of the human mind itself. Finally Nietzsche prophesied the death of God, and the theistic God-image considered synonymous with Christianity itself began its final descent from being an object of attack to being a concept considered irrelevant.

Even as the human mind reached the point of rejecting Christianity and the theistic notion of God, human hands constructed a weapon that represented total nihilism, complete anti-God, complete anti-Christ. Human beings were now confronted, for the first time in history, with not only the prospect of personal death but the distinct possibility of the death of the species. What had been started by Christ as the light of the world, the salvation of humanity, had now turned into its polar opposite: Christ had engendered Antichrist, and one royal brother replaced the other. Humanity is now confronted with the prospect of annihilation even as 2000 years before it was offered salvation.

Herein lies another oppositional parallelism. We were challenged to *accept* Christ. We did not, choosing rather to *reject* him. The result: *crucifixion* – the death of one human being. Out of death came the risen Christ, however, and *salvation* for all humanity. We are today being challenged to *integrate* Antichrist within a Christ-oriented consciousness. We are not, choosing rather to *accept* him in place of Christ. The result: potential *planetary annihilation* – the death of the species. Out of this annihilation may come a few survivors. Christ came to save; Antichrist comes to destroy. The tragedy of our time is that we are rejecting the saviour to embrace the destroyer, using our life's energies to build the weapons of our death.

Hiroshima, the possibility of planetary devastation and human annihilation, has become our new God-image. All nations seek for it, they lust for it, depriving themselves of simple human needs in order to build more weapons of mass destruction to offer on the altar of the new god. When God became incarnate as Christ the Magi came offering gifts of gold, frankincense and myrrh. Today a new God-image appears as a result of our Faustian ego-inflation since the decline of theism, and we offer vials of plutonium which we have named after him – Pluto, the god of hell. We even ignited the first atomic bomb on the day commemorating the transfiguration of Christ, thus unconsciously signalling that we intended likewise to transform the world, only not after the light but after darkness – with a blast that shone brighter than a thousand suns.

Yet we do not recognize Antichrist for what he is any more than we recognize Christ for what he was, for many who are looking at all, continue to look beyond the world to a fatherly God to break through nature to save them. Yet God is already here, living amongst us, coming from within us, acting in our midst incognito save to those who discern the mysteries of incarnation and revelation.

The question then was: how could God be appearing in a suffering servant? He had no form nor comeliness, and when people saw him there was no beauty that they should desire him (Isa. 53). He was despised and rejected by humanity, a man of sorrows, acquainted with grief, whom people esteemed not and finally crucified, bruised not only by them but by the will of the Lord (Isa. 53.10).

The question now is: how can God be appearing in plutonium? It causes cancer and genetic damage and is the essential ingredient in fast breeders and nuclear bombs. It must be stored for tens of thousands of years. Yet it is attracting the wealth of Babylon to its service and the minds and hearts of the people who are constructing and maintaining the military industrial complexes around the world. Can what the whore of Babylon is worshipping truly be called God? Can the weapons of mass destruction we are building each day come from the same source as the suffering servant of God?

The book of Revelation depicts such a situation; it describes such a God. The Lamb of God that first came to take away the sins of the world, now calls down destruction upon humanity he formerly came to save. The Lamb of God who was at first in conflict with death and the forces of Satan, now commands the angel of the bottomless pit. The Lamb of God who came first to give his blood for a ransom for many, now rides forth and treads the winepress of the wrath of God, spilling the blood of millions. And the God of the *Summum Bonum* pours out vial after vial of wrath, destruction and torment upon a defenceless humanity, seeking now to destroy the very world this same God sought to save through Christ. God is in Christ, God is in Antichrist; 'The Lord gave and the Lord has taken away; blessed be the name of the Lord' (Job 1.21).

Indeed, Antichrist is the feeling of God-forsakenness, even as Christ is the feeling of God-acceptedness; it is the symbol of hell even as Christ symbolizes heaven, the negative God-image even as Christ is the positive God-image. To quote Moltmann's description of the rejection of Jesus by God, I would say that Antichrist

> is the experience of abandonment by God in the knowledge that God is not distant but close; does not judge, but shows grace. And this, in full consciousness that God is close at hand in his grace, to be abandoned and delivered up to death as one rejected, is the torment of hell.[264]

The final point that needs to made is that God and humanity co-creating the apocalypse in our day bring about the interweaving of the wrath of God with the Faustian ego-inflation that arises after the death of a God-image. Their intermingling is complex and their result empirically one. As the crucifixion of Christ served to demonstrate the implacable demands of an antinomial God ('I will strike the shepherd'), as well as to bring into focus the worst human sin, so Hiroshima is demonstrating the absolute perversity of the human personality following the 'death of God' while simultaneously revealing the wrath of a living God as never before. Thus the paradox of co-creation: on the one hand, Hiroshima humanizing the apocalyptic possibilities previously ascribed only to God; on the other hand, at that point where humanity believes it has totally secularized the world and gained full autonomy and mastery of its fate, even of the end of historical time, God appears, deep within our psychic depths, working in and through our sin, indeed, creating evil through the manifestation of the archetype of the Antichrist, and challenging us once again to recognize that all of history is 'in God'.

J. THE PARADOX OF APOCALYPSE

The interface between the abandonment of God and the acceptance of God, between God becoming incarnate in Christ and God as revealed in Antichrist is a difficult one, for it means that we must see 'the mighty acts of God' as spanning the pleroma of reality from the heights of heaven to the depths of hell. It is an understanding that lifts God beyond the confines of our morality, leaving us with the question of what is good and what is evil, where is God and where is God not. It is an understanding that can easily lead to cynicism and despair, for it is one that must be intuitively grasped, not logically constructed. Above all, recognizing God in Antichrist along with God in Christ challenges the notion we have been discussing throughout this thesis: namely, what is the meaning of the 'mighty acts of God' in our midst for our salvation? How can Antichrist, the bringer of our destruction, be an instrument in our election to grace?

A symbol which I believe is helpful in understanding the Christ/ Antichrist complex is that of baptism. The crucifixion and resurrection of Christ are symbolized by this sacrament, as are the events of our day laden as they are with the revelation of Antichrist.

It is generally agreed that to be baptized 'into Christ' not only symbolizes public acceptance of Christ and admission into his body (the church) but means to be 'baptized into his death' (Rom. 6.3), to be 'circumcised with Christ' (Col. 2.11). It signifies the death of the believer to his or her natural self and the resurrection into the spirit of truth.

If we are truly to appreciate the hand of God in Hiroshima and the approaching annihilation, then it is imperative that we see a baptism in what is happening, otherwise we shall have no choice but to give up hope, and despair. The left hand of God can only be understood within the context of God's right hand.

Robinson, in his study of baptism in *Twelve New Testament*

Studies, is helpful in discerning the baptism motif in the Apocalypse itself.

The final conflagration in which the vials of the wrath of God consume the world and the armies of the one riding forth with a garment dipped in blood vanquish the Satanic host, he says, is

> the great universal Baptism in which in Christ the whole world has been plunged – a baptism of blood, in fire of judgment, yet a baptism nevertheless from which the nations may finally find healing, through the 'river of the water of life, bright as crystal, proceeding out of the throne of God and of the Lamb' (22.1f).[265]

Citing the Psalmist, that the enemies of God have poured out the blood of the saints 'like water round about Jerusalem' (Ps. 79.2), Robinson offers the further insight that in the Apocalypse it is not the enemies of God spilling the blood but the Divine itself. The pouring out of the seven vials of the wrath of God in Revelation 16

> is given them by God – poured out in the Cross like water round about Jerusalem. So . . . once more the bath of blood and the bath of baptism are one; and in the work of redemption so understood we have a category of interpretation among the most profound and universal in the New Testament.[266]

In baptism one can see the left and right hands of God working as closely as in Christ crucified and Christ resurrected. It is clear that they form a complementary whole in which both death and life, crucifixion and resurrection play a part. Therefore, our trust and hope in God is not shattered when God appears in Antichrist, for we know that it is in death and through death that life comes.

However, the Apocalypse, even when seen within the symbol of baptism, presents us with a paradoxical concept of God, one which orthodox Christian theology evaded so long as it asserted the notion of God as the *Summum Bonum* and of evil as the *privatio boni*.

These concepts are adequate for prophetic times when consciousness can afford to be one-sided. We are in apocalyptic times, however, when it is not only the enemies of God that are making the blood to 'flow round the city' but God as well. We are experiencing a side of God peculiar to the time just prior to the termination of history, a side that is dark, brooding, destructive, merciless: the polar opposite of all that was manifested of God's incarnation in Christ. We are in a universal religious nightmare where all our old concepts and notions, made almost indelible by the heavy weight of a long tradition, have been shattered. Our old skins have been filled with the new wine of Hiroshima and have been burst asunder. We have been placed in the position of Job where what we have heard with our ears about God is being contradicted by what we are seeing with our eyes of God.

How do we reconcile Hiroshima, the symbol of the negation of existence, with Jesus Christ, the symbol of the perfection of existence? Moreover, how do we reconcile these polarities within the totality of the one Godhead, especially when the antinomial and paradoxical nature of God that emerges seems to tear us asunder and deliver us over to insoluble conflict?

Ever since John experienced the conflict into which Christianity inevitably leads, humanity, whether consciously or unconsciously, has been weighted with this burden. The profundity of it is that it does not involve humanity alone but God as well.

Jung asserts that God incarnated the light side of the Divine first in order to create a durable basis for a later manifestation of the dark side.[267] Given the 'evil inclination' of the human heart, the manifestation of the dark side of God is meeting with far more acceptance than the light side did, even though this acceptance means our self-destruction. Because of this, Jung asserts that

> We therefore need more light, more goodness and moral strength and must wash off as much of the obnoxious blackness as possible, otherwise we shall not be able to assimilate the dark God . . . and at the same time endure him without perishing. For this all the Christian virtues are needed . . .[268]

This is a crucial point, for it means that we can only successfully deal with the dark side of God if we have adequately integrated the light side of God: we need to be deeply grounded in Christ in order to integrate Antichrist. Otherwise, we shall perish. The opposites, Christ and Antichrist, therefore, rather than repelling one another, in fact form a complementary whole, and we must integrate both into ourselves.

What must be recognized is that the integration of these opposites must take place in the human psyche, for Hiroshima has humanized the eschaton and therefore it is our own psyches in which the cosmic battle is being fought.

What Jung emphasizes is that

> Everything now depends on man: immense power of destruction is given into his hand, and the question is whether he can resist the will to use it, and can temper his will with the spirit of love and

wisdom. He will hardly be capable of doing so on his own unaided resources. He needs the help of an 'advocate' in heaven, that is, of the child who was caught up to God and who brings the 'healing' and making whole of the hitherto fragmentary man.[269]

The child referred to is the child of Revelation born of the woman pursued by the dragon. Most commentators assert that the child represents Christ. Without his aid, without his Spirit of love and wisdom, we are lost in dealing with the Antichrist. Put more concretely, we shall only be able to integrate the Hiroshima event into our understanding of God's action in history by first truly integrating the Christ event into our own psychic depths.

As I have pointed out, this work of the Spirit is a slow and complex process. It requires first that we recognize that the light side of God was incarnate in Christ; second, that we be genuinely transformed by the salvific power of God in Christ and at the same time gain in consciousness and moral power sufficient resilience and strength to enable us to deal with the polarities of ordinary life; and third, that we be thus in some way prepared to grapple with the ultimate polarities in human experience: the antinomial character God at work in the cross and in Hiroshima.

With the challenge of Antichrist comes the spirit of wisdom which can lead us into a deeper understanding of Christ crucified. The cross, therefore, is an event in which God has taken the deepest polarities possible and woven them together for a higher good. With the sending of the Holy Spirit, there is at work in us that which brings to our remembrance the whole paradoxical reality of God's action in Christ. It is a spirit of wisdom which comes to our aid through the depths of our unconscious nature, and it is the task of consciousness to respond to this work of the Spirit. Only then will we survive and continue our slow, painful advance towards wholeness.

VII

Conclusion: Hiroshima as Gateway to Christ Crucified

Again the question: *Why is it that after several thousand million years of life on planet earth, our species, in our generation, has brought this life to the point of self-extinction through thermonuclear war?*

This is a question no other generation has had to ask, and yet the simple fact we must face is that the impact of the atomic bombing of Hiroshima on 6 August 1945 has transformed our world. Before this date, every human being had to live with the prospect of his or her own individual death; since Hiroshima, however, we have all had to live under the omnipresent spectre of species death. We have entered the Age of Overkill where there is enough nuclear megatonnage to kill each person on the planet not just once but scores of times over. Not content with even this degree of power, the superpowers and their allies are involved in an escalation of both quantity and sophistication of their nuclear arsenals that simply boggles the mind: neutron bombs that kill people but leave property untouched; Trident submarines capable of launching over four hundred city-destroying missiles; cruise missiles that can fly at treetop levels for thousands of miles before coming to within ten metres of their targets; killer satellites that can destroy 'enemy' satellites in outer space; bombs only the size of grapefruits but which can devastate a city of millions; and finally, huge multi-megaton nuclear bombs that if exploded from high in the atmosphere can ignite an area the size of Europe into a raging fire storm. Complementing these various types of nuclear weapons are different categories of nuclear warfare, ranging from 'limited surgical' nuclear strikes on specific targets to complete 'wargasm' – that category calling for the total destruction of the world. And all this is happening while most of the world goes hungry and lives in need. $870,000 is spent every minute arming ourselves[1] while every twenty-four hours

50,000 people die of either starvation or some other hunger-related disease.[2]

We are all survivors of Hiroshima; we are all *hibakusha*: 'explosion-effected persons'. All of us, whether immediately present at the blast or a half a world away, have participated in the death immersion Hiroshima signifies: we have all been involved in the vast breakdown of faith in the larger human matrix supporting each individual person and therefore have experienced the loss of faith in the very structure of human life. Hiroshima replaced the natural order of living and dying with a macabre and unnatural order of death-dominated life.

The psychic mutation this caused on the *hibakusha* was that of 'a death spell' which inaugurated in their lives a syndrome of death guilt, psychic numbing, impaired mourning, counterfeit nurturance and paranoia. All of us, because we all live under the omnipresent threat of annihilation, must see ourselves as organically and indelibly stamped with the same syndrome. Our participation can be most clearly seen in the fact that we, like most *hibakusha*, refuse to come to grips with either the enormity of the experience or the guilt that the experience has instilled in us. Rather, the overwhelming response has been that of the cessation of feeling, which only serves to deepen the guilt and magnify our paranoia. Thus we continue to arm ourselves with weapons of such mass destruction that in the event of a nuclear war, according to Lord Mountbatten, 'there will be no chances, there will be no survivors – all will be obliterated'.[3] Our deadening of feelings, our heightening of guilt and paranoia, our huge and ever expanding nuclear arsenals only serve to give proof to Einstein's words, that when we split the atom we changed everything in the world – except for human consciousness. And thus we drift towards 'unparalleled catastrophe. . .'

The paralysis of the Christian church in particular has been more deep than anywhere else owing to the fact that it is in the throes of the aftermath of the 'death of God' and therefore has not yet articulated a new God-image relevant to a secular age while remaining consistent with the distinctive claims of the Christian faith. Moreover, given the traditional doctrines of the *Summum Bonum* and *privatio boni*, the church does not have adequate concepts with which to deal with the problem of evil. Because of this, the church has been unable to help the world make the leap in consciousness necessary to keep pace with the leap in technology which Hiroshima represents.

This is not to say that the annihilation is inevitable; we shall only make it so if we refuse to come to grips with what Hiroshima signifies. There were *hibakusha* who did, in fact, achieve a reformulation of the death immersion experience through a psychic opening up. They were able to keep their minds focussed, even with death and carnage all around them, upon what Lifton terms 'a vision of ultimately indestructible human continuity'.[4] They were able to maintain a perception predicated upon an inner confidence that no matter what the level or intensity of death, they would be able to integrate it, while looking beyond the event itself towards a reassertion of life. The Japanese word 'akiramu' is used to denote the type of reformulation they experienced.[5] It connotes an active encounter and involvement with powerful forces, not passive submission. The notion of illumination implied is that of giving the evil forces significant inner form. It is an understanding by which the individual ego can blend with, and be acted upon, by the numinous forces and events surrounding and engulfing it. It is a vision in which there is infinite strife and change on the one hand, and yet a simultaneous harmony of all the parts on the other, even the parts representing death and destruction. By psychically opening up to the evil around them, the *hibakusha* could integrate it because of their deeper connection to the good, and go forward with a sense of mission. The challenge of mission, as E. H. Erikson puts it, is to 'increase the margin of man's inner freedom by introspective means applied to the very centre of his conflicts'.[6]

Properly perceived and integrated, therefore, the Hiroshima experience offers us a way into a reconnection to the very goodness of life.

> The paradox is an ultimate one: the existence of weapons that can annihilate man and his history could also, however indirectly, be a stimulus towards a deeper and more humane grasp of the same. Hiroshima was the prelude to all this – an expression of technological evil and madness which could, but will not necessarily, be a path to wisdom.[7]

As I stated in the Introduction, it is the 'path to wisdom' that Hiroshima represents that I have focussed upon, rather than the death and nihilism it also implies. Like those few *hibakusha* who were capable of opening up the psyche to appreciate its numinosity, so Christians must recognize that in Hiroshima can be discerned the mysterious workings of the hand of God.

In order to come to terms with discerning Hiroshima as a 'mighty act of God', however, we needed a discussion of an ontology of

God. I offered such an ontology under the term 'process panen-theism'. This entails an understanding of God as a dipolarity, meaning that God possesses both an abstract, independent, tran-scendent dimension and a consequent, dependent, relative dimen-sion. The consequent aspect of God involves God in the created world in an intimate and inseparable way. God and the world co-inhere together in a relational encounter that changes both. God and humanity co-create history together, God instilling within us the divine lure that gives us our subjective aim, we concretizing this lure according to our degree of freedom. What we do and how we act affects God directly. This co-inherence and this co-creativity place both God and humanity in an evolutionary process of change in which each is involved with and vulnerable to the activity of the other. It is a process of creative novelty.

In the hermeneutic of engagement, I argued that this co-inherence between God and humanity can be seen in the intersection of two aspects: the historical event, meaning that point in history in which God is experienced as being numinously present; and the confes-sional heritage, which is typologically constructed and therefore enables us to understand the new event according to old patterns by which we have discerned the hand of God in our midst before. The prophecies of Deutero-Isaiah were offered as a paradigm by which the hermeneutic of engagement should be understood. In these prophecies, new events were understood as 'mighty acts of God' because they were typologically the same as events deep in Israel's past in which God had been numinously present.

The hermeneutic of engagement stresses the co-inherence be-tween confessional heritage and historical event in the same way as process panentheism stresses the co-inherence of God and the world. Both aspects are understood to be necessary ingredients in the ontology of 'the mighty acts of God'.

It is my assertion that the dropping of the atomic bomb on Hiroshima is an event in which the hand of God can be seen. The momentousness of its impact is such that we can now terminate the life functions not only of the human race but of the planet itself. The 'end of time' is now an omnipresent reality. In the hermeneutical model I set forth, Hiroshima represents the historical event.

The typological category that we as Christians have used to speak of the final consummation of history has been that of apocalypse. It was basic to apocalyptic thought that the magnitude of evil in the world had become so intense that none of the old categories with which the believing community had dealt with it in the past was any longer capable of doing so. The historical situation was believed to have degenerated to the point that all hope was lost for any deliverance coming from the historical realm; instead, the apocalyptists looked to God for their salvation, believing that God and God alone would be powerful enough to destroy the evil and bring justice and a restoration of the elect to a place of supremacy. Apocalyptic was rigidly deterministic, asserting God to be in control of history, having ordained its beginning, its duration, the limit and degree in which evil would be allowed to hold sway, its termination, and the establishment of a new heavenly and earthly order. All things being ordained by a sovereign God, the only realm in which human free will had meaning was in terms of whether to repent or not.

In explaining the presence of evil, the apocalyptists appealed to both the 'evil inclination' of human heart and the demonic and angelic forces who were in rebellion against God. These evil forces were led by an angelic prince named Satan or Beliar who came down to the earth after the heavenly rebellion and caused humanity to sin. Having dominion on earth, although still under the control of God to be sure, these evil forces made war against God, endeavouring with all their power to corrupt, infect and destroy. Common throughout apocalyptic writings is the theme of a great last battle between the forces of darkness and the hosts of light, when, led by an Antichrist figure who is usually seen as a historical satanic being the forces of evil do battle with the angelic forces of God. The Antichrist is ultimately vanquished, and God ushers in the new age.

Perhaps the most dominant motif in apocalyptic was the awareness that God was coming and coming in wrath. I noted several characteristics concerning this wrath: first, that it was integral to the overall personhood of God; second, that the wrath of God and the evil of the forces in rebellion were not dissimilar – both were involved in wanton destruction of nature and humanity alike; third, that the wrath of God frequently took little account of covenantal morality, frequently blinding people and keeping them blind so that God's wrath could flow forth unimpeded. This was seen particularly in the Exodus account of the Ten Plagues and in the life and death of Jesus. Job's experience also culminated in the awareness that God's expression of the Divine Self takes precedence over the moral judgments and wants of individual peoples and nations. Finally, I stressed that while God's behaviour did not conform to covenantal morality and was therefore experienced as an antinomy of dark and light dimensions, this did not lead Israel or the believers to despair. In every instance, the wrath of God served a specific function within an over-all plan of election. God is equally comfortable in using the left hand of darkness and the right hand of light, creating evil as well as good (Isa. 45.7), but more than this, God is able creatively to integrate all aspects of life into an organic whole which demonstrates a final purpose in divine love. It is in this sense that I have argued we must understand God as *Summum Bonum*.

Apocalyptic, then, focusses on the end of time, on that point in history when the wrath of God and the evil of the world, generally epitomized by an Antichrist figure, come together in an orgy of violence and destruction that obliterates the world. Out of this judgment God ushers in a new age.

With the advent of the nuclear age, what the apocalyptists formerly ascribed to God's sole control and discretion is now within human power. In this sense, Hiroshima has humanized the eschaton. The referent for the destruction of the world and the termination of human history is no longer to be seen only in terms of an all-controlling God outside ourselves, but also in terms of a powerful urge to enact the apocalypse from within history. Since Hiroshima, we must speak of God and humanity co-creating the apocalypse: God instilling within us the divine lure to do so while we fashion the instruments of destruction that will historicize this subjective aim.

What Hiroshima demands of us, therefore, is a re-examination of apocalyptic both in terms of humanity now being able to bring down the final curtain of human history, and in terms of dark and hidden dimensions of God never clearly discerned before.

The locus where both these dimensions can be explored is the human psyche. In this discussion I utilized the depth psychology of Jung, not only because he clearly affirms the objective reality of the psyche, but also because he was very much aware of the presence of God within our psychic depths. His delineation of the psychoid nature of the archetypes offers an empirically verifiable way in which the divine lure of God can be seen to affect our innermost depths; and in his assertions concerning the empirical synonymity of God and the unconscious and of God and the image of the Self, it becomes clear that our path of individuation is integral to our co-creation with God of our next creative advance. Moreover, Jung's empirical data on the interface between our ego and God in the psyche parallel the process panentheistic assertions concerning a God who works in us to effect our salvation. Process panentheism asserts that God and humanity co-create reality; depth psychology explains a way in which we can see how this co-creation is actualized.

The exploration via depth psychology into our psychic depths gives further clarification to the two dimensions which Hiroshima makes it imperative that we explore: that we have humanized the eschaton and that there are hidden reaches within our potential experience of the Godhead that must be known.

This attempt at a 'psycho-theology' is one which, while utilizing the structures which Jung presents in his depth psychology, is still deeply resonant with the fundamental claims of Judaeo-Christianity. The Jungian notions we have used concerning the interaction of the ego and the Self, in terms both of their respective freedom and of their mutual dependence, can be formulated as the relation between humanity and God, for God-images and the images of the Self, while certainly not identical, are experientially synonymous. In speaking of the ego arising out of the Self, therefore, or concerning the fact that the Self emerges into consciousness in order to actualize itself, one could equally say of the Divine that it creates human beings and seeks humanity in order to actualize itself in the encounter with its creatures. One can equally say that God is revealed in humanity and that human awareness is deepened by its encounter with and recognition of God. This reciprocal relationship between the ego and the Self, and between humanity and God, is not only the focus of depth psychology but also the impetus to the development of the Judaeo-Christian tradition concerning a God who acts in human history and concerning human beings who are dramatically transformed by that action.

What I have endeavoured to put forward is that the impetus for the interaction of God with humanity is not so much due to an altruistic love of an impassible Being outside the human space/time who could just as easily not have acted as acted, as it is due to a God who is compelled to interact with the creation because the very antinomial nature of God demands it. God must interact with humanity because only through interacting can God be actualized. As discussed earlier, the interaction between us and God, as between ego and Self, is that of us reaching from our finitude towards the Infinite, and the Infinite reaching from Infinity towards the finite. Again, however, the impetus for this is not so much the polarity between God and humanity as it is the 'oppositeness' within God and humanity – in the antinomy of the God-image. I have argued that this was the fundamental insight of Job, the recognition that if we receive good from the hand of God, 'shall we not receive evil?' and that, paradoxically, while enduring this evil we can still appeal to the same God as our Redeemer.

This recognition of a God beyond the God of covenant, of a God who uses darkness as well as light to effect the divine will, resulted in such a transposition of values that the very foundations of the Mosaic covenant were shaken. This began the movement in both God and humanity for a new covenant through the incarnation and crucifixion of Jesus Christ. When Christ hung in agony from the cross ridiculed by humanity as blasphemer and rebel and forsaken by God, then it was that Divinity itself drank of the same cup that Job was forced to drink of, and the Godhead experienced the anomie of being made to be sin who knew no sin. Christ crucified is God's answer to Job.

Taken psychologically, the incarnation of God into human form is a symbol of the Self (God-image) penetrating into humanity's expanded consciousness to become actualized. When consciousness engages with an archetypal image emerging from the unconscious, the power and meaning of that image become actual in consciousness and the psyche is transformed. A new aeon begins.

This transformation of the relationship between God and humanity, like the relational encounter between the Self and ego-consciousness, leads to a new equilibrium that mutually empowers both. Initially, of course, the Self has an overwhelming impact on the ego, and if the ego stands firm and is able to engage consciously with this experience, it is transformed; once transformed, the ego is then in turn empowered to penetrate deeper into the unconscious due to its now greater acuity of perception and cognition.

This is a process that never stops: individuation is a continual process involving the enantiodromia of opposites, in which it is essential that contact with both poles be maintained. Consciousness is forever in danger of becoming too one-sided, and the unconscious is continually in need of compensating for this. Thus the movement of God towards humanity and the reaching of humanity towards God did not stop with the incarnation of God in Christ. The Self becomes actual in consciousness in two stages, actualizing first one half of its polarity, then the other. In the person of Christ, God's light side became incarnate but the apocalypse of John prophesied that at the end of the Christian aeon the love of God would be balanced by the wrath of God, and the love of the Lamb of God would be balanced by the vengeance of the Lamb of God. Like Job, John was given to see the terrible double aspect of God.

Traditional Christian theology did not find it easy to deal with this polarity in our experience of reality and so was led to affirm the irreconcilability of good and evil, light and dark. The character of God was seen as totally manifested in the person of Christ; therefore, because the person of Christ was taken as the measure of perfection, God was understood to be perfect in the same way. This led quite logically to the doctrines of the *Summum Bonum* and the *privatio boni.*

In this connection I might point out that although the doctrine of the person of Christ depends ultimately on what we understand God to be doing in and through the cross, the church in fact separated the two in its development of doctrine. It found it easier to deal with the person of Christ than with the meaning of the cross. This may be a clue towards understanding why the church could find it possible to lay down what it considered to be clear teaching about the person of Christ and the *Summum Bonum* and *privatio boni* and yet never found it possible to arrive at a commonly accepted doctrine of the atonement.

The approach of traditional theology to the question of evil is in keeping with a fundamental psychological law: that in the first instance consciousness can only relate to one pole of an archetype and in so doing ensures that the opposite pole is projected on to the external world and is reflected back to consciousness as 'the enemy'. That this process, for all practical purposes, cannot be avoided is due, at least in part, to the length of time it takes for an individual consciousness to grow sufficiently strong and resilient to enable the ego to deal with polarities on the level of ordinary life. Only with this behind it can the ego then go on to grapple with the ultimate polarities in its experience of reality and relate them to the antinomial character of God. What is true for an individual is even more true for a community, especially one as diverse and widespread as the church.

This suggests that the past two millennia have been the indispensable preparation for the radical transformation in our experience and understanding of God to which Hiroshima points. Further, and at an even deeper level, the integration of the clear goodness of God as manifested in the person of Christ is essential if we are to grapple with the darkness of God without being destroyed.

In our theological understanding of God and of the Christian vocation, we can only really go, as individuals and as a community, as far as our moral and psychological development can stand the steadily increasing tensions that arise from integrating more and more deeply into consciousness our experience of the polarities at work in the heart of reality.

In this process we need to recognize that there is an inertial force which militates against the desire for transformation and greater consciousness, making the struggle to individuate and become more conscious extremely arduous. The inhibiting and decelerating propensity of the unconscious is strong enough to overcome all but the most determined. Christ learned obedience through what he suffered. As Jung puts it:

> God acts out of the unconscious of man and forces him to harmonize and unite the opposing influences to which his mind is exposed from the unconscious. The unconscious wants both to divide and unite. In his striving for unity, therefore, man may always count on the help of a metaphysical advocate, as Job clearly recognized. The unconscious wants to flow into consciousness in order to reach the light, but at the same time it continually thwarts itself, because it would rather remain unconscious. That is to say, God wants to become man, but not quite. The conflict in his nature is so great that the incarnation can only be brought by an expiatory self-sacrifice offered up to the wrath of God's dark side.[8]

The impetus to individuate, for God to actualize in history and for humanity to be willing to be transformed by that actualization, is the fruit of the ubiquitous yet subtle working of the Holy Spirit. It is the Holy Spirit which draws humanity into the life process of God even as it actualizes God into the historical matrix of humanity. The point of contact between the Holy Spirit and humanity is in the Self, and yet at the same time it is the Holy Spirit which empowers the ego to engage with the Self.

In the archetypal image of 'God in humanity', therefore, the symbolism of the Self and the symbolism of the Holy Spirit are united, for the continuing activity of God and the continuing indwelling of the Holy Spirit correspond, God and the Self being empirically synonymous in terms of the indwelling of the Self in the psyche and the continual interaction of the Self with ego-consciousness. The dawning of more consciousness in humanity, then, which is brought about by the confrontation and integration of consciousness by the Self in order to be actualized, represents 'part of the divine life-process'.[9] The work of the Holy Spirit can therefore be understood as 'the Self's actualization in man'.[10]

The Holy Spirit as the continuing indwelling of God was not only the impetus behind the original incarnation of God in Christ. It is the catalytic factor in the revelation of the other side of God – the Antichrist. Thus when God 'slipped us the atom bomb' and for the first time in human history global apocalypse became a real possibility, the Holy Spirit was at work. In Christ, the Holy Spirit brought about an incarnation of God, full of grace and truth. Today, the apocalyptic darkness of God as foretold in the Revelation of John has been actualized, full of vengeance and judgment. Now we can annihilate humanity and terminate history just as efficaciously as Christ could save humanity and redeem history. The seals of the Lamb of God and the bowls of the wrath of God have become historicized; all that remains is for them to be emptied – by us.

As in Christ God became human, so now in revealing Antichrist so starkly in Hiroshima God is again compelling us to search out more deeply the antinomial character of Christ crucified. As in Christ, while it was God's will that he die, it was nevertheless the Romans and the leaders of the Jews who crucified him; so now, while it was the Holy Spirit that gave us the mathematical secrets of the bomb, the vision as it were, it is the US and Soviet missiles that will, if the end must come, destroy us all. In co-creation, God joins with the human and humanity joins with the divine in the exercise of power, thus blurring the normal distinctions between sacred and profane, infinite and finite. It is a dynamic that transforms, links and empowers both, intermingling God and humanity together for a brief moment in time. Thus Christ walked the earth totally human, fully divine, breaking the old traditions, bringing down the kingdom of God. Now Antichrist also stalks the earth, the bombs that can destroy our entire planet being fully human-made yet daemonically divine, thrusting history into the trans-historical, threatening the kingdom of God with annihilation. Christ came from above, issuing forth from the Godhead; Antichrist comes from the bowels of the bottomless pit, spewing plutonium the world over.

The work of the Holy Spirit in bringing about this enantiodromia should not be seen as producing something antithetical or irreconcilable; quite the contrary, in the course of individuation, good and evil, light and shadow, are essential aspects of the Self which must be actualized and integrated one with the other if we are to become fully conscious. With Christ humanity was challenged to realize itself as never before in terms of its potential goodness; now with Antichrist we are being challenged to know ourselves as never before in terms of our depravity. This we can only do in the strength of, and without losing touch with, the goodness Christ has wrought in us. It is a precondition of individuation that we become aware of our shadow, even as we develop the good. Indeed, even as Christ was received by the sinners and socially rejected, so Jung points out that the guilty man is eminently suited and therefore chosen to become the vessel for the continuing incarnation, not the guiltless one who holds aloof from the world and refuses to pay his tribute to life, for in him the dark God would find no room.[11]

Even as it is true that sinners are peculiarly suited to receive the salvific light of Christ, it is also true that the darkness of our shadow can be integrated without ill effects only if we remain sufficiently conscious of the light. Darkness can only be integrated without it destroying us if that integration is into light. Moreover, it must be carried out by an ego that continually bears in mind the cost of moral goodness and purity. God's revelation of Antichrist does not negate God's incarnation in Christ; the opposite is true, the Holy Spirit must keep in our remembrance all the deeds and teachings of Christ in order that we may integrate the Antichrist without our being destroyed. While the light side of God had to be crucified in order to shine, the dark side must be illumined and integrated in order to enable us to survive. Thus while Christ's death saved humanity, only Antichrist's life will prevent our annihilation. God and humanity had to be anti-Christ to Christ, demanding his blood sacrifice, rejecting him as blasphemer and rebel; only in this way could the love of Christ fully be shown to the world. Today, God and humanity must be Christ to Antichrist, accepting the evil as a real, legitimate, part of Divinity and humanity; only in this way will the shadow side of ourselves be confronted, acknowledged and integrated. Only the light of Christ can truly illumine the night of the Antichrist, and therefore the Holy Spirit is needed as never before to bring to our remembrance the power and grace of Christ.

The paradox Hiroshima confronts us with, therefore, is this: On the one hand we must accept the message and person of Christ with an intensity we have never had to before, for if we fail to integrate the darkness Hiroshima represents into a deeply lived Christian consciousness we face our own annihilation. On the other hand, Hiroshima demands that we recognize the darkness of God and come to grips with the antinomial character of a God who creates both good and evil. In this sense, Hiroshima is the gateway to Christ crucified even as Christ crucified is the key to understanding Hiroshima. This paradox can be a path to wisdom for us if we realize that the action of God in Hiroshima, like the action of God in Christ crucified, points not to our destruction but to a deeper commitment and experience of the resurrection. The goal is not annihilation but wholeness.

The image of baptism and the image of the cross have been offered to help explicate this paradox of darkness serving the light and of both being integral to a single totality. Death and life are integral to each other. Without their complementarity there is no wholeness. Both are necessary aspects of the creative integration of a God who is Lord of all history, all vicissitudes of life, all possibilities of self-expression.

With the advent of the nuclear age, when God 'slipped us the atom bomb', God has revealed in new ways the darkness of the Divine. We must integrate this antinomy within ourselves in the same manner in which some of the *hibakusha* did: by opening ourselves up to it and integrating it within a consciousness already deeply-rooted in life. Christ is the receiver of Antichrist even as Hiroshima is the gateway to Christ. Like baptism and the cross, both must form a unity for the experience of integration to be complete. If we fail to do this, even as Wotan, whom the Germans failed to integrate, rose up and destroyed them, so the dark wrath of God will consume us, even as we will destroy ourselves by our own ego inflation and sin.

If we recognize Emmanuel in our midst, however, and integrate the darkness of God into what we have already received of divine light in Christ, we shall be empowered to enter into a new era of human understanding. Herein lies both the paradox and challenge of Hiroshima: God with us, to be integrated by us so that not only can the Divine become more human but humanity more divine.

Athanasius spoke long ago about God becoming human in order that humanity might become divine. St Paul before him spoke of redeemed humanity being hidden with Christ in God and also that God made Christ to be sin who knew no sin that in him we might become the righteousness of God. This 'ingoddedness' is a critical dimension to be understood if we are to appreciate the process panentheistic claim that all of human history is indeed 'in God'. It can also provide us with a clue to a contemporary meaning of Jesus' words to those who were blind to his signs and deaf to his teaching: 'Is it not written in your law, "I said, you are gods"?' (John 10.34).

If we can appreciate the numinosity of Hiroshima and take seriously its demand that we grapple anew not only with the light of Christ but with the antinomial character of God, we shall be empowered to 'transcend and divinize our humanity using it as an instrument for the energizing and illumination of the divine within'.[12]

This is the work of the Holy Spirit in the present age, for the Holy

Spirit is the 'mute, eternal, unfathomable One in whom God's love and God's terribleness come together in wordless union'.[13]

T. S. Eliot gives yet deeper insight into this unfathomable mystery:

> The dove descending breaks the air
> With flame of incandescent terror
> Of which the tongues declare
> The one discharge from sin and error.
> The only hope, or else despair
> Lies in the choice of pyre or pyre –
> To be redeemed from fire by fire.
>
> Who then devised the torment? Love.
> Love is the unfamiliar Name
> Behind the hands that wove
> The intolerable shirt of flame
> Which human power cannot remove.
> We only live, only suspire
> Consumed by either fire or fire.[14]

It is this shattering paradox from out of the depths of Judaeo-Christianity that Eliot is addressing: Love bringing torment, forcing humanity to wear 'the intolerable shirt of flame'; Christ the giver of life confronted by Antichrist the taker of life. It is a paradox that can only be resolved within the movement of the human psyche. We must integrate the antinomial polarity within our experience of the Godhead we worship; we must choose between 'pyre and pyre'. Only if we do this, only if we meet the 'high calling of God in Christ' and the 'high calling of God in Antichrist' will we be able to say with Eliot that

> All shall be well and
> All manner of thing shall be well
> When the tongues of flame are in-folded
> Into the crowned knot of fire
> And the fire and the rose are one.

NOTES

I Introduction: The Darkness of God

1. Henry Wieman, *The Source of Human Good*, London 1946, p. 40.
2. Ibid., p. 41.

II The Inherited Tradition

1. Arnold Loen, *Secularization: Science without God*, SCM Press 1967 p. 8. See also Heinz Zahrnt, *What Kind of God? A Question of Faith*, SCM Press 1971, p. 19.
2. Zahrnt, *What Kind of God?*, p. 17.
3. Henri de Lubac, *The Discovery of God*, Darton, Longman & Todd 1960.
4. Quoted by Zahrnt, in op. cit., p. 17.
5. Nicholas Berdyaev, *The Beginning and the End*, Geoffrey Bles 1952 p. 9 (my italics).
6. Quoted by Zahrnt in op. cit., p. 21.
7. Hegel, *Early Theological Writings*, Gloucester, Ma. 1970, p. 159.
8. Lessing, *Werke*, ed. Witkowski, VII, p. 214, quoted by Zahrnt in op cit., p. 24.
9. 'Über Bedingungen und Möglichkeiten eines neuen Humanismus', in *Rechenschaft und Ausblick*, Munich 1958, p. 340, quoted by Zahrnt in op cit., p. 25.
10. Ludwig Feuerbach, *The Essence of Christianity*, London 1854, p. ix
11. Ibid., pp. 13–14.
12. Gabriel Vahanian, *The Death of God: The Culture of Our Post Christian Era*, Brazillev, New York 1961, p. xiii.
13. Ibid., p. 187.
14. Thomas Altizer, *The Gospel of Chrisian Atheism*, Collins 1967 p. 136. 'If there is one clear portal to the twentieth century,' Altizer asserts 'it is a passage through the death of God, the collapse of any meaning o reality lying beyond the newly discovered radical immanence of modern man, an immanence dissolving even the memory or the shadow of tran scendence' (p. 22). Cf. William Hamilton, *The New Essence of Christianity* Darton, Longman & Todd 1966, *passim*; by both authors, *Radical Theology and the Death of God*, Penguin Books 1968, *passim*. For a good discussion of this viewpoint, see R. M. Brown, '*Theology Today*', Vol. XXIII, No. 2 July 1966, pp. 279–290; also *The Theology of Altizer: Critique and Response* ed. J. B. Cobb, Westminster Press, Philadelphia 1970, *passim*; in Europe

Dorothee Sölle, *Christ the Representative: An Essay in Theology After the 'Death of God'*, SCM Press 1967. For an interpretation of secularism from a more sociological perspective, see Harvey Cox, *The Secular City*, SCM Press 1965; from a more existentialist viewpoint, R. G. Smith, *Secular Christianity*, Collins 1966.

15. Paul M. van Buren, *The Secular Meaning of the Gospel*, SCM Press 1963, p. 102. 'The basic presuppositions we have about the world are not verifiable and yet everything we do depends on them, as Hume has taught us,' says van Buren (p. 85). Blaikie observes here that while devastatingly critical of the theistic system in Christianity, accepted without proof, van Buren accepts Hume without proof either (op. cit., p. 38).

16. Ibid, p. 84. 'It is not only the case that, as Nietzsche said, "God is dead",' says van Buren, 'but the problem now is that the *word* "God" is dead' (p. 103). For an excellent critique of van Buren, coming from another secular theologian, see R. G. Smith, *The Doctrine of God*, Collins 1970, pp. 148–151.

17. Schubert Ogden, 'Faith and Secularity', *God, Secularization and History: Essays in Memory of Ronald Gregor Smith* ed. Eugene T. Long, Columbia, SC 1974, p. 14.

18. Ibid., p.15; cf. Zahrnt, II, also John Macquarrie, *Thinking about God*, SCM Press 1975, p. 104.

19. Karl Rahner, *The Church after Council*, London 1966, p. 390.

20. Loc. cit.

21. Loc. cit.

22. Martin Buber, *The Eclipse of God: Studies in the Relation Between Religion and Philosophy*, Gollancz 1953, p. 34.

23. R. G. Smith, *The Doctrine of God*, p. 22.

24. Ogden, 'Faith and Secularity', art. cit., p. 17.

25. Paul Tillich, *Systematic Theology*, Vol I, Chicago University Press 1951, p. 175. All 3 vols were reissued by SCM Press in 1978.

26. C. A. van Peursen, 'Man and Reality – The History of Human Thought', in *The Student World*, vol. lvi (1963), no. 1, pp. 13–21. Cf. F. Ferré, *Language, Logic and God*, Eyre & Spottiswoode 1961, *passim*.

27. De Lubac, *The Discovery of God*, p. 16.

28. Zahrnt, *What Kind of God*, p. 16.

29. Rahner, *The Church After Council*, p. 26.

30. The accumulated evidence gathered by scholarly research strongly indicates that the appelative 'Yahweh' is a causative imperfect of the Canaanite/Proto-Hebrew verb 'to be', a verb meaning 'to cause to be', 'to create'. See Frank Cross, *Canaanite Myth and Hebrew Epic*, Cambridge, Ma. 1973, pp. 65ff. See also W. F. Albright, *Yahweh and the Gods of Canaan*, Athlone Press 1968, pp. 146ff.

31. G. E. Wright, *God Who Acts*, SCM Press 1952, p. 11.

32. John Baillie, *The Idea of Revelation in Recent Thought*, OUP 1956, p. 50.

33. John Hick, *Evil and the God of Love*, Macmillan 1966, p. 18.

34. See David R. Griffin, *God, Power and Evil: A Process Theodicy*, Westminster Press, Philadelphia 1976, pp. 21ff.

35. See below, Chapter VI, Section F.

36. Hick divides Christian theodicies into two main camps: the Augustinian (which he rejects) and the Irenaean (which he is more sympathetic with). After discussion of these he articulates his own theodicy, making great use of the notion that humans are in a condition of 'epistemic distance' from God such that it is not only possible but tempting to explain the world in purely scientific terms, without recourse to the 'God hypothesis'. For a discussion of the traditional theodicies, including Hick's, from a process perspective, see Griffin, *God, Power and Evil, passim.*

37. Origen, *De principiis,* II, ix, 2; in J. P. Migne, *PG(=Patrologia Graeca),* Vol. 11, cols. 226–227; in C. G. Jung, *Collected Works,* Routledge & Kegan Paul, 20 vols 1953–79, Vol. IX, ii, p. 45, n. 28. (Hereafter only volume and paragraph numbers will be given.)

38. Irenaeus, *Adv. haer.* II, 4.3; in Jung, ibid., p. 46, n. 29.

39. Tatian, *Oratio ad Graecos,* in Migne, *PG* , Vol. 6, col. 829; in Jung, ibid., 81.

40. In Jung, IX, ii, 89. For complete discussion of Augustine's notion of the *privatio boni,* see Hick, *Evil and God of Love,* pp. 44–64.

41. Aquinas, *Summa Theologia,* trans. Fathers of the Dominican Province, London 1912, I, q.48, a.2.

42. Ibid., I, q.49, a.1; also q.48, a.3.

43. Ibid., I, q.48, a.1.

44. Ibid., I, q.48, a.2; *Topics,* iii, 4.

45. See Hick, op. cit., pp. 94–104.

46. Charles Journet, *The Meaning of Evil,* Geoffrey Chapman 1963, p. 35.

47. Hick, *Evil and the God of Love,* p. 121.

48. Loc. cit.

49. See Hick, op. cit., pp. 151–174.

50. Hick, op. cit., p. 253.

51. Sergius Bulgakov, *The Wisdom of God: A Brief Summary of Sophiology,* Williams & Norgale 1937, p. 116, n.1.

52. See below, pp. 125f.

III The 'Mighty Acts of God'

1. Victor Lowe, 'Whitehead's Metaphysical System', in *Process Philosophy and Christian Faith* ed. D. Brown et al., Indianapolis 1971, p. 3.

2. John Cobb and David Griffin, *Process Theology: An Introductory Exposition,* Christian Journals, Belfast 1976, p. 21; see Norman Pittenger, *Alfred North Whitehead,* Lutterworth Press 1969, p. 13.

3. Ivor Leclerc, *Whitehead's Metaphysics: An Introductory Exposition,* Allen & Unwin 1958, pp. 55f.

4. For further discussion of this point see Peter Hamilton, who observes that relativity theory along with quantum theory 'form the very foundation of Whitehead's philosophical system' (*The Living God and the Modern World,* Hodder 1967, p. 396). Cf. John Wilcox, 'A Question from Physics for Certain Theists', in *Journal of Religion,* Vol. 40, No. 4, Oct. 1961, pp. 293–301; Lewis S. Ford, 'Is Process Theism Compatible with Relativity

Theory?' in *Journal of Religion,* Vol. 48, No. 2, April 1968, pp. 124–135. For particular reference to Hartshorne, see Frederick F. Fost, 'Relativity Theory and Hartshorne's Dipolar Theism', in *Two Process Philosophers: Hartshorne Encounters Whitehead* ed. Lewis S. Ford, Tallahassee, Florida 1973, pp. 89–99. See also Pittenger, *Process Thought and Christian Faith,* James Nisbet 1968, p. 13.

5. Alfred North Whitehead, *Process and Reality: An Essay in Cosmology,* New York 1929, pp. 33, 113; revised edition Collier-Macmillan 1979. (Hereafter referred to as *PR.*) Whitehead's bare statement of his theory of actual entities takes the form of thirty-six principles: twenty-seven under 'Categories of Explanation' (pp. 33–39) and nine under 'Categoreal Obligation' (pp. 39–42). According to Hartshorne, we experience about ten 'occasions' per second. ('The Development of Process Philosophy', in *Process Theology* ed. E. H. Cousins, Paulist Press, New York 1971, p. 60.) Cobb and Griffin offer the example of a motion picture to clarify what Whitehead means here: the movie appears to be a continuous flow while in reality it is composed of still frames moving in rapid succession, one after the other (op. cit., p. 15). Elsewhere, Cobb, uses the term 'energy-event' to describe an 'actual entity' *(God and the World,* Westminster Press, Philadelphia 1965, p. 72); cf. Cobb, *A Christian Natural Theology: Based on the Thought of Alfred North Whitehead,* Westminster Press, Philadelphia 1965, pp. 28–39.

6. In Lowe, 'Whitehead's Metaphysical System', art. cit., p. 4. Cf. also Hartshorne, loc. cit.

7. See Bernard M. Loomer, 'Christian Faith and Process Philosophy' in *Journal of Religion,* Vol. XXXIX, No.3, July 1949, p. 188.

8. *PR,* p. 31.

9. Ibid., pp. 27–28.

10. Ibid., p. 31.

11. Ibid.

12. Ibid. For a good discussion of the plurality of actual entities, see Ivor Leclerc, *Whitehead's Metaphysics,* pp. 53–58.

13. *PR,* pp. 31,32.

14. Ibid, pp. 43,339, 340.

15. Ibid., pp. 34, 35; see Leclerc, *Whitehead's Metaphysics,* pp. 59–63.

16. Hartshorne, 'The Development of Process Philosophy', p. 58.

17. *PR,* pp. 36, 37.

18. Ibid. p. 521.

19. Tillich, *Systematic Theology,* I, p. 281.

20. *Dialogues with Alfred North Whitehead,* New York 1956, p. 297; cf. *Essays in Science and Philosophy,* pp. 89, 90. For discussion, see Hamilton, op. cit., pp. 142ff.

21. Norman Pittenger, *Process Thought and Christian Faith,* p. 110.

22. Norman Pittenger, *Alfred North Whitehead,* p. 34.

23. *PR,* pp. 519–520. For further discussion of Whitehead's critique of classical theism, see D. D. Williams, 'Deity, Monarchy and Metaphysics: Whitehead's Critique of the Theological Tradition', in *The Relevance of Whitehead* ed. I. Leclerc, Allen & Unwin 1961, esp. pp. 353–359.

24. *PR*, p. 343.

25. William Christian, *An Interpretation of Whitehead's Metaphysics*, Yale University Press New Haven 1959, reprinted Greenwood Press 1977, pp. 318, 319.

26. John Cobb, *God and the World*, p. 43.

27. Whitehead, *Adventures in Ideas*, Cambridge University Press 1933, p. 214.

28. Loomer, 'Christian Faith and Process Philosophy', art. cit., p. 193.

29. D. D. Williams, 'How Does God Act?', art. cit., pp. 370–371.

30. In Lowe, art. cit., p. 19.

31. *PR*, p. 523.

32. Ibid., p. 524. In Whitehead's thinking, the primordial nature of God is correspondent to the conceptual pole of an actual entity, the consequent nature to the physical pole of an actual entity (ibid., p. 54). For comment, Lewis S. Ford, 'Whitehead's Categorical Derivation of Divine Substance', in *The Monist*, Vol. 54, No. 3, Chicago, July 1970.

33. *PR*, pp. 523f.

34. Ibid., p. 530.

35. Ibid., p. 525.

36. Ibid., p. 529.

37. Loc. cit.

38. Ibid., p. 532.

39. Loc. cit.

40. Loc. cit.

41. Williams L. Sessions maintains that Hartshorne 'did not derive most (nor perhaps the most basic) of his philosophical tenets from Whitehead. Historically or biographically speaking, therefore, Hartshorne is not a Whiteheadian.' Sessions asserts that it was instead nineteenth-century Idealism which provided the form, language and a good deal of the polemical ammunition of Hartshorne's Harvard dissertation in which he formulated his basic thoughts. ('Hartshorne's Early Philosophy', in *Two Process Philosophers*, op. cit., pp. 11f.) For discussion of Hartshorne's differences with Whitehead, see Hartshorne, 'On Some Criticisms of Whitehead's Philosophy', in *The Philosophical Review*, Vol. 44, No. 4, July 1935, pp. 335f.; David R. Griffin, 'Hartshorne's Differences from Whitehead', in *Two Process Philosophers*, pp. 37–40; and Lewis S. Ford, 'Whitehead's Differences from Hartshorne', in ibid., pp. 58–65.

42. Alan Gragg, *Charles Hartshorne*, Word Books, Waco, Texas 1973, p. 43.

43. Charles Hartshorne, *Reality as Social Process: Studies in Metaphysics and Religion*, Glencoe, Ill., Boston 1953, p. 18 (hereafter: *RSP*); see also Hartshorne and Reese, eds, *Philosophers Speak of God*, Chicago 1953, p. 512 (hereafter: *PSG*). As Hartshorne understands it, classical metaphysics were built primarily upon the impetus given by Plato and Aristotle, both of whom depreciated the notion of change. This understanding reached its peak in mediaeval theology which denied change on the grounds that it was logically excluded by the assertion of the omnipresence and immutability of God who was unchangeable in all aspects. Aquinas, as well as Kant

later, defined God in essentially the same manner, maintaining that there was no possibility of change, no unactualized potentiality in the reality of God. In more modern times, Tillich modified this notion of Being as the fundamental referent with his concept of God as 'the Ground of Being', asserting that it does in fact entail movement and rest. He maintained with Plato, however, that being is a more inclusive category than becoming and wrote critically of process thinking *(Systematic Theology,* I, p. 200; III, pp. 430–432). To his criticisms, Hartshorne replies: 'When (Tillich) says that being comprises movement and rest, process philosophy can only reply: "Movement itself (process, actualization) comprises elements of rest, and this is all the rest we have reason to talk about. Motion is never a mere aspect or constituent of motion." ' ('Tillich's Doctrine of God', in *The Theology of Paul Tillich* ed. C. W. Kegley and R. W. Bretall, Macmillan, NY 1952, p. 169). For his part, Whitehead, while agreeing with Hartshorne, said that 'the essence of the universe is more than process. The alternative metaphysical doctrine, of reality devoid of process, would never have held the belief of great men, unless it expressed some fundamental aspect of our experience' *(Modes of Thought,* Cambridge University Press 1938, p. 137). For further discussion of the relationship of permanence to change in process philosophy, see Hamilton, *The Living God,* pp. 26–32.

44. Charles Hartshorne, *Aquinas to Whitehead: Seven Centuries of Metaphysics of Religion,* Milwaukee 1976, p. 22 (hereafter: *AW*).

45. Loc. cit.

46. Loc. cit. Cf. Hartshorne, 'Whitehead's Idea of God', in *Alfred North Whitehead; Essays on His Philosophy* ed. P. A. Schilpp, Evanston, Chicago 1941, p. 530f.

47. *AW*, p. 50.

48. Loc. cit. Hartshorne apparently has derived his notion of a dipolar Divinity from Morris Cohen's 'Law of Polarity', which states that 'ultimate contraries are correlative, mutually independent . . .' (*PSG*, p. 163). Cf. *RSP*, p. 86; for discussion, see Eugene H. Peters, *Hartshorne and Neo-Classical Metaphysics, An Interpretation,* Lincoln, Neb. 1970, p. 79f.

49. *PSG*, p. 3.

50. Ibid., p. 4.

51. Ibid., p. 8.

52. Gragg, *Charles Hartshorne,* p. 86.

53. Hartshorne, 'The Dipolar Conception of Deity', in *The Review of Metaphysics,* Vol. XXI, No.2, Issue No.82, Dec. 1967, p. 285.

54. Loc. cit. What Hartshorne has in mind in terms of the 'proper meaning' of worship is a 'consciously unitary response to life'. For him, God is 'the One Who is Worshipped', the all-inclusive being of universal love. If God were not the all-inclusive wholeness of the world, then worshipping the Divine would be disintegrative rather than integrative dynamic. See Hartshorne, *A Natural Theology for Our Time,* Open Court, LaSalle, Ill. 1967, pp. 3–7 (hereafter: *NTOT*).

55. Hartshorne, *AW*, p. 43.

56. Hartshorne, *The Divine Relativity: A Social Conception of God,*

Yale University Press, New Haven and OUP, London 1948, p. 48 (hereafter: *DR*).

57. Loc. cit.
58. John A. T, Robinson, *Exploration Into God,* SCM Press 1967, p. 66.
59. Martin Buber, *I and Thou,* T. &. T. Clark, revd edn 1970, p. 124.
60. *Exploration into God,* p. 67.
61. John A. T. Robinson *Honest to God,* SCM Press 1963, pp. 48–49.
62. L. Feuerbach, *Essence of Christianity,* p. 98.
63. Robinson, *Honest to God,* p. 49.
64. Robinson, *Exploration into God,* p. 71.
65. Ibid., p. 72.
66. Ibid., p. 110.
67. Gustav Fechner, *Zend Avesta,* in *PSG,* pp. 249–250.
68. R. G. Smith, *The Doctrine of God,* p. 250.
69. Second edn, ed. by F. L. Cross and E. A. Livingstone, OUP 1974, p. 1027.
70. Robinson, *Exploration into God,* p. 93.
71. Pittenger, *Process Thought and Christian Faith,* p. 40.
72. Loc. cit.; see also Cobb, *God and the World,* p. 105.
73. Hartshorne, *Man's Vision of God and the Logic of Theism,* Willet, Clarke & Co., Chicago/New York 1941, p. 348 (hereafter: *MVG*); see also *DR,* p. 90; see Pittenger, Ibid., p. 42.
74. Christian, *An Interpretation of Whitehead,* p. 407 f.
75. Hamilton, *The Living God,* pp. 165f.
76. Cobb, *God and the World,* pp. 79, 80.
77. *DR,* p. 89.
78. Ibid., p. 142.
79. Nikos Kazanzakis, *Report to Greco,* Faber 1965, pp. 291–292.
80. In Robinson, *Exploration into God,* p. 102.
81. Pittenger, *Process Thought and Christian Faith,* p. 41.
82. *DR,* p. 142.
83. *PSG,* p. 142.
84. Ibid., p. 163.
85. *MVG,* p. 30: Cf. Cobb, *God and the World,* pp.. 87–102.
86. Hartshorne, 'The Dipolar Conception of Deity', p. 285.
87. Loc. cit.
88. *NTOT,* p. 123.
89. David Griffin, *God, Power and Evil: A Process Theodicy,* p. 278. Griffin defines genuine evil as an event without which the universe would be a better place (p. 22).
90. D. M. Baillie, *God Was in Christ: An Essay on Incarnation and Atonement,* Faber 1948; paper edn. 1961, p. 108.
91. Schubert Ogden, *The Reality of God,* SCM Press 1967, p. 164.
92. Gerhard von Rad, *Genesis: A Commentary,* SCM Press 1956, pp. 45–49.
93. Ibid., p. 47.
94. See below, pp. 161ff.
95. This term is also used by Paul Hanson in his 'model of dynamic

transcendence' by which he articulates an ontology of divine events. See his *Dynamic Transcendence,* Fortress Press, Philadelphia 1978, pp. 76–90.

IV The Historical Event: The Atomic Bombing of Hiroshima

1. Henry L. Stimson, 'The Decision to Use the Atomic Bomb', *Harper's Magazine,* Vol. 194, No. 1161, New York/London, February 1947, pp. 101–105.

2. Ibid., p. 105.

3. W. F. Craven and J. L. Cate, eds, *The Army Air Forces in World War II,* Vol. IV: *The Pacific – Matterhorn to Nagasaki,* Chicago/London 1953, p. 716.

4. Herbert Feis, *The Atomic Bomb and the End of World War II,* Princeton University Press 1968, p. 48.

5. In Robert J. Lifton, *Death in Life: Survivors of Hiroshima,* Simon & Schuster, New York 1967, p. 18; (hereafter: *DL*).

6. In *Children of the A-Bomb: The Testament of the Boys and Girls of Hiroshima* ed. Arata Osaka, London 1959, pp. 129, 130.

7. Gordon Thomas and Max Morgan-Witts, *Ruin From the Air: The Atomic Mission to Hiroshima,* Hamish Hamilton 1977, pp. 326, 324.

8. Dr M. Hachiya, *Hiroshima Diary,* Chapel Hill, NC 1955, p. 69.

9. In Lifton, *DL,* p. 19.

10. In ibid., p. 29.

11. In ibid., p. 79.

12. Feis, *The Atomic Bomb,* p. 23.

13. Len Giovannitti and Fred Freed, *The Decision to Drop the Bomb,* Methuen 1967, p. 265.

14. Ibid., p. 269.

15. Frank Chinnock, *Nagasaki: The Forgotten Bomb,* Allen & Unwin 1970, p. 90.

16. Henry Wieman, *The Source of Human Good,* p. 37.

17. Arthur Koestler in *The Observer,* 1 January 1978.

18. Lifton, *DL,* p. 256.

19. Ibid., p. 30.

20. Ibid., p. 479.

21. Loc. cit. Emphasis is mine.

22. Pedro Arrupe, *A Planet to Heal,* Rome 1975, p. 26.

23. Lifton, *DL,* p. 21.

24. Ibid., p. 479.

25. *The Guardian,* 4 December 1980, p. 13.

26. Jim Garrison, *From Hiroshima to Harrisburg,* SCM Press 1980, pp. 186–189.

27. Ibid., pp. 189–190.

28. As reported in *The Guardian,* 15 May 1979, p. 3.

29. Thomas Mancuso, Alice Stewart and George Kneale, 'Radiation Exposure of Hanford Workers Dying from Cancer and other Causes', *Health Physics,* Vol. 33, No. 5, 1977, pp. 369–384.

30. Garrison, *From Hiroshima to Harrisburg,* pp. 86f.

31. BEIR Committee (Biological Effects of Ionizing Radiation), 'The Effects on Populations of Exposure to Low Levels of Ionizing Radiation', Washington DC, National Academy of Science, November 1972.

32. L. C. Whyte, *The Next Development in Man*, New York 1948, p. 122.

33. Ananda Coomaraswamy, *Am I My Brother's Keeper?*, New York 1946, p. 30.

34. Thomas Merton, *Gandhi on Non-Violence*, New York 1964, p. 3.

35. Alvin Toffler, *Future Shock*, The Bodley Head 1970, pp. 4, 5.

36. Ibid., p. 15.

37. Hans Küng, *On Being a Christian*, Collins 1977, p. 34.

38. Max Lerner, *Age of Overkill*, Heinemann 1964, p. 26.

39. *North-South: A Programme for Survival* (The Brandt Report), Pan 1980, p. 16.

40. Lifton, *History and Human Survival*, Simon & Schuster, New York 1961, p. 151.

41. *DL*, p. 157.

V The Confessional Heritage: Apocalyptic and the Wrath of God

1. S. B. Frost, *Old Testament Apocalyptic: Its Origins and Growth*, (The Fernley-Hartley Lecture 1952), Epworth Press 1952, p. 4 (hereafter: *OTA*).

2. W. Schmithals, *The Apocalyptic Movement: Introduction and Interpretation*, Abingdon 1975, p. 1 (hereafter: *AM*).

3. See especially Isa. 52.1–12; 54.11–17, 55.12,13.

4. Otto Plöger, *Theocracy and Eschatology*, Blackwell 1968, pp. 26–52; see also Paul Hanson, *Dawn of Apocalyptic*, Fortress Press 1975, pp. 12–16; Frost, *OTA*, p. 5ff.; Schmithals, *AM*, p. 134f.

5. Schmithals, *AM*, p. 135.

6. Frost, *OTA*, p. 5.

7. Loc. cit.

8. Ibid., p. 6.

9. Josephus, *Complete Works, Antiquities*, XIII, 372–376, Loeb Classical Library, Heinemann 1926.

10. Paul Hanson, *Dawn of Apocalyptic*, p. 397.

11. Ibid., p. 12; see also D. S. Russell, *The Method and Message of Jewish Apocalyptic 200 BC–AD 100*, SCM Press 1964, pp. 264ff. (hereafter: *MMJA*). For an excellent and concise summary of the continuity between prophetic eschatology and apocalyptic eschatology, see Hanson, op. cit., pp. 12–16; *contra:* Gerhard von Rad, *Old Testament Theology*, Vol. II, SCM Press 1965, pp. 306ff.

12. Hanson, *Dawn of Apocalyptic*, pp. 399, 398.

13. Frost, *OTA*, p. 33.

14. Ibid., p. 40. For his discussion of the four dominant myths in apocalyptic: Conflict, Saviour, Golden Age and Judgement, see 35ff. See also Ladislav Cerny, *The Day of Yahweh and Some Relevant Problems*, Prague 1948, *passim*; von Rad, *Old Testament Theology*, II, pp. 119–125.

15. Rudolf Otto, *The Kingdom of God and the Son of Man*, new and revised edition, London 1943, p. 39.

16. Russell, *MMJA*, p. 220.

17. Loc. cit.

18. Loc. cit.

19. See Frost, *OTA*, p. 146, n. 14.

20. Russell, *MMJA*, p. 105.

21. E. Stauffer, *New Testament Theology*, SCM Press 1955, pp. 19, 258.

22. Russell, *MMJA*, p. 106.

23. Schmithals, *AM*. p. 23. Also see Frost, *OTA*, pp. 25, 26.

24. H. H. Rowley, *The Relevance of Apocalyptic: A Study of Jewish and Christian Apocalypses from Daniel to Revelation*, Lutterworth Press 1946, pp. 157f. (hereafter: *RA*).

25. Ibid., p. 163.

26. Abraham Heschel, *The Prophets*, Harper 1962, p. 222; cf. Jurgen Moltmann, *The Crucified God*, SCM Press 1974, p. 262.

27. Ibid., pp. 222, 223.

28. Ibid., p. 224.

29. Ibid., pp. 223, 224.

30. Ibid., p. 229.

31. Ibid., p. 283.

32. Moltmann, *The Crucified God*, p. 272; cf. Heschel, *The Prophets*, pp. 284ff.

33. Elie Wiesel, *Night*, MacGibbon & Kee 1960, pp. 75–76.

34. W. Eichrodt, *Theology of the Old Testament*, Vol I, SCM Press 1961, p. 286. (Eichrodt's italics.)

35. See Brevard S. Childs, *Exodus: A Commentary*, SCM Press 1974, p. 170.

36. Ibid., p. 174.

37. I Chron. 21.1 is one of only three passages where Satan is used as a proper name of an angel. The other two are Job 1 and Zech. 3.1–9. In Job 1 and Zech. 3.1–9, the word 'satan' is used with the definite article and denotes 'the tester' or 'the adversary'. In I Chron. 21.1, Satan is used as a proper name and is revealed in his most antagonistic form: tempting David to disobey God.

38. See H. W. Hertzberg, *I and II Samuel*, SCM Press 1964, p. 411.

39. Karl Barth, *The Epistle to the Romans*, OUP 1935, p. 400.

40. Rudolf Otto, *The Idea of the Holy*, OUP 1928, p. 18.

41. Ibid., p. 19.

42. Eichrodt, *Theology of the Old Testament*, Vol. I, p. 260. See Ex. 9.14; I Sam. 6.4; II Sam. 24.21, 25; Num. 14.37; 25.8f.; Ps. 91.10; 106.29.

43. In Eichrodt, op. cit., p. 261, n. 2.

44. Ibid., pp. 262, 263. (Eichrodt's italics.)

45. Ibid., p. 263.

46. Loc. cit.

47. Karl Barth, *The Epistle to the Romans*, p. 77.

48. Loc. cit.

49. Otto, *The Idea of the Holy*, p. 83.

50. Karl Barth, *The Epistle to the Romans*, p. 77.

51. Loc. cit.

52. Loc. cit.
53. See Hos. 13.13; Mark 13.8; Matt. 24.8; Rev. 12.1–6.
54. See Jub. 1.29; I Enoch 45.4; 72.1; 91.16f.; II Enoch 65.7; II Baruch 32.6; 57.2; Manual of Discipline IV.25; Hymns of Thanksgiving XI.13–14; XIII.11–13; Matt. 19.28; II Peter 3.13; Rev. 21.2.
55. Frost, *OTA*, p. 22.

VI The Synthesis of Hiroshima and Apocalyptic

1. See above, pp. 70f.
2. *Jung's Contribution to Our Time: the Collected Papers of Eleanor Bertine* ed. Elizabeth C. Rohrbach, New York 1967, p. 3.
3. Victor White, *God and the Unconscious*, London 1952, p. 47. See also Antonio Moreno, *Jung, Gods and Modern Man*, Sheldon Press 1970, p. 78 (hereafter: *JGMM*).
4. Jung, *Collected Works*, XI, 334.
5. James Heisig, *Imago Dei: A Study of C. G. Jung's Psychology of Religion*. Ph.D. dissertation submitted to Cambridge University 1973, p. 148.
6. Ibid., p. 181.
7. Ibid., pp. 189ff.
8. Aldous Huxley, *Adonis and the Alphabet*, Chatto & Windus 1956, p. 172.
9. Heisig, *Imago Dei*, pp. 150, 151.
10. Hans Schaer, *Religion and the Cure of Souls in Jung's Psychology*, Routledge 1951, p. 21 (hereafter: *RCS*). For Schaer's discussion of psyche and soul see esp. pp. 21ff;
11. Martin Rees, 'The Origins of the Universe', in *New Scientist*, 2 Dec. 1976, *passim*. See also Jan Darius, 'Superclusters: Fact or Fancy?', in *New Scientist*, 19 May 1977, *passim*.
12. Schaer, *RCS*, p. 23; cf. Jung, VIII, 356.
13. Jung, X, 528. See Schaer, *RCS*, pp. 23ff.; also Goldbrunner, *Individuation: A Study in the Depth Psychology of Carl Gustav Jung*, Hollis & Carter 1955, pp. 8–11; (hereafter: *Individuation*).
14. Jung, X, 528.
15. Schaer, *RCS*, p. 24; Ira Progoff, *Jung's Psychology and its Social Meaning*, Routledge 1953, pp. 73–77 (hereafter: *JSPM*).
16. Jung, VI, 37–50.
17. IX, i, 150; cf. Aniela Jaffé, *The Myth of Meaning in the Work of C. G. Jung*, Hodder 1970, p. 40 (hereafter: *MM*). For criticism of Jung on this point, see Raymond Hostie, *Religion and the Psychology of Jung*, Sheed & Ward 1957, p. 92 (hereafter; *RPJ*). Hostie concurs with Goldbrunner in calling Jung an 'agnostic positivist' (*RPJ*, p. 140; Goldbrunner, *Individuation*, p. 161). For other discussion see Moreno, *JGMM*, p. 105.
18. Jung, XI, 769.
19. According to Werner Heisenberg, 'Natural science does not simply describe and explain nature; it is part of the interplay between nature and ourselves; it describes nature as exposed to our method of questioning'

(Physics and Philosophy: The Revolution of Modern Science, Allen & Unwin 1954, p. 75). Cf. Heisenberg, *The Physicist's Conception of Nature,* Hutchinson 1958, p. 24; also Jung, XIV, 787; VIII, 437. Modern physics has discerned that the observer, in setting up the method of measurement, determines to some extent the properties of the observed object. If the arrangement of the experiment is altered, the properties of the observed phenomenon will change as well. Physicist John Wheeler argues that this involvement of the observer is *the* critical feature of quantum theory and has suggested that 'one has to cross out that old world "observer" and put in its place the new word "participant". In some strange sense the universe is a participatory universe' ('From Relativity to Mutability', in *The Physicist's Conception of Nature* ed. Jagdish Nehra, Dordrecht, Holland/Boston 1973, p. 244.) As von Weizäcker puts it: 'Man tries to penetrate the factual truth of nature, but in her last unfathomable reaches suddenly, as in a mirror, he meets himself' *(The History of Nature,* Routledge 1951, p. 63). For an excellent discussion of the impact of quantum theory on epistemology, see Northrop's 'Introduction' to Heisenberg's *Physics and Philosophy, passim.*

20. Jung, VIII, 421.
21. Jung, XI, 769.
22. Jung, VIII, 421, 422.
23. Ibid., 423.
24. *Psyche: Zur Entwicklungsgeschichte der Seele,* Stuttgart 1851, *passim*; cf. Schaer, *RCS,* pp. 31ff.
25. Quoted in Jolande Jacobi, *The Psychology of C. G. Jung,* Routledge 1969 p. 7 (hereafter: *PJ*).
26. Loc. cit.
27. Ibid., p. 8; for analysis of the structure of consciousness see pp. 10–30; Schaer, *RCS,* pp. 54–57; Progoff, *JPSM,* Chapter III, for particular emphasis on the autonomous complexes; and Goldbrunner, *Individuation,* pp. 41–51.
28. Jacobi, *PJ,* pp. 30f.; Schaer, *RCS,* p. 31; Goldbrunner, *Individuation,* pp. 12–19; Avis M. Dry, *The Psychology of Jung: A Critical Interpretation,* Methuen 1961, p. 90.
29. Jacobi, *PJ,* pp. 31ff; Dry (op. cit., pp. 90ff.) has a critical discussion, pointing to the ambiguities of Jung's concept.
30. Ibid., p. 51; for discussion of will as purposive libido, Schaer, *RCS,* pp. 28ff; libido in personality and culture, Progoff, *JPSM,* pp. 176–180; discussion of contrast in Freud's and Jung's description of libido, Hostie, *RPJ,* pp. 26–35.
31. Quoted in Jacobi, *PJ,* p. 34; cf. Jung, V, 28.
32. Jung, loc. cit. Mircea Eliade shares this view. See *Cosmos and History,* New York 1959, xiii; also *Images and Symbols,* Harvill Press 1961, pp. 34–45. Both Jung and Eliade quote Nietzsche on this point. See F. Nietzsche, *Human All Too Human,* in *The Complete Works of Frederick Nietzsche* ed. Oscar Levy, New York 1921, pp. 24–47.
33. XVI, 204.
34. Ibid., 356, n. 12.

35. Goldbrunner, *DPJ*, pp. 61, 62.

36. Ibid., pp. 77ff.

37. Schaer, *RCS*, pp. 36ff.; Jacobi, *PJ*, pp. 35ff; E. A. Bennet, (*C. G. Jung*, Barrie & Rockliff 1961, pp. 126–138) has an interesting discussion of the transforming power of dreams; Progoff, *JPSM*, pp. 135–156, discusses how dreams integrate the psyche.

38. IX, i, 118.

39. L. Stein, 'Language and Archetypes', in *Contact with Jung*, ed. Michael Forham, London 1963, p. 77; cf. Igor Caruso, *Existential Psychology*, New York 1964, p. 101; Jane Singer *(Boundaries of the Soul: The Practice of Jung's Psychology*, London 1973, pp. 73–84) has an excellent discussion of archetypes and how they differentiate Jung from Freud.

40. Scott, *Hermetica*, Vol. I, 140, 12b.

41. *De Divinis Nominibus*, trans. Ed. of the Shrine of Wisdom, Fintry, Surrey 1957, Chap. 2, par. 61 (p. 21). The oldest known usage of the term occurs in Cicero (106–43 BC). He translated it into Latin so the term was in usage in late antiquity.

42. Augustine, *Liber de diversis quaestionibus*, XLVI, 2.

43. Moreno, *JGMM*, p. 23.

44. Jung in Jacobi, *PJ*, pp. 45, 46.

45. There are several analogies to the psychological concept of archetypes in the natural world. Jaffé discusses analogies in the area of crystallography, biology and physics in *MM*, pp. 29ff.

46. Jung, IX, i, 187.

47. Jaffé, *MM*, pp. 17, 18.

48. Jung, VIII, 414; cf. VI, 565; VIII, 115, 118, 130, 135, 158, 200, 201; IX, i, 43, 44.

49. Jacobi, *PJ*, pp. 43–44.

50. For short discussion of his research see Jaffé, *MM*, p. 30f.

51. Jung, III, 565.

52. Wolfgang Hochheimer, *The Psychotherapy of C. G. Jung*, Barrie & Rockliff 1969, p. 33.

53. Jung, VIII, 263–282.

54. Jung, VIII, 406.

55. Jung, in a foreword to Esther Harding, *Woman's Mysteries*, New York 1955, p. x.

56. Jung, VIII, 405; cf. IX, i, 34ff, for examples of this.

57. Jung in Harding, op. cit., pp. ix, x.

58. Jung, XVI, 177.

59. Jaffe, *MM*, p. 22.

60. Jung, VIII, 439.

61. Ibid., 420.

62. Jung, IX, i, 291.

63. Jacobi, *PJ*, pp. 42ff.

64. Ibid., pp. 52ff.

65. Jung, VII, III; cf. Schaer, *RCS*, p. 53.

66. Bennet *(C. G. Jung)* lists the psychic indications of the interplay of opposites, pp. 139ff.

67. Ralph Waldo Emerson, in ibid., pp. 138, 139.
68. Jung, V, 581; cf. IX, i, 178.
69. In Jacobi, *PJ*, p. 53.
70. Schaer, *RCS*, p. 45.
71. Ibid., pp. 64, 65.
72. Moreno, *JGMM*, p. 34; cf. Jung, IX, i, 350; X, 299, 344.
73. In Jacobi, *PJ*, p. 19.
74. Ibid., pp. 47, 48.
75. Moreno, *JGMM*, p. 24.
76. Jung, VIII, 729.
77. Jung, *Memories, Dreams, Reflections*, ed. and recorded Aniela Jaffé, Routledge 1963, p. 310. For discussion of mana, see Schaer, *RCS*, p. 100; Hostie, *RPJ*, p. 126.
78. Jung, XI, 757.
79. Jung, X, 565.
80. Jung, XIV, 787.
81. Jung, XI, 757. For critique of Jung's method of articulating *imago dei*, see Heisig, *Imago Dei*, pp. 187ff.
82. Jung, XII, 15.
83. Ibid., 247.
84. Loc. cit.
85. On God as 'Ground of being' see Paul Tillich, *The Shaking of the Foundations*, SCM Press 1949, pp. 56, 59, 63. For discussion of 'infinite holiness' and 'finite holiness', see *The Courage to Be*, Nisbet 1952, pp. 177f.
86. Jung, XI, 556; cf. 749, n. 2. See Schaer, *RCS*, p. 149, for further discussion of this point; also Jaffe, *MM*, p. 49.
87. Jung, XIV, 781; see Singer, *Boundaries of the Soul*, pp. 336f. for discussion.
88. Goldbrunner, *Individuation*, p. 146; see pp. 146–156 for further discussion of the religious experience of God.
89. H. L. Philp, *Jung and the Problem of Evil*, New York 1959, p. 225; cf. Jung, VII, 266; VIII, 430; IX, i, 490.
90. Jung, VIII, 432.
91. Singer, *Boundaries of the Soul*, p. 140.
92. Hostie, *RPJ*, p. 70.
93. Moreno, *JGMM*, p. 34; cf. Hostie, *RPJ*, p. 71ff.
94. Schaer, *RCS*, p. 48; cf. Singer *(Boundaries of the Soul*, pp. 187–202), who says that the 'persona is oriented toward society or, more precisely, toward the expectation of society that an individual may have'. She points out that *persona* was the name given to masks which actors of antiquity wore to simplify the roles they played.
95. Jung, VII, 103, n. 5; IX, ii, 266, 28; XI, 131ff, 292.
96. Jung, IX, ii, 8–10; XII, 38.
97. Jung, IX, i, 567; X, 81; XII, 38.
98. Jung, IX, ii, 14.
99. Aquinas, *Summa Theologia*, II-III, q. 60, a. 3. Cf. ibid., 8.
100. Moreno, *JGMM*, p. 43.
101. Jung, X, 301; 22–223; XI, 76, 83, 198; XII, 29.

102. Jung, XI, 129.

103. Jung, *The Integration of Personality*, Routledge 1963, p. 153.

104. Loc. cit.

105. Moreno, *JGMM*, pp. 45, 46.

106. Jung, X, 883; XI, 13111.

107. Moreno, *JGMM*, pp. 32, 33.

108. Jung, VII, 186, 274, 275; IX, i, 523, 524; XI, 345.

109. Jung, V, 198; VII, 394, 395; XI, 82; XII, 28–34; cf. Eliade, *The Two and The One*, Harvill Press 1965, pp. 205–206.

110. Progoff, *JPSM*, p. 166.

111. Bertine, *Jung's Contribution to Our Time*, p. 6.

112. Jung, XI, 233; cf. 156–157; 272; 198; *Man's Search for Meaning*, New York 1968, p. 196; V. White, *Soul and Psyche*, Harvill Press 1960, pp. 164–165; Eliade, *Cosmos and History*, p. 96; Aquinas, *Summa*, I, q. 48, a. 6.

113. Ibid., 233.

114. Jung, Letter, June 1949, in Jaffé, *MM*, 89; cf. XI, 156–157, 272, 198.

115. Jaffé, MM, p. 89.

116. Jung, XI, 391.

117. Loc. cit.

118. Jung, IX, ii, 125.

119. Ibid., 126.

120. This whole issue is thoroughly discussed by David Cox in his work, *Jung and St Paul: A Study of the Doctrine of Justification by Faith and its Relation to the Concept of Individuation*, Longmans 1959, *passim.* See particularly pp. 15–114; 337–341, for similarities between Jung and Paul; pp. 341–356 for a summary of the differences.

121. See Jung's 'Psychology and Religion', in XI, esp. 1–55.

122. Ibid., 74, See Schaer, *RCS*, p. 63; Moreno, *JGMM*, p. 73.

123. Ibid., 75.

124. Otto, *The Idea of the Holy*, 2nd edn, London 1950, p. 7.

125. Loc cit.

126. Ibid., pp. 12, 13.

127. Schaer, *RCS*, p. 76.

128. In Schaer, *RCS*, pp. 148, 149.

129. VI, 412.

130. Ibid., 413.

131. Jung, X, 290.

132. Ibid., 413.

133. Loc. cit.

134. Loc. cit.

135. Loc. cit.

136. Ibid., 373.

137. *New Larousse Encyclopedia of Mythology*, London/New York 1959, pp. 253–258.

138. Jung, X, 385.

139. Ibid., 386.

140. Ibid., 389.
141. Ibid., 395.
142. Ibid., 389.
143. Loc. cit.
144. Ibid., 385.
145. Ibid., 400–457.
146. Ibid., 423.
147. Ibid., 432.
148. Ibid., 433.
149. Ibid., 437.
150. Loc. cit.
151. Ibid., 439.
152. Loc. cit.
153. Jung, V, 341.
154. XI, 86.
155. X, 441.
156. Ibid., 485.
157. Loc. cit.
158. Jung, IX, ii, 67.
159. Jung, X, 487.
160. Jung, XI, 562; see Jaffé, *MM,* pp. 101–111.
161. Authorized Version.
162. See above, p. 57.
163. *Hebrew and English Lexicon of the Old Testament.* OUP 1952, pp. 947–9.
164. Claus Westermann, *Isaiah 40–66: A Commentary,* SCM Press 1969, p. 162.
165. Ex. 4.24 speaks of the Lord attempting to 'kill' Moses. Only when Zipporah cut Moses' foreskin and said 'surely you are a bridegroom of blood to me!' did the Lord 'let him alone'. This strange incident took place after the Lord had commanded Moses to deliver Israel from the hand of Pharaoh. The incident ends without explanation, and Moses carries on his way to Egypt.
166. See above, pp. 107–112.
167. W. Eichrodt, *Man in the Old Testament,* SCM Press 1951, p. 54. See Gen. 32.25ff. and Ex. 4.24ff.
168. Ibid., pp. 54, 55.
169. Hartshorne, *ANTOT,* p. 122. See also Jack Kahn, *Job's Illness: Loss, Grief and Integration: A Psychological Interpretation,* Oxford/New York 1970, *passim.*
170. Gerhard von Rad, *Wisdom in Israel,* SCM Press 1972, p. 211. Cf. E. Dhorme, *A Commentary on the Book of Job,* Nelson 1967, p. xli.
171. See Job 5.8f; 8.20f; 11.13–15; 22.21–30; 36.8–11.
172. Von Rad, *Wisdom in Israel,* pp. 196ff; 212f. Cf. Dhorme's treatment of retribution, *Commentary,* pp. cxxvii-cli; Robert Gordis, *The Book of God and Man: A Study of Job,* Chicago/London, 1965, pp. 135ff., 156.
173. Dhorme, *Commentary,* p. xxx.
174. cf. Job 9.21; 23.10–12; 27.2, 4–6.

175. Martin Buber, 'A God Who Hides His Face', in *Dialogues of Job: A Study and Selected Readings* ed. Nahum N. Glatzer, New York 1969, p. 62.

176. Leonard Regaz, 'God Himself is the Answer', in *Dialogues of Job*, p. 129.

177. Dhorme, *Commentary*, pp. CXVI, CXVII.

178. Ibid., p. CXLVI.

179. Von Rad, *Wisdom in Israel*, p. 217.

180. Paul Weiss, 'God, Job, and Evil', in *Dialogues of Job*, p. 183.

181. Dhorme, *Commentary*, p. CLI.

182. Eichrodt, *Man in the Old Testament*, pp. 65, 66.

183. Von Rad, *Wisdom in Israel*, p 226.

184. Samuel Terrein discusses Job in the context of other Mesopotamian laments about evil in *The Book of Job: Introduction and Exegesis, (Interpreter's Bible, Vol. 3)*, Abingdon, Nashville 1954, pp. 878–84.

185. Eichrodt, *Man in the Old Testament*, pp. 64, 65.

186. H. H. Rowley, *Job,* Oliphants 1970, p. 20.

187. Francis Anderson, *Job: An Introduction and Commentary*, IVP 1976, p. 66.

188. See von Rad, *Wisdom in Israel*, p. 239.

189. Loc. cit.

190. Paul Ricoeur, *The Symbolism of Evil,* Boston 1967, p. 314, see below pp. 185–187.

191. Cross, *Canaanite Myth and Hebrew Epic*, pp. 343–346. Terrien observes at this point that 'when orthodoxy becomes a source of theological sin . . . it fulfills a paradoxical function: it sharpens the quest of the heretic into a frantic search for light; and it transforms him, writhing as he may be in the midst of his rebelliousness, into a herald of truths hitherto concealed or unborn' *(Job*, p. 900).

192. Moltmann, *The Crucified God*, p. 151.

193. See pp. 115–7.

194. See pp. 99–103.

195. See pp. 107ff.

196. See pp. 100, 101.

197. This interpretation follows the order of the Greek text and the translation of the Authorized Version.

198. See Jung, XI, 659.

199. Jung has an interesting discussion of the paradox of redemption from a psychological perspective. See loc cit.

200. H. Benedict Green speaks for many in stating that 'God does not tempt in the sense that Satan does . . . by actual enticement to evil; but he does permit his elect to undergo trials which are a severe test of their faithfulness . . .' *(The Gospel According to Matthew*, OUP 1975, p. 91). Cf. George A. Buttrick, *The Gospel According to St Matthew (Interpreter's Bible, Vol. 7)*, pp. 314, 315; also Norval Geldenhuys, *Commentary on the Gospel of Luke,* Marshall, Morgan & Scott 1950, p. 321. Several commentators speak of this petition being part of the apocalyptic tradition from Daniel onwards which anticipated a trial of cosmic proportions at the end

of time. Jesus inherited this outlook, and spoke in Luke 22.28 of life being a sequence of trials. See Green, loc. cit.; and E. J. Tinsley, *The Gospel According to Luke,* Cambridge 1965, p. 127. Only E. Earle Ellis approximates Jung's position in his assertion that this petition entails an understanding of temptation as from 'God (Ex. 17.7 LXX; Ac. 5.9; I Cor. 10.9; Heb. 3.9) and/or a severe testing *(peirasmos)* by Satan resulting in one's destruction' *(Gospel of Luke,* Oliphants 1966, p. 163).

201. Jung also questions the orthodox position. See XI, 651.

202. Matt. 6.9–13; Luke 11.2–4.

203. See Zech. 13.27.

204. There is a striking parallel between the description of Abraham's action in Gen. 22.6 and the description of the crucifixion in John 19.17.

205. See Jung, XI, 691.

206. See pp. 50–4.

207. See Jung, XI, 693.

208. Jung, XI, 708. For a discussion of origin and use of the term and symbol 'Lamb of God' in the Johannine tradition and also for an explanation of how the Lamb of God as depicted in the Book of Revelation is consonant with the apocalyptic expectation of a Messiah which would vanquish all enemies of God, see C. E. Douglas, *The Last Word in Prophecy: A Study of the Revelation of St John the Divine,* Faith Press 1938, pp. 188–205. Austin Farrer sheds further light on the divine intent in the devastations wrought by the Lamb of God by drawing parallels to OT passages *(The Revelation of St John the Divine: Commentary on the English Text,* OUP 1964, pp. 116–126). H. M. Feret emphasizes that with the canticle in Rev. 5.9ff. it is impossible to distinguish between God and the Lamb: 'thus we know, at the end of this great vision . . . that it is through Christ triumphant that history renders glory to God . . .' *(The Apocalypse of St John,* Blackfriars 1958, p. 68). cf. John Walvoord, *The Revelation of Jesus Christ: A Commentary,* Marshall, Morgan & Scott 1966, pp. 113–121; also Jacques Ellul, *Apocalypse: The Book of Revelation,* Seabury Press 1977, pp. 100–124.

209. Ibid., 732.

210. Ibid., 733. Most commentators completely miss this point. Walvoord, e.g., after an exegetical discussion of the seven vials of the wrath of God, states that the 'utter perversity of human nature, which will reject the sovereignty of God in the face of such overwhelming evidence, confirms that even the lake of fire will not produce repentance on the part of those who have hardened their hearts against the grace of God' (op. cit., p. 242); cf. Ellul, op. cit., pp. 171–213. G. R. Beasley-Murray draws attention to the parallels between the spilling of the vials of the wrath of God in 15.1–16.21 and the ten plagues God inflicted upon Egypt *(The Book of Revelation,* Oliphants 1974, pp. 232–233).

211. Loc. cit. George E. Ladd has something of this in mind when he states that the pouring forth of the vials of the wrath of God, like the judgments of the Lamb of God, 'have the oblique purpose of bringing men to their knees before God in the last opportunity for repentance (16.8)' *(A*

Commentary on the Revelation of John, Eerdmans, Grand Rapids, Michigan 1972, p. 203).

212. Space does not permit a discussion of the historical development of the concept of the antinomial nature of God. For this discussion, see Jung, IX, ii, 99–126.

213. Petru Dimitriu, *Incognito,* Collins 1964, p. 407.

214. Ibid., p. 404.

215. Ibid., p. 458.

216. John A. T. Robinson, *But That I Can't Believe!,* Collins 1964, p. 64.

217. John A. T. Robinson, *Truth is Two-Eyed,* SCM Press 1979, p. 26.

218. John A. T. Robinson, *Exploration into God,* SCM Press 1967, p. 109.

219. Robinson, *Truth is Two-Eyed,* p. 30.

220. Charles Davis, *Body as Spirit,* Hodder 1976, pp. 116, 117.

221. Robinson, *Truth is Two-Eyed,* p. 31.

222. Ibid., p. 31; internal quotation from Davis, p. 124.

223. Ibid., p. 32; cf. *The Human Face of God,* SCM Press 1973, pp. 88–98.

224. Davis, *Body as Spirit,* p. 117.

225. Loc. cit.

226. Paul Ricoeur, *The Symbolism of Evil,* pp. 257, 258.

227. Loc. cit.

228. Ibid., p. 313.

229. Ibid., p. 240.

230. Ibid., p. 314.

231. Frederick Sontag, *The God of Evil: An Argument from the Existence of the Devil,* New York 1970, p. 130. Emphasis his.

232. Ricoeur, *The Symbolism of Evil,* p. 316.

233. Robinson, *Truth is Two-Eyed,* p. 35.

234. Cf. 'Answer to Job'; 'A Psychological Approach to the Dogma of the Trinity', in XI; 'A Psychological View of Conscience' and 'Good and Evil in Analytical Psychology', in X; and Jung's Foreword to Erich Neuman, *Depth Psychology and the New Ethic,* Harper & Row 1973. For a good summary of Jung's thought on the matter of evil, see L. Frey-Rohn, 'Evil from the Psychological Point of View' in *Evil: Studies in Jungian Thought,* Evanston, Ill. 1967, *passim.*

235. Jung, IX, ii, 84.

236. Loc. cit; cf. 97.

237. *Hexaemeron,* II, 5; in Migne, *PG,* Vol. 31, col. 341; in Jung, IX, ii, 82–85.

238. Ibid., 97, 98.

239. Ibid., 113.

240. Bertine, *Jung's Contribution to Our Time,* p. 50.

241. Jung, IX, ii, 76.

242. Irenaeus, *Adversus Haereses,* II, 5, 1; in Jung, ibid., 75.

243. Loc. cit.

244. Ibid., 77.

245. Loc. cit.

246. Loc. cit; cf. 271.
247. See ibid., Chap. VI, for discussion of the fish symbolism, perhaps the most important symbol Christ and Satan hold in common.
248. Ibid., 127ff.
249. Ibid., 79.
250. Origen, *Contra Celsum*, VI, 45; in Migne, *PG*, Vol. 11, col. 1367; cf. Jung, ibid., p. 44, n. 28.
251. Ibid., VI, 45; in Migne, *PG*, Vol. 11, col. 878; in Jung, ibid.
252. Jung, XI, 733.
253. See above Chapter III, Section A.
254. Jung, IX, ii, 68.
255. See above, pp. 144–47.
256. Jung, IX, ii, 170.
257. White, *God and the Unconscious*, pp. 16, 17.
258. Jung IX, ii, 170.
259. Jung *The Secret of the Golden Flower*, Routledge 1957, pp. 112, 113.
260. White, *God and the Unconscious*, p. 21.
261. See above, p. 160.
262. Jung, XI, 733.
263. Jung, IX, ii, 78.
264. Moltmann, *The Crucified God*, p. 148.
265. John A. T. Robinson, *Twelve New Testament Studies*, SCM Press 1962, p. 174.
266. Ibid., p. 175.
267. Jung XI, 740.
268. Ibid., 742.
269. Jung, XI, 745. Cf. Dimitriu, *Incognito*, pp. 431, 459.

VII Conclusion: Hiroshima as Gateway to Christ Crucified

1. Lord Philip Noel-Baker, 'An Idea Whose Time is Come', in *Pugwash Newsletter*, July and October 1980, p. 42ff.
2. See Garrison, *From Hiroshima to Harrisburg*, pp. 100–103.
3. In *Apocalypse Now?* published in World Disarmament Campaign London 1980, p. 10.
4. Lifton, *DL*, p. 369.
5. See Garrison, *From Hiroshima to Harrisburg*, pp. 57ff.
6. E. H. Erikson, *Young Man Luther*, Faber 1958, p. 252.
7. Lifton, *DL*, p. 157.
8. Jung, XI, 740.
9. Ibid., 238.
10. Ibid., 289.
11. Ibid., 746.
12. Athanasius, *Orat.* iii. 53.
13. Jung, XI, 260.
14. 'Little Gidding', *Four Quartets*, Faber 1944, ll. 200–213, 255–59.

INDEX

Altizer, Thomas, 14
Anaximander, 48
Anderson, Francis, 171
AntiChrist, 101, 102, 106, 142,
    153, 160, 178, 182, 190–201,
    206–7, 211–15
Antinomy, 25, 52, 53, 60, 146,
    168–70, 172–4, 183, 192, 197,
    199, 201, 208, 212, 214
Apocalypse, 5, 7, 60, 92–117, 118,
    136, 168, 193–201, 205–7
Aquinas, Thomas, 23, 125, 142
Archetypes, 129–37, 152–60, 192,
    207, 209
Aristotle, 24, 125
Arrupe, Pedro, 70, 71
Athanasius, 214
Augustine, 23, 130, 171

Baillie, D. M., 52
Baillie, John, 20
Barth, Karl, 1, 27, 111, 115, 116
Basil, 188, 189
Berdyaev, Nicholas, 10
Bertell, Rosalie, 81
Bertine, Eleanor, 120, 145, 189
Bonhoeffer, Dietrich, 10
Brezizinski, Zbigniew, 86
Buber, Martin, 16, 42, 43, 167
Bulgakov, Sergius, 25, 52
van Buren, Paul, 14

Calvin, John, 24, 25
Carus, C. G., 126, 127
Cesium-137, 67, 80, 84
Childs, Brevard, 108
Christian, William, 33, 45
Cobb, John, 29, 33, 45, 46
Consciousness, 123, 125, 127, 129,
    130, 133, 134, 146, 149, 209,
    210, 214
Coomaraswamy, Ananda, 86

Cross, Frank, 171

Davis, Charles, 185, 186
Descartes, 11
Dewey, John, 13
Dhorme, E., 166, 168, 169
Dimitriu, Petru, 183, 184
Dreams, 129

Ego, 127, 134, 142, 144–7, 162,
    209–10
Eichrodt, Walther, 106, 113, 114,
    165, 170, 171
Einstein, Albert, 1, 48, 124, 203
Eliot, T. S., 215
Emerson, Ralph Waldo, 134
Enantiodromia, 134, 135, 155,
    160, 192, 193, 209
Enlightenment, 10ff, 193
Evil, 21–3, 50–4, 57, 60, 99–103,
    106, 112–117, 143, 161–6,
    170–8, 183–93, 198, 200, 205–7,
    210

Faust, 156–8, 193, 197
Fechner, Gustav, 44
Feuerbach, Ludwig, 12, 13, 42
Freud, Sigmund, 13, 127–9
Frost, S. B., 93, 94, 97, 117

Goldbrunner, J., 128, 129, 140
Griffin, David, 29, 52
Groves, Leslie, 61

Hamilton, William, 45
Hanson, Paul, 95, 96
Hartmann, Edward von, 127
Hartshorne, Charles, 31, 37–53,
    120–22, 148, 166
Hegel, Georg Wilhelm, 11, 12
Heisenberg, Werner, 124, 125
Heisig, James, 121

Heraditus, 48, 134
Hermeneutic of engagement, 7, 57, 58, 60, 123, 136, 151, 152, 205
Heschel, Abraham, 103
Hibakusha, 69–71, 120, 203, 204, 214
Hick, John, 22–4
Hiroshima, 3, 5–7, 20, 61–92, 118, 136, 152, 197, 201–5, 208, 210, 213–15
Hochheimer, Wolfgang, 131
Hume, David, 13

Individuation, 140–7, 209, 211, 212
Iodine-131, 80
Irenaeus, 23

Jacobi, Jolande, 127, 129, 131, 133, 136
Jaffé, Aniela, 131, 132, 145
Jaspers, Karl, 12
Johnson, Carl, 84
Journet, Abbé Charles, 24
Julian of Norwich, 54
Jung, 7, 28, 47, 120–160, 188–93, 200, 201, 207, 208

Kahn, Herman, 1
Kant, Emmanuel, 10, 26, 52, 125, 138, 139
Kazanzakis, Nikos, 47
Koestler, Arthur, 69
Küng, Hans, 87

Leibniz, 30
Loen, Arnold, 9
Lerner, Max, 88, 89
Lessing, 12
Libido, 127
Lifton, Robert, J., 69, 70, 91, 120, 204
Lindblom, J., 98
Logical positivism, 12
Loomer, Bernard, 33
Lowe, Victor, 29
de Lubac, Henri, 10, 17
Luther, Martin, 24

Maccabaeus, Judas, 95
Mancuso, Thomas, 82, 83
Manhattan Project, 61, 72, 85

Merton, Thomas, 86, 87
Moltmann, Jurgen, 105, 172, 197
Moreno, Antonio, 135, 136, 142–4
Mysterium tremendum, 113, 115, 148, 163, 168

Nagasaki, 66–8, 73, 79
Najarian, Thomas, 83
Neo-platonism, 24, 25
Nuclear power, 72–85

Ogden, Schubert, 14–16, 54
Oppenheimer, Robert, 77
Origen, 23, 191
Otto, Rudolf, 97, 113, 131, 148

Panentheism, 32, 44–50
Pauli, Wolfgang, 72
van Peursen, C. A., 16, 21, 55
Philip, H. L., 140
Pittenger, Norman, 32, 45, 48
Plato, 125, 131
Plöger, Otto, 94
Plutonium-239, 80, 83–5
Polarity, 37–44, 48, 49, 122, 123, 134, 141, 143, 175, 191, 200, 201, 208–10
Price, Lucien, 32
Privatio boni, 3, 23–27, 173, 183, 185, 186, 188–10, 195, 199, 203, 210
Process panentheism, 6, 27, 46, 48, 49, 147–52, 205, 207, 214
Progoff, Ira, 145
Psyche, 7, 28, 119, 120–47

von Rad, Gerhard, 57, 166, 169–71
Rahner, Karl, 15, 16, 18
Regaz, Leonard, 167
Ricoeur, Paul, 171, 186, 187
Robinson, John A. T., 42–5, 184–6, 199
Rowley, H. H., 102, 171
Russell, D. S., 97–99

Santayana, George, 13
Schaer, Hans, 124, 129, 135, 149
Schmithals, W., 93, 94, 101
Secularization, 10, 11, 13–15, 55
Self, 133, 138–40, 144, 162, 207–9, 211
Shadow, 141, 142, 212, 213

Singer, Jane, 141
Smith, Ronald Gregor, 16, 44
Sontag, Frederick, 187
Spinoza, 30
Stauffer, E., 99
Stein, L., 129
Sternglass, Ernest, 82
Stimpson, Henry, 61
Strontium-90, 67, 79, 80, 84
Summum Bonum, 3, 5, 23–27, 44,
    53, 54, 60, 119, 170, 172–6, 183,
    185, 186, 188–10, 195, 197, 199,
    203, 207, 210

Tatian, 23
Technotronic society, 86, 87
Teilhard de Chardin, 48, 54
Tibbetts, Paul, 61
Tillich, Paul, 16, 31, 139, 140
Toffler, Alvin, 87
Truman, Harry, 61

Unconscious, 122, 123, 126–29,
    130, 133–5, 137–9, 149, 207, 209

Vahanian, Gabriel, 14

Weber, Max, 11
Weiman, Henry, 4, 13, 68
Weiss, Paul, 169
Westermann, Claus, 162
White, Victor, 120, 193
Whitehead, Alfred North, 29–36,
    47, 52, 58, 121, 148
Whyte, L. L., 86
Wiesel, Elie, 105, 106
Williams, D. D., 33, 52
Wrath of God, 5, 103–117, 161–6,
    206, 209
Wright, G. E., 20

Zahrnt, Heinz, 10, 18